THE ETHICS OF DEVELOPMENT

EDINBURGH STUDIES IN WORLD ETHICS

THE ETHICS
OF
DEVELOPMENT

FROM ECONOMISM
TO HUMAN DEVELOPMENT

Des Gasper

EDINBURGH UNIVERSITY PRESS

Edinburgh University Press Ltd
22 George Square, Edinburgh

Reprinted 2005

Typeset in Times
by Koinonia, Manchester, and
printed and bound in Spain by
GraphyCems

A CIP record for this book is available
from the British Library

ISBN 0 7486 1058 8 (paperback)

CONTENTS

ANALYTICAL TABLE OF CONTENTS

LIST OF TABLES AND FIGURES

PREFACE

This book offers one introduction to the field of ethics and development – 'development ethics' – for students, practitioners, and others who are interested. Development ethics looks at meanings given to societal 'development' in the broad sense of progress or desirable change, at the types, distribution and significance of the costs and gains from major socio-economic change, and at value-conscious ways of thinking about and choosing between alternative paths and destinations. It aims to help in identifying, considering and making ethical choices about societal 'development', and in identifying and assessing the explicit and implicit ethical theories.

There are many defensible foci for a relatively short book in the ethics of development, in part because the term 'development' is used in various fundamentally distinct ways. These include: long-term economic growth and change; societal progress; planned intervention; what happens in the world's 'South'; and what agencies in or from the world's 'North' do to, with and in the South. One could thus equally validly focus such a book on the professional ethics of planned interventions and development cooperation, or on theories and approaches concerning human rights, including economic and social rights.

Priority is given here to clarity on what is meant by development, in the general sense of 'progress, improvement'. Since the idea of development has been and is universalist, it would be strange to have a book on development ethics that was confined to the South alone. This is not an evasion, let alone a post-modern betrayal, of burning issues about the poor and suffering. On the contrary, by asking who benefits from economic growth, it will direct our attention to the situation of the poor.

'Economism' refers to the ideas that most of life should be understood, valued and managed in terms of economic calculation, and/or that there is a separate and foundational economic sphere, 'the economy', which must be run according to its own universal technical requirements, and whose growth is the essence of development. (The concept of economism will be discussed more fully in section 3.6.) The central thread of the book, reflected in its sub-title, concerns the reassessment of economic growth, and its supersession as lead policy criterion, intellectually though not yet so much in practice, by a self-consciously normative and more broadly theorised conception of 'human development'.

In terms that will be explained further in Chapter 1, the book covers issues in first- and second-stage development ethics: that is, it presents ethical concerns about development experiences and policies, and then examines major valuative concepts and theories used to guide, interpret or critique those experiences and actions. It comes only briefly to the third stage, the ethics of policy planning and professional practice, devising and negotiating and trying to execute value-sensitive action. Those topics require a further book or books. 'Ethics of development' is thus a deliberate title, since the main focus is on ideas about the meaning and content of development, rather than the perhaps broader labels 'development ethics' or 'ethics and development' which cover all three stages.

Nigel Dower's opening book in this EUP series on world ethics concluded that the reconceptualisation of development is central to world ethics. He suggested that 'we need to re-evaluate our commitment to material affluence, for the sake of the environment, for the sake of peace and for the sake of the poor' – and for the sake of ourselves, residents of the rich industrialised countries, his primary audience. This 'is not a call for self-sacrifice, though it may involve a re-evaluation of what is important in our lives … We … need to fundamentally re-evaluate our idea of well-being and thus the idea of development … [Happily,] doing what we ought can be self-affirming rather than self-denying' (Dower 1998: 196). My book centres correspondingly on ideas of development and aspects of well-being.

We will consider the debated meanings of improvement of human lives in a world which is both one and multiple. The book contains a critique of (1) liberal–utilitarian forms of ethics and political philosophy, which predominate in the contemporary world (whether or not also in the academy) but which contain Eurocentric and/or economistic and/or over-individualistic presumptions that undermine their claims to universal validity and often local validity too; and of (2) forms of communitarian or post-modernist anti-universalism. The latter often converge with Old and New Right positions on world ethics. I query monism, meaning doctrines where there is only one correct understanding of goodness and rightness – such as that economic growth is always to the good – but query also relativist doctrines that there are no criteria for moral judgement other than the inherited habits which help to define particular cultural traditions, which allegedly can never be ranked. The book tries to speak constructively to defenders of such views.We will consider the reasons why both economic growth and respect for diversity are widely considered good, and thereby examine the moral implications and insights of those sets of views, which can be different from their practice or proclamations. The book attempts this constructive critique partly through a qualified defence of a basic needs approach, drawing on the refinement of basic needs thinking in the theories of Len Doyal & Ian Gough, Amartya Sen and Martha Nussbaum, and (although in the background) from the political assertion of basic needs thinking under the banner of basic rights in the international human-rights movement. While having such a point of view, the book attempts to deal carefully and sympathetically with a range of viewpoints. Its primary purpose is to present those viewpoints in a way that contributes to intelligently selective use of them and to their improvement.

The chapters proceed as follows:

- Chapter 1 clarifies the rationale, meanings, methods and scope of 'development ethics'. Chapters 2 to 8 then form a continuous line of argument on the normative content of 'development'.
- Chapters 2, 3 and 4 ask directly: 'what is development?' and show how inadequate it is to *equate* development, in the sense of societal improvement, with economic growth and its social concomitants, which are more usefully described as 'modernisation'. Chapter 2 in particular clarifies the variety of concepts of development, and the typical pattern of conflation of descriptive concepts, such as industrialisation or economic growth, with a normative interpretation of development. We should keep these analytically separate, so that we can normatively assess any particular case of industrialisation, economic growth or modernisation.
- Chapter 3 examines in more detail two influential ideas whose standard usage sustains the identification of development with growth of economic activity: 'effectiveness' and especially 'efficiency', when dangerously defined to include only measures of economic impact. 'Equity' is often objectionably treated as a subjective concern lying outside 'efficiency', and then left invisible, like people.
- Chapter 4 highlights various interpretations or aspects of equity, to counteract its marginalisation and to clarify choices. Each interpretation proves to be a different face of equality, with its own legitimate claim at least in certain circumstances. Often several aspects are relevant in a situation, and we have to consider how to combine them. Attention to only some aspects of equity and marginalisation of the others is then also a danger.

- Chapter 5 investigates further the conflation of the concepts of economic growth, modernisation and development, by examining the possible relationships of violence and insecurity to growth and modernisation. This discussion illustrates the dramatic broadening of the concept of development in the past generation.
- Chapter 6 looks at the ideas of 'human needs' and 'basic needs' which underlie many concepts of development and equity. It shows how basic needs theory of the 1970s has been upgraded by concepts formed by Amartya Sen, and the related and in certain ways perhaps deeper work of Len Doyal, Ian Gough and others. This provides a core of some universal basic human priorities and a shared framework for a substantial part of ethical discourse. But it also ensures space for major variation between cases and cultures: in operationalising basic priorities, in prioritising for beyond a basic level, and in some cases in interpreting what is basic.
- Chapter 7 presents some influential siblings or offspring of needs ethics: the United Nations Development Programme's work on 'human development', which draws on Sen's capability approach; Sen's generalisation of such ideas into a philosophy of 'development as freedom'; and the work of Martha Nussbaum, who has created an enriched capabilities ethic based on a fuller theory of human personhood.
- Chapter 8 takes further the question of how far do well-argued conceptions of what is good 'development' (whether seen as outcome or process or intervention) contain universally shared, universally valid, elements; how far are they instead culturally relative? It looks at whether there are moral constraints also in prioritising beyond a level of basic material needs, and supports the view, as in human rights discourse and basic human needs ethics, that there are some.
- Finally, Chapter 9 reviews themes of the book as a whole, and refers on to further issues in development ethics.

I have oriented myself to students, professionals and interested general readers, and not written exclusively for an advanced academic audience. (A few sections or subsections in Chapter 3 and Chapter 6 are indicated as optional reading.) The book tries to be a largely self-contained introduction, accessible for both (post)graduate and higher undergraduate levels. It discusses early on what ethics is and what methods it can use, and provides illustrations, discussion questions, and reading suggestions. The individual chapters can, in my experience, fit as the main teaching material for two- to three-hour sessions with an emphasis on participatory discussion: perhaps first in small groups and then in a plenary which begins with reporting back by some of the small groups. The topics can also be treated more gradually, with two or more sessions per chapter.

The book focuses on concepts, but with ongoing reference to cases, contexts, and individuals. The emphasis throughout is on probing and clarifying the meanings, uses and areas of relevance of some key concepts: notably 'development', 'efficiency' and 'effectiveness', 'equity', 'needs', 'freedom' and 'choices', 'culture' and 'community'. Examination of concepts is partnered by examination of cases and contexts, including from famine and other emergencies, land alienation and land reform, industrialisation, globalisation, and international debt; and by reference to the relationships in colonialism, post-colonialism, and international aid.

My thanks go to Nigel Dower for his invitation to write this book, and to him and the staff at Edinburgh University Press for their helpfulness and patience during its completion. A study group of the Development Studies Association (UK and Ireland), formed in 1991, has been an important stimulus to me in thinking about development ethics. I learnt from participants in the group, especially Sabina Alkire, John Cameron, Raff Carmen, Nigel Dower, Ananta Giri, Charles Gore, Mozaffar Qizilbash, and Hugo Slim. I also benefited from contact with my Institute of Social Studies (ISS) colleagues (past and present) Thanh-Dam Truong, Irene van Staveren, Jan Nederveen Pieterse, Cristobal Kay, Shanti George and Raymond Apthorpe; and from contacts with Dave Crocker, Asunción St Clair and others in the International Development Ethics Association, notably at its conferences in Aberdeen and Chennai (Madras). A further stimulus has come from teaching, especially to many batches of masters students at the ISS. I gained too from trying out ideas in lectures and presentations in Britain, Denmark, India, Namibia, the Netherlands, Norway, South Africa, Spain, the USA and Zimbabwe. Raymond Apthorpe, John Cameron and Nigel Dower each very kindly and usefully commented on a full draft or drafts, and Mozaffar Qizilbash and Irene van Staveren on selected chapters. To Raymond I owe a special debt, for his suggestions and friendship ever since my student days. Finally, my deep thanks go to Shanti and Anisa for their support and company during the years in which I have been working on development ethics and especially on the ideas in this book.

Des Gasper
Institute of Social Studies, The Hague
The Netherlands

ACKNOWLEDGMENTS

Part of Chapter 4 is adapted from my paper 'Equity, Equality and Appropriate Distribution – Multiple Interpretations and Zimbabwean Usages', in Carty and Singer (eds 1993), pp. 35–62.

Part of Chapter 5 is based on material from my paper 'Violence and Suffering, Choice and Responsibility: Issues in Ethics and Development' (1999), *European Journal of Development Research*, 11(2), 1–22.

Chapter 7's subsection on the Human Development Report 2000 is based on my contribution to Gasper & St Clair (eds 2000). Parts of section 7.3 are based on my paper 'Development as Freedom' (2000), *Journal of International Development*, 12(7), 989–1001.

CHAPTER 1

WHAT IS THE ETHICS OF DEVELOPMENT?

Are there really any ethical questions about development – is it not an uncontentious category? Who, it might be asked, could possibly be against development? So why is there a field of work called development ethics? What sorts of concerns and problems have led to it?

This chapter looks at the 'why? what? how? and for-by-and-with whom?' of development ethics. Firstly, it examines the field's rationale, through introducing a series of concerns including, amongst others, the prevalence of extreme and undeserved poverty in a world of great riches; and the huge extent and huge neglect of diseases which make many poor people's lives miserable and lock them into their poverty. The range of concerns also illustrates the progressive extension and deepening of the concept of 'development'. The second half of the chapter then looks at the emergence, scope and character of the resulting field of thought, discussion, and practice. What are the boundaries and extent of the particular area called development ethics? What sorts of methods can and should ethics, and in particular development ethics, use? What is or should be the field's character, in terms of purposes, roles, participants, and audiences? How do practitioners, academics, and different disciplines figure? Different answers about the appropriate shape of the field reflect different perceptions of its central roles, questions, and methods.

1.1 WHY DEVELOPMENT ETHICS? CASES AND QUESTIONS

The range of concerns in development ethics reflects the gradually widening scope of the concept of 'development' over the past thirty or forty years. A first set of concerns arises from the perceived feasibility of reducing and removing extreme *poverty*. The moral urgency of doing so – given the suffering and life restriction which such poverty brings, and its typically *undeserved* and inescapable nature for the persons concerned – has been part of the genesis and rationale for development studies. We

1

then see added a series of further concerns, beyond conventional poverty reduction (i.e. raising of incomes), which include the following:

- the central importance in particular of health, yet the enormous scale of *sickness*;
- the importance similarly of peace and security, yet the frequency of *violence*, often planned;
- the unbalanced distribution of the costs of change, and the frequency of processes of *impoverishment*, particularly involving infliction of the costs of change upon the weak;
- the importance of the *natural environment* yet its rapid and perhaps even fatally accelerating despoliation;
- the questions of whom do *obligations* fall on, and what ethical statuses attach to *national boundaries*;
- even if national boundaries are not considered absolute ethical divisions, the question of the ethical status and content of differences between *cultures*;
- the importance of sources of *meaning,* yet the spread of meaninglessness and of searches for meaning in ways that involve aggression towards others.

Let us take an introductory look at some of these areas.

EXTREME POVERTY AMIDST IMMENSE RICHES

Around one-third of all children under the age of five in [the forty-two highly indebted poor countries] are malnourished and physically stunted, with profound consequences throughout their lives. (Sachs 1999: 19)

Globalisation is generating great wealth. This could be used to massively reduce poverty worldwide and to reduce global inequality. The world's richest 225 people have a combined wealth equal to the annual income of the poorest 47 per cent of the world's people … [Almost] one in four of the world's population (two-thirds of them women) lives in abject poverty without access to adequate food, clean water, sanitation, essential healthcare or basic education services. That's 1.3 billion people whose lives are blighted by poverty, robbed of their dignity, deprived of the opportunity to fulfil their potential. (Short 2000: 10)

Clare Short, as UK Secretary of State for International Development, was citing recent United Nations Development Programme (UNDP) *Human Development Reports*, which stated too that the average African household consumes 20 per cent less today than twenty-five years ago, whereas over that period average consumption in the advanced industrial countries rose almost 75 per cent. Although comparing a stock of wealth with a flow of income is inappropriate, when we compare income with income the comparison remains dramatic: the world's richest 225 people equate to the poorest 450 million (a calculation amended from Dasgupta 2001).

Alternative uses of the wealth were highlighted in a 1993 World Development Movement brochure. It sported a photograph of a fighter pilot, with the sarcastic caption 'It's a matter of life or death. For the price of vaccinating just three million children, your money buys this man a new jet fighter.'

Rich-country aid to poor countries as a net flow has been of the order of perhaps $25 billion annually. In gross terms it is around double that since much is in loan form, and it is due to increase by 20 per cent or so as a result of the Monterey conference in 2002. This is not large compared to the costs of the Kosovo or Afghanistan interventions, the foreign subsidisation and bailout of the Russian economy, the $75 billion credit mobilised to support South Korea alone in 1997–8, or rich countries' farm subsidies of over $360 billion a year (even before a massive US raise in 2002), which is a sum $30 billion more than Africa's entire GDP (*The Economist*, editorial 23 February 2001). American military expenditure is around $400 billion per year and increasing annually by amounts very much greater than the total of US development assistance. In many years net public aid to poor countries was far exceeded by the net transfer on private debt by those countries (the excess of interest payments and principal repayments over new loans; Hanlon 2000). Even existing aid levels might, if strongly targeted, serve better to reduce absolute poverty, argue some. But most American aid goes to two high- or middle-income allies, Israel and Egypt. Rich countries could, for instance, have offered long ago to pay the costs of vaccinating Africans against malaria, in order to encourage pharmaceutical companies to develop a vaccine (*The Economist*, editorial 23 February 2001).

We will see that various types of poverty exist, not only material poverty. But here we must stress a different point. Besides the huge scale of absolute poverty in a world of vast wealth and inequality, nearly all of the suffering involved is undeserved. It is borne by people – half of them children – who have had no chance of anything better. They face not merely bad conditions but often no opportunities to change them. Muhammad Yunus, who founded the Grameen Bank in Bangladesh in the 1970s, gives examples. Let us look at one of them, in which (lack of) shelter and women's rights, illness and climate all figure. It shows the potential for betterment if there is well-directed support.

> The life story of Ammajan Amina, one of our first borrowers, illustrates what micro-credit can do for a street beggar. Of her six children, four had died of hunger and disease. Only two daughters survived. Her husband, much older than her, was ill. For several years, he had spent most of the family assets on trying to find a cure. After his death, all that Amina had left was the house. She was in here and had never earned an income before. Her in-laws tried to expel her and

her children from the house where she had lived for 20 years, but she refused to leave.

She tried selling home-made cakes and biscuits door-to-door, but one day she returned to find her brother-in-law had sold her tin roof, and the buyer was busy removing it. Now the rainy season started, and she was cold, hungry and too poor to make food to sell ... Because she was a proud woman, she begged but only in nearby villages. As she had no roof to protect her house, the monsoon destroyed her mud walls. One day when she returned she found the house had collapsed, and she started screaming: 'Where is my daughter? Where is my baby?'. She found her older child dead under the rubble of her house.

When my colleague Nurjahan met her in 1976, she held her only surviving child in her arms. She was hungry, heartbroken and desperate. There was no question of any money-lender, much less a commercial bank, giving her credit. But with small loans [from Grameen Bank, with no collateral required] she started making bamboo baskets and remained a borrower to the end of her days. Now her daughter is a member of Grameen. Today, we have more than 2 million such life stories, one for each of our members. (Yunus 1998; see also Yunus & Jolis 1998)

Large-scale, extreme, remediable, undeserved suffering demands a response. Counter-views hold that aid fatally discourages local efforts or exceeds the duties of any potential donor nation or its members – but is permitted if it furthers their interests or as purely discretionary charity (see e.g. Bauer 1981; discussed in Gasper 1986).

Equally important are debates over the ethical and other assumptions behind rules and barriers in international trade. Often, while rich-country markets are tightly managed, poor-country markets are forced open, as we will see in the case of priority drugs.

HEALTH AND SICKNESS, NEEDS AND PROFITS

The World Health Organisation estimated in 1998 that there were forty-five million blind people worldwide and another 135 million with seriously impaired vision. For 80 per cent of the blind, the affliction can be cured or could have been prevented. Cataracts (opaque membranes on the surface of the eye) are responsible for half of all blindness, yet are relatively easily removable. In Africa, of the approximately 3,000 cataract removals required per million people per year, only 200 occur, due to shortage of resources (*Development and Cooperation*, 1998(6)). Well over a million extra operations a year are needed.

An estimated two million people died of AIDS-related illnesses in Africa in 1999. This included a disproportionate number of women, weakened by childbirth, and around 450,000 children under the age of fifteen. Mother-to-child transmission of HIV has been greatly reduced in rich countries by anti-retroviral drugs, avoidance of breast-feeding, and caesarean delivery. The cost of such measures for very poor countries is prohibitive for local budgets. By 2010 average life expectancy in Malawi

is projected to have fallen to thirty years. Meanwhile the country has been
congratulated warmly by foreign funders for its record in paying off debts
to the IMF and World Bank, reports O'Kane (2000). Malawi at last
qualified in 2000 for $1 billion HIPC (highly indebted poor countries)
debt relief. The suffering, anguish and disruption caused by the AIDS
epidemic affects the future in indirect ways too. In Zambia in 1998, for
example, the number of teachers who died due to HIV/AIDS (around
1,500) was equal to two-thirds of the number of new teachers trained
(*Developments*, 2000(3)). In some other countries teacher deaths exceed
the numbers of entrants to the profession.

Despite their immense profits and assets, pharmaceutical corporations
have rarely accepted any obligation to assist those in need who cannot
pay. Prices have been set far above the marginal costs of production.
World trade agreements permit poor countries to themselves produce
patented medicines in emergency situations, but the corporations have
declined to accept as emergencies long-term situations in which hundreds
of thousands or millions suffer and die. They and the US government
have pursued punitive legal action against those countries which
attempted to supply key patented drugs at more affordable prices. A huge
global campaign during 1999–2001 was required to defeat this placing of
super-profits above health.

In much of sub-Saharan Africa over 10 per cent of the adult population
is HIV positive; in several countries the figure is over 20 per cent. Faced
with pharmaceutical companies able to charge around £150 a month per
patient in Britain for anti-AIDS drugs, South Africa turned to Southern
sources which could supply the drugs at a fraction of the price: India,
Brazil and especially Argentina. The USA first imposed tariffs on some
South African exports, then appealed to World Trade Organization (WTO)
regulations to block Argentina from pursuing free trade in medicines and
threatened it with trade sanctions. Under pressure during its 2000 elections,
the US government then offered South Africa compensating loans of $1
billion a year (to be repaid at commercial interest rates) to buy the drugs
exclusively from American companies at a 75 per cent discount on the list
price – implicitly to match the Brazilian/Argentinian price (Palast 2000).

The WTO regulations are supposedly to compensate pharmaceutical
producers for the risk and expense of creating new medicines. Yet since
the corporations focus on products for rich-country markets, should poor
countries pay huge mark-ups on anti-AIDS drugs, to fund future research
and development which is largely irrelevant to their needs? Further, who
in fact bears the risk and expense? GlaxoSmithKline's anti-AIDS drug
AZT, for example, was invented in 1964 by a professor funded by the US
government's National Institutes of Health (NIH).

A Glaxo unit bought the formula to use on pet cats. In 1984 an NIH lab discovered the HIV virus ... NIH spent millions inventing a method to test [anti-retroviral drugs]. When the tests showed AZT killed the virus, the government asked Glaxo as the compound's owner, to conduct lab tests. Glaxo refused ... [because] HIV could contaminate labs ... So NIH's Dr Hiroaki Mitsuya ... per-formed the difficult proofs ... In February 1985 NIH told Glaxo the good news and asked the company to conduct human trials. Glaxo refused again, but within days of the notice the company got inventive by filing a patent in Britain for its 'discovery'. Glaxo failed to mention the US government work. (Palast 2000)

Expensive drugs that delay the arrival or transfer of AIDS are not the ideal measure. A vaccine is the health priority, but not a priority for profit-making. Also during 2000, Bill Gates of Microsoft, under pressure from the US government for monopolistic practices, raised the capital of his charitable foundation by some billions of dollars. The declared priority for the funds is to promote development and distribution of new vaccines against diseases such as AIDS and malaria. In 2001, worldwide pressure led the drug giants to drop their lawsuit against the South African govern-ment and to negotiations around a UN-initiated fund for combatting AIDS in poor countries. The WTO meeting in Doha in 2001 reendorsed the priority of cheap supply in emergencies, with much fanfare, as if this was a new concession.

Economists are increasingly recognising what others have long known, that besides being wretched in itself ill health is an enormous brake on pro-gress in much of the world. Yet treatments for many poor-country diseases are antiquated, absent, or unaffordable, since pharmaceutical giants have seen no profit in research to create, upgrade or replace them. Of the thou-sands of new drugs developed in recent years, only 1 per cent have been for tropical diseases (*The Courier*, 2000). No vaccination has existed for major afflictions like sleeping sickness, kala azar, or malaria. The prominent Harvard economist Jeffrey Sachs highlighted these issues in a feature article in the influential pro-market journal *The Economist* (14 August 1999):

Recent advances in biotechnology, including mapping the genome of the malaria parasite, point to a possible malaria vaccine. One would think that this would be high on the agendas of both the international community and private pharma-ceutical firms. It is not. A Wellcome Trust study a few years ago found that only around $80m a year was spent on malaria research, and only a small fraction of that on vaccines ... The [AIDS] vaccine research that is being done focuses on the specific viral strains prevalent in the United States and Europe, not on those which bedevil Africa and Asia ... Tuberculosis is still taking the lives of more than 2m poor people a year and, like malaria and AIDS, would probably be susceptible to a vaccine, if anyone cared to invest the effort. (Sachs 1999: 18, 19)

The Economist's accompanying editorial trumpeted economists' (belated) recognition of the economic impacts of ill health as taking aid discussions beyond 'mere altruism' and 'a purely emotional pitch'. Ill health *per se* is apparently a purely emotional consideration. Sachs, in contrast, compared the dominance of the finance- and economics-based International Monetary Fund (IMF) and World Bank with the underfunding and neglect of the United Nations organisations for health and science (including the WHO, the Food and Agriculture Organization (FAO) and UNESCO):

> [These lack] even access to the key negotiations between poor-country governments and the Fund at which important strategies get hammered out ... The malaria problem reflects, in microcosm, a vast range of problems facing the [highly indebted poor countries] in health, agriculture and environmental management. They are profound, accessible to science and utterly neglected. [Temperate country research is typically inapplicable to the tropics, semi-tropics, and high mountain environments.] A hundred IMF missions or World Bank [country] health-sector loans cannot produce a malaria vaccine ... Monsanto, a life-sciences multinational based in St Louis, Missouri, has a research and development budget that is more than twice the R&D budget of the entire worldwide network of public-sector tropical research institutes ... The World Bank ... does not finance global public goods. America has systematically squeezed the budgets of UN agencies, including such vital ones as the World Health Organization. (Ibid.: 17, 19, 20)

Similar arguments have been advanced for decades by the UN specialist agencies and by development NGOs. Their recent recognition by insider economists like Sachs has started to have some impact. In early 2001, British ministers announced plans for an international fund to provide cheap vaccines against childhood diseases in developing countries, aimed at reducing the figure of ten million deaths each year of children under five. The fund would guarantee a market for drugs produced by the pharmaceutical industry and subsidise research costs. The mid-1990s United Nations summit meetings targets to cut infant mortality by two-thirds by 2015 were otherwise en route to being only 30 per cent fulfilled.

TOWARDS A 'CALCULUS OF PAIN': RECOGNISING VARIETIES OF SUFFERING AND VIOLENCE

Most sickness was not consciously planned. But wars, including civil wars, bring large-scale deliberate wounding, hardship and, indirectly, sickness; and some forms of socio-economic development can stimulate such conflicts, as we will see in Chapter 5. Further, all forms of socio-economic development involve choices, explicit or implicit, about the priority to give to reducing suffering versus other objectives such as the growth of aggregate wealth or of national power, and about the weight given to the suffering of some groups compared to others. Sustained economic growth and the associated modernisation in low- and middle-income countries have nearly always involved huge amounts of directly

Table 1.1 Varieties of suffering on paths of development

VARIETIES OF SUFFERING	*PLANNED SUFFERING (planned by major holders of economic and political power, as part of economic development)*	*'UNPLANNED' SUFFERING, 'COLLATERAL DAMAGE' (unplanned as part of economic development strategy)*
SUFFERING FROM (PHYSICAL) VIOLENCE INFLICTED BY OTHER PEOPLE	As in many past and some present development strategies; e.g. via slavery, forced labour, expropriation, 'ethnic cleansing' or other forced removals	'Side effects'; e.g. suffering from domestic violence or civil wars triggered by economic pressures, or diversion of emergency aid to continue the civil wars
SUFFERING OTHER THAN FROM PHYSICAL VIOLENCE INFLICTED BY OTHERS	E.g. from forced savings, economic adjustment. [In these cases, violence is not applied but may remain as a threat, a potential enforcer.]	E.g. from natural hazards and harsh environments; from societal dysfunction, including other side effects of market forces, such as some famines; and from global environmental change

(Adapted from Gasper 1999a.)

associated suffering. The prominent American sociologist Peter Berger emphasised this in his *Pyramids of Sacrifice: Political Ethics and Social Change* (1974), one of the foundation stones of development ethics as a conscious field. In Berger's terms, the political ethics of development involves a 'calculus of pain'. Some types of development policy involve conscious sacrificing of the well-being of certain groups, for example, stigmatised out-groups such as indigenous peoples whose lands and resources are taken from them for more intensive use by the more power-ful, or labourers in sectors which are deemed uncompetitive and due to be replaced by cheaper supplies from elsewhere.

The table above indicates examples of unintended and intended suffer-ing, both through violence and other paths. Much suffering is from planned physical violence: manifest, intentional, and large scale, by governments and their opponents, by vigilantes, by traffickers in people and now even traffickers in parts of people (see e.g. Truong 2001). Some other physical violence may be deemed 'side effects', like increased levels of domestic violence and civil conflict. Here the violence when it occurs is in general intended by the perpetrators but not as part of a long-term development strategy. The classification in the table is imperfect; the boundaries between planned and unplanned, physical and non-physical, are not sharp. It conveys, however, the breadth of the areas of suffering.

'Collateral damage' is a euphemistic military term for injuries inflicted on groups besides those who are intended to be harmed. Economists speak similarly of 'negative externalities', harm that is not reflected in market calculation of the costs of an enterprise. These are anodyne, distanced terms for damage to people and to social and ecological systems. Perhaps the greatest example of such damage is the steady onslaught on the natural environment. Not only ecosystems but people suffer from this – usually disproportionately people in poorer groups and in poorer countries. For example, global warming, which is now established as very likely a side effect mainly of fossil fuel-based economic growth, will have its main negative effects on low-income tropical and sub-tropical countries, notably those in low-lying areas. Yet as of 2000 it was estimated that the 20 per cent of world population living in countries with the *highest* average incomes produced 53 per cent of all carbon dioxide emissions, which contribute to global warming; while the 20 per cent living in the poorest countries produced only 3 per cent. This sort of pattern applies in numerous other instances.

THE INFLICTION OF COSTS ON THE WEAK: THE EXAMPLES OF DAMS, FAMINES, DEBT AND STRUCTURAL ADJUSTMENT

Who bore the suffering mentioned by Peter Berger? In many cases the main costs of structural change are imposed on the weak. Let us consider four examples. Two are dramatic: the impacts of dams and of famines. The next two are more insidious: economic structural adjustment programmes, and the bleeding of many of the lowest-income countries since 1980 through debt repayments.

Giant dams, such as at Aswan or Kariba, had in the mid-twentieth century a status as 'the cathedrals of development', a phrase used by India's first prime minister, Jawaharlal Nehru. The film version of Boris Pasternak's *Dr Zhivago*, about the human costs of the Russian Revolution, memorably opened and closed at a great dam, symbol of the transformative brutal industrialisation unleashed by Stalin and of the energy extolled by Lenin when he declared that Communism equalled Soviet (local workers' councils) power plus electrification. Such dams often come at major human and environmental cost, whether or not they involve forced labour as in the Soviet case. In order to generate maximum power they are frequently located where a large river with a rapid flow is about to fall markedly: typically at the end of a highland valley or canyon, below the mountains and above the plains, often in remote areas populated by peoples who are relatively marginal in terms of national politics and power. These low-income groups lose their lands once the valley is flooded – not to mention their homes, their livelihoods, and their way of life – for the benefit of urban power-consumers and irrigation water-users downstream. Typically in the past they were not compensated substantially or at all, regardless of whether or not provisions for compensation existed; their losses were treated as their contribution to national development (Cernea 1999). The worldwide movement against the mega-dams under construction on the Narmada river in India, and many similar actions, forced these issues onto the table from the 1980s. Some defenders declare that the movement and its insistence on compensation for displaced persons represent a Northern conspiracy to keep poor countries poor, by the imposition of standards never applied during the North's own industrialisation. There are potentially also conflicts here between aggregate poverty reduction and the protection of particular groups' ways of life. However, other means exist which arguably would balance these goals better, such as the use instead of many small dams (Alvares & Billorey 1988). But large dams represent large gains (and administrative convenience) for large contractors, suppliers, financiers, and the politicians whose approval must be obtained.

While irrigation should help to counter the threats of malnutrition and famine, many of the greatest modern famines have been caused less by declines in food availability than by collapses in the acquisition power of vulnerable groups. During the Irish famine of 1845–9, in what was a part of the United Kingdom, then the wealthiest country in Europe and probably the world, food continued to be exported from Ireland while hundreds of thousands died. In Bengal under British rule during 1943–5 around three million people died prematurely when food prices soared due to wartime military spending, government procurement, speculative hoarding, and restrictions on trade (Sen 1981). Marginal groups who relied on buying food, such as fishermen and landless labourers, suffered a catastrophic collapse of their purchasing power. In two other cases – the Soviet Union (specifically the Ukraine) in 1931–3 and China in 1959–61 – during wastefully rapid and poorly planned industrialisation drives (see e.g. Granick 1967 and Gray 1974), import priority was given to machinery, not food, despite major declines in food availability and large-scale starvation. Millions died while food was compulsorily procured domestically and transferred away from shortage areas.

Many low-income countries in the 1980s and 1990s had a similar combination of widespread and increasing suffering amongst poorer and even formerly middle-class groups at the same time as large-scale extraction of resources to metropolises. But in this case the resources were not channelled into national industrialisation or a world war. Instead the period saw the greatest ever consumer boom in the North. Low-income countries had acquired debts in the 1970s following the first great oil price hike, and had been encouraged to do so by banks looking to recycle OPEC surplus funds. The second oil price hike at the end of the 1970s, followed by a borrowing-based American military spending drive, sent many countries into crisis as world interest rates soared and took their debts out of control.

> Developing country debt increased tenfold in the 1970s. This was followed by a debt crisis in the early 1980s, in which many countries were unable to meet repayments ... In the period 1984–91, developing countries ... gave creditors $209 billion more in interest payments and principal repayments than they received in new loans. Yet total debt doubled again in the 1980s, not because of new lending but because old debts were being rolled over [with ever more interest payments due] ... For the 38 countries defined by the World Bank as 'severely indebted low income', total debt rose from 5 per cent of GNP in 1970 ... to 139 per cent of GNP in 1990, and [was] at the same level in 1999. Many of the poorest countries pay more in debt service than they spend on education or health. (Hanlon 2000: 877–8)

One topic of discussion concerns what would be the *effects* of writing off debts. We look in Chapter 3 at which types of effects are usually considered and in which ways. A prior issue, relatively neglected, concerns the *moral status* of the debts. Hanlon (2000), from the Jubilee 2000 campaign for debt write-offs, queried the moral priority of repayment:

- The Universal Declaration of Human Rights, endorsed by all the creditor countries, gives priority to fulfilment of basic needs, contrary to the massive cutbacks enforced on poorer countries in order for them to service and repay foreign debt.
- Much of the debt was contracted corruptly, with no benefit to the borrower country population. It fits the legal category of 'odious debt', fit for repudiation.
- The repayment terms applied in the Third World debt crisis since 1982 have been much harsher than those applied after 1945 to Germany, a considerably richer country. (Yet Germany was long in the forefront of insisting on rigorous repayment by the South.)
- The major present creditors have in the past themselves defaulted or received debt forgiveness.

Infliction of costs on poorer people is not as coldly intentional in the case of debt repayment as in forced displacement for dams. It is in part an unintended effect of the systematisation of world capitalism, its tightening up on debtors. The Jubilee 2000 campaign contributed significantly to the offer by the rich nations in 2000 of debt relief to twenty-two of the poorest countries, most of them African – after two decades of damage.

'Many of Jubilee 2000's assertions have been essentially moral and politically strategic, rather than based on economic analysis,' remark n & Weinhold (2000: 870). 'Essentially moral' could refer to talking ..., about what would be desirable, as opposed to what is feasible or what would actually happen as a result of measures proposed. In drawing prescriptions from moral arguments we must consider economic analysis, including analysis of constraints and the likely effects from debt relief (such as the effects on future investors), in order to judge how to effectively advance chosen values. We will see, however, in Chapter 3 how mainstream economic analysis when extended to giving policy prescriptions largely hides its own debatable moral presumptions. It is frequently presented – despite a narrow field of vision and narrow set of values – as a sort of hard truth, a set of laws of nature; and can then ignore or denigrate other perspectives. Too often 'essentially moral' becomes a dismissive label for concerns for poor people, and 'economic analysis' becomes the prestigious codeword for concern for people with purchasing power. We saw *The Economist* celebrate economists' sadly late recognition of the economic impacts of ill health. Concern for the suffering of the sick, *per se*, was labelled 'a purely emotional pitch'. Such denigratory labelling is the real 'purely emotional pitch'.

Characteristic of work in development ethics have been an insistence on *clarifying* the values behind evaluative and prescriptive arguments from economics; a rejection of the *narrowness* of the set of values from the marketplace, and a stress instead on increasing the range of values to be considered; and a rejection therefore of an *automatic* superior status for economics arguments. Do economics arguments trump human-rights arguments, for example? For many people, the reverse will often be true. Most of the work that sees itself as development ethics has aimed to use a broad, not narrow, vision, to look with an open heart and open mind at real experience, real joys and suffering, and at interconnections besides those captured by markets and the categories of economics.

The debt crisis forced the door open for externally imposed economic structural adjustment in many lower- and middle-income countries. Structural adjustment programmes in turn enforced priority to debt servicing and repayment, above health and education and universally proclaimed human rights. Economic decline, opportunities in new export sectors and growing shortages of fuel and fodder have placed additional burdens on already overloaded women, as home-makers, care-givers, fuel- and water-collectors, and increasingly also as income-earners (see e.g. Dasgupta 1993; Elson ed. 1995). The programme designers – economists and financiers in a few Northern metropolises, remote from Southern realities – failed to foresee the massive damage that would be done to human development, and also to natural environments, as indebted countries' incentives to export soared. Even less did they foresee, although they should have, their contribution to tipping some unstable states into civil war, bringing immense costs especially for the weakest, to which we will come in Chapter 5.

GLOBAL OBLIGATIONS AND UNIVERSAL VALUES?

We have seen the frequency of distress in a world of wealth. What obligations arise, if any, and for whom? The answers offered can vary according to stances on many matters. Is there shared responsibility for the problems? Is there, for example, Northern co-responsibility and sometimes lead responsibility for partly failed development strategies of capital-intensive industrialisation and later of neo-liberal structural adjustment? Is there a shared status as members of a global community, with equal rights to a common global environmental heritage?

- In the case of debt, we see arguments for risk- and responsibility-sharing, the priority of basic human rights, and repudiation of 'odious' debts. These responses clash with an insistence that contracts entered into must be adhered to, regardless: as a duty and also because otherwise the whole edifice of contractual agreements may be jeopardised.
- In the case of global warming, we see a clash between one predominantly American view, that damage inflicted on common resources which are the property of none is not culpable, and a majority world view now that damage to environmental resources which are a common heritage (e.g. the ozone layer) brings overriding obligations to reduce that damage and its harmful effects for people.
- In the case of international aid, we see multiple clashing positions on whether it has any right to exist at all and with what status – only as an exercise in (mutual) self-interest; or as charity; or as an obligation-cum-right – and relatedly, disputes over who should provide it, what should be its priorities, and what should be its style of operation and cooperation. The issues concern what it means to help, and whether to help, as well as about what helps and how to help.
- In the case of trade too we see burning ethical issues and conflicting positions, for example over intellectual property rights and the attempted acquisition by Western corporations of legally backed control over genetic information, including information long held informally by communities in low-income countries. We see the emigration too from low-income countries of a high proportion of their most trained persons, often trained with public funds.

In such debates we repeatedly encounter issues about the moral status, if any, of national boundaries; and whether or to what degree there are universal values, such as propounded in the United Nations Universal

Declaration of Human Rights from 1948, or how far values – for example on women's rights – are and should be culturally specific. We consider some of these issues later in the book.

WHAT IS DEVELOPMENT?

Underlying or leading out of most of the above debates are questions of the meaning of well-being and 'development', matters which are disputed within cultures too. A recurrent issue concerns the often experienced emptiness of material 'development'. This was a major source of the 'cruel choice' identified by Denis Goulet: does the way of life required to achieve material affluence also require abandonment of life's meaning? Peter Berger wrote in similar terms of the need for political ethics to undertake a 'calculus of meaning', in addition to the 'calculus of [physical] pain'. Is 'development' material advance, or something else, or a combination of material advance and something else?

The book *Ethical Dilemmas of Development in Asia* (1983), edited by Godfrey Gunatilleke and others, centred on the competition between two compelling, conflicting societal visions: a traditional 'transcendental model', which interprets our material world in terms of a metaphysical world and a belief in life beyond death; and on the other hand a modern 'secular model' which refers only to, and offers, (dramatic) improvements in terms of comfort, security and (aspects of) freedom in this life, which it sees as either the only things that are important, or as favourable conditions for whatever other things one considers important. In Chapter 2 we will look at the various meanings of 'development', and Chapters 6 to 8 will consider aspects of well-being.

1.2 WHAT? ON MEANINGS AND AGENDA

THE CORE AGENDA OF DEVELOPMENT ETHICS

Development ethics as a field, as formulated in Lebret (1959), Goulet (1971) and Berger (1974) and elsewhere, arose thus from the following insights.

First, the very idea of development as societal improvement is *value relative*. So the direction of the path ahead demands to be discussed rather than taken for granted; otherwise it will be determined solely and tacitly by power, including the power to make others carry most of the costs and to determine which costs and benefits will be counted and which ones ignored. Behind market calculations in particular, and most economic evaluations, lies money power: those with more money are considered more, those with no money are ignored (unless the moneyed wish to spend on the moneyless); values with no monetary representation are ignored too. Development ethics attempts clarification, assessment and widening of the values which are given power.

Second, development strategies and paths typically involve major human *costs* and suffering. Their nature and distribution, nationally and internationally, must be taken into account and responded to. Even in development ethics there is sometimes danger of over-absorption in theorising the good and specifying requirements for human flourishing, as compared to analysing and counteracting the bad. In Berger's terms, some of the costs are physical and obligate a 'calculus of pain'; others are psychic, and require a 'calculus of meaning' – a theme also probed by Goulet. (Berger's terms unfortunately could suggest, contrary to his intention, that meanings bring no pain.) The common infliction of a disproportionate share of costs and suffering on the weak occurs precisely because they are weak. Assiduous updating throughout the past generation of the mushrooming debts, even the odious debts, of many wretchedly poor, disease-stricken countries has ground on for so long because in contrast to post-Nazi Germany they were not seen as forces to be reckoned with or major strategic partners to be invested in.

Third, non-development too can have terrible costs, as in the case of Ammajan Amina described in the previous section. Wolfgang Sachs's bald claim that 'development does not work' (1992: 1) is an insufficient account of the experience of East Asia's third of humanity or the doubling or near-doubling of life expectancy in much of the South. Hence people may face *cruel choices*, where each option involves tolerating or causing great bads, and which call for Berger's 'calculi of political ethics' or, less grandly put, for intense and systematic discussion.

Fourth, we must identify and compare *alternatives*. Each prevailing orthodoxy – Eurocentric 'stages-of-growth theory', 'the Washington consensus', 'Human Development', whatever – deserves value-critical examination, because there were or are serious empirical alternatives and value alternatives to it. The issue is to reconceive development to give it a more adequate value direction and make it more equitable, and try to find or create alternative means that will do this. Anti-developmentalists declare this impossible. Chapter 2 suggests that they use a particular historically specific meaning of 'development' by which their proposition becomes true by definition.

Since Goulet and Berger presented these four propositions at the level of national and agency policy choices, others have formulated parallel issues for the level of individual conduct by professionals and citizens.

Development ethics is in large part about choices: choices about values and about strategies. Ethical discussion about development only has much point because there are real, serious choices to make. If there were but one development path that could be taken seriously – because all others quickly proved on examination to be impossible or grievously flawed by instrumental and/or value misconceptions – there would not remain much to discuss; only the propounding of the one true way. But the options do not consist of one robust path to heaven plus innumerable roads to hell. Similarly, while Lebret, Berger and especially Goulet helped to create a field of development ethics, not all those who then work in the field share their particular views. It is unlikely, however, that the options are all equally defensible paths to their own incomparable destinations. At least in some cases we can conclude that certain alternatives are better and others inferior; and amongst the better alternatives we may find shared features as well as areas of acceptable variation.

Partha Dasgupta argues similarly, recommending the perusal of comparative data on national and regional development performance. Seeing the dramatic differences in performance counteracts the tendency to believe that because everything is caused, and is one sense inevitable, therefore we have no choices. We would end up 'condoning the most predatory of political regimes and oppressive of social practices. [This] is to overlook the existence of choice, and thus responsibility. And that is to deny persons the respect that is owed to them' (Dasgupta 1993: 128). While everything is caused, we have the ability to cause ourself to act on causes.

EMERGENCE AND CONTRIBUTORS

We can identify a series of phases and arenas in thought on development ethics. There has long been, and continues to be, important work which does not use this label but covers some of development ethics' concerns. Much social and political philosophy and other writing fits here. Parts of the work of major modern European philosophers such as John Locke (1632–1704), Jeremy Bentham (1748–1832), John Stuart Mill (1806–73) and Karl Marx (1818–83) speak directly to those concerns. So do the writings and practice in the twentieth century of a series of political leaders from 'the South', like Mahatma Gandhi (1869–1948), Mao Tse-Tung (1893–1976) and Julius Nyerere (1922–99); and the work of the international human rights movement, especially on economic and social rights. The inter-church and inter-religion work on global ethics led since the 1980s by the dissident Catholic theologian Hans Küng is also relevant.

Deserving mention as a bridging figure is the Swedish economist (Nobel prize winner in 1974), sociologist and administrator Gunnar Myrdal (1898–1987). His widely disseminated writings from five decades, both theoretical and case-based, revived systematic attention to the value choices in social science and policy, especially in economics (e.g. Myrdal 1958). The focus on development in the South which he added in the last thirty-five years of his life helped to spread this concern into development studies (e.g. Myrdal 1968).

The label 'development ethics' appeared in the 1950s, in the work of Louis-Joseph Lebret, a French economist (1897–1966; see e.g. Lebret 1959). Both the label and the core agenda acquired wider attention in the 1970s due in considerable part to Denis Goulet (1931–), especially through his book *The Cruel Choice: A New Concept in the Theory of Development* (1971). Goulet is an eloquent multi-disciplinary American existentialist thinker with strong Brazilian links – an earlier version of *The Cruel Choice* appeared in Portuguese – who researched also in France, Spain, North Africa and South Asia. Complementary to his contribution was *Pyramids of Sacrifice* (1974) by the sociologist Peter Berger (1927–). Lebret, Goulet and Berger did not originate the questions in development ethics but they did generate a conscious coherent field of work. Goulet in particular defined and sustained the project.

There were other important influences in the 1960s and 1970s towards crystallisation of the field. E. F. Schumacher (1911–77), founder of the Intermediate Technology movement, wrote on the themes 'small is beautiful' and 'Buddhist economics' (Schumacher 1973). Deeper attention was paid to the moral premises of redistributive public action and international aid, following attacks from the New Right (see e.g. Bauer 1971; Lal 1976; and the commentary in Gasper 1986).

In the 1980s Amartya Sen (1933–), the Indian economist and philosopher well known for work on social choice theory, welfare economics and famine, began to elaborate his capability theory of human welfare. This culminated in a 1999 book, *Development as Freedom*. The capability approach has grown into a major focus in development ethics, including through research programmes in the United Nations' World Institute for Development Economics Research and the UNDP's annual *Human Development Reports*. Within this framework, the American classicist and moral philosopher Martha Nussbaum (1947–) has expounded a related but distinct capabilities ethic of Aristotelian inspiration, notably in her *Women and Human Development* (2000). A less publicly prominent but also influential voice has been the British Kantian philosopher Onora O'Neill (1941–), in *Faces of Hunger* (1986) and later books.

The growing body of work is reflected in various university courses and academic conferences, for example since the late 1980s through the International Development Ethics Association (IDEA), headed by the American social philosopher David Crocker (1937–) and from 2002 by the British moral philosopher Nigel Dower (1942–). While its membership and activities have been mainly in the Americas, notably Central

America, IDEA has also held large conferences in India and Britain and stimulates other work.

More importantly, the 1990s saw a growing explicit ethical thrust in forums for development policy and practice: in the debates on aid, trade and development cooperation, for example on ethical trading, child labour, debt relief, intellectual property rights, environmental sustainability and humanitarian relief, and in growing attempts to establish and apply norms and codes of practice in relief and development work. This was not only through NGOs and citizens' movements. Some governments in the South, notably South Africa's, installed many human rights as constitutional principles; some Northern governments sought a human rights-based approach in development cooperation; and from the end of the 1990s even the World Bank under James Wolfensohn and the Inter-American Development Bank under Enrique Iglesias gave some programmatic attention to issues of development ethics (e.g. Serageldin & Martin-Brown eds 1998).

DEFINITIONS

The range of acute and debated ethical and value questions in or associated with development policy and practice leads us to the definition of development ethics provided a generation back by Denis Goulet. Development ethics (DE) is the examination of *'ethical and value questions posed by development theory, planning, and practice'* (Goulet 1977: 5). The definition's meaning depends naturally on how we interpret 'development', which we discuss more fully in Chapter 2.

David Crocker, another leading figure in the field, defined DE similarly as *'the normative or ethical assessment of the ends and means of Third World and global development'* (1991: 457). Constituent questions which he highlighted include: the meaning of 'development'; what are appropriate development choices, ends and means, in low-income countries; rich–poor relations, including what responsibilities do the rich (persons, countries) have to the poor; and who is to be involved in deciding on such questions and using what methods.

In both these definitions, development ethics is a field of study. However, the concept can be specified in rather different ways, just like 'ethics' more generally:

1. A person's or group's 'ethic' or 'ethics' is their set of *substantive beliefs about what is good or bad and right or wrong* in relations between people (and between societies, and humans and other life), i.e. their morality or morals. The words 'ethics' and 'morals'/'morality' are sometimes given different meanings, with for example morals presented as rules or commands, or referring to actual behaviour; but the original difference is only that 'ethics' is

a word of Greek origin and 'moral' has a Latin origin. People often use them interchangeably in the sense stated here; thus both 'ethical' and 'moral' can mean correct or right in relations between people. ('Normative' is a broader term than 'ethical' or 'moral', because it covers other types of values also, e.g. aesthetic values.)

2. 'Ethics' can also refer to *theories and principles* which guide morals ('ethics' in sense 1 above).

3. 'Ethics' is also *a field* (in fact a set of fields) *of study* which considers, and generates, such sets of substantive ethical beliefs and associated theories:
(a) descriptive (and explanatory) ethics is work that tries to identify, describe, and explain the features in and variations between sets of ethical beliefs; this is part of sociology, social anthropology, social psychology and cultural studies;
(b) prescriptive (or first-order or substantive) ethics is work that proposes and tries to justify ethical beliefs;
(c) methodological (or second-order) ethics is work that tries to identify, assess, and/or propose methods in first-order ethics.

Fields 3(b) and 3(c) cover 'ethics' (or 'moral philosophy') as a branch of philosophy. Academic philosophy often neglects descriptive and explanatory ethics, which weakens its basis for work in prescriptive and methodological ethics. This criticism has been forcefully made by sociologists, feminists and others. The danger is perhaps less extreme in development ethics, given its strong links to policy and to the social science-based field of development studies; but it remains substantial.

Each of the definitions for 'ethics' could be used for development ethics: (1) a set (or sets) of beliefs/ideas about morality in issues of development; (2) a theorised set of such beliefs; (3) the study of sets of such beliefs and the issues they concern. The third type, development ethics as a field of study, is the major sense used in this book.

1.3 HOW? ON METHODS AND ROLES

METHODS

Many readers may hold doubts about the meaning of 'development' and the justification of some things done under its name, but also have doubts about ethics. Is it not subjective or at least culturally relative? A better moment to consider this will be towards the end of the book, when the reader can judge on the basis of the analyses of specific questions in the intervening chapters, rather than only from general claims. However, it is worth highlighting that development ethics, like most or all ethics, makes reference to experience, to feelings, to logic and reasoning, to principles which actors themselves espouse or acknowledge, and to principles proffered by various theorists and leaders.

We can broadly distinguish three necessary, complementary stages of work: first-stage reactions to experience; second-stage abstracted systematisation of ideas; and third-stage application, including adaptation and also negotiation and compromise, in the face of a reality richer than any of the multiple available intellectual systems (Gasper 1996a).

The first stage involves what we can call a 'look and feel' phase. Writers and speakers ask us (or we ask ourselves): 'Look at this experience! – think and feel about it'. They ask for our attention, widen our experience, even open our eyes, and in the process perhaps broaden our categories. Often they ask us also to 'look at these claimed ethical principles and categories [autonomy, for example]; and consider how you view with them existing and new experiences'. The more intensively we examine cases, using such new or sharpened ideas and feelings, the more we can distinguish this as a separate type of work (Gasper 2000a).

The stage of systematising of ideas flows out of the first stage. It can begin with an 'identify and describe' phase of descriptive ethics. One seeks to clarify the values and value choices encountered in situations, and to describe any formalised systems of values present and any societal systems for making choices and articulating values. This phase blends into the next, trying to further systematise and assess. Activities here include clarifying concepts and checking logic, including the mutual consistency of different values, asking: 'What do you think your stated values will bring if fulfilled? And how can your higher values in fact be furthered?' Next, when considered necessary, follows a phase of innovation and even system-building: to establish new or modified concepts and schemata; to draw new analogies, connections, and comparisons; and to adjust both these and older ideas in the light of their implications. At the intersection of the second and third stages comes the activity of applying systematised ideas to draw conclusions about the adequacy of certain values, valuations, practices, and systems of values or value choice.

In the third stage, of practice, one has to use imperfect general ideas together with typically imperfect data about a range of relevant factors in often idiosyncratic real cases. One has to face the fact of limitations of any system of ideas when applied, and often the need to negotiate and compromise with other systems. Since theories are inherently limited, practical ethics is more than just 'applied' ethics, more than just applying general theories. One has to reflect on how to deal with uncertainty (some people prefer to deny it), and with the certainty of weaknesses in one's own conceptual schema (though again some people officially reject the possibility). How to deal with factors outside one's schema? How to deal with conflicting ethical viewpoints? And how to acquire sufficient support from across partly conflicting views in order to influence decisions?

'Stage' here can be thought of as like a theatre stage: an arena of thought and expression. 'Stage' also suggests a sequence, but with the provisos that we always need all three stages, and that there are feed-backs as well as feed-forwards. 'Stage' in ordinary language can also suggest that later levels could rank higher than those earlier, but here that connotation is weaker. Reacting to experience is far from necessarily being a primitive and preliminary stage. The way we see experience, and the experience we seek out, will depend on the ideas and skills we have developed. The three stages are instead complementary.

POSSIBLE ROLES OF DEVELOPMENT ETHICS

What realistically is the role of such a field of work? Development ethics could be seen first as *an academic sub-discipline*. This appears to be a more North American concern, reflecting the much greater scale of pro-fessional philosophy there. The field is, however, closer in structure and potential to an inter-disciplinary field than an academic sub-discipline (Gasper 1994). So it becomes seen differently (even with different views on which are its core topics) by different groups involved in it, say from the North and the South; but each group gains from the interaction with the others.

Next it can be seen as *a field of professional ethics*, comparable to business ethics, medical ethics, and so on. Its terrain covers: What should those working in 'development theory, planning and practice' do with and to and for their principals, clients, advisees, students, research sub-jects, and constituencies? What should they/we work on, whom should they/we work for, which criteria should they/we use in assessing and evaluating situations and policies? What sorts of 'vision' and motivation can sustain such prescriptions?

Thirdly and probably of most relevance and importance, it can be conceived as *a forum for serious reflection (including feeling), on a broader scale than implied in the traditional model of professional ethics*: amongst development policy-makers, planners, practitioners and activists, and their major clients, and amongst development studies academics and students. The main audience traditionally assumed in political philosophy was the state or, in other respects, individuals. But many collectives besides the state must be seen as moral agents, having agency and respon-sibility, including NGOs, community associations, international aid organisations, mass media, universities and private companies, especially large corporations.

For playing these roles effectively, especially the third role, I have argued (Gasper 1994) that development ethics should consciously:

- be an inter-disciplinary field: to involve philosophers, practitioners and social scientists of many types. From the introduction above of some

of its foci, origins and contributors, we can see that it has been fed by
a rich mixture of ideas and experiences, from many countries,
professions and disciplines;

- be an international field, including Southerners as well as Northerners,
East as well as West. There is important work in development ethics
by Latin Americans, Africans and Asians (such as Max-Neef 1989;
Shivji 1989; Gunatilleke et al. eds 1983);

- take a global view, looking at North as well as South and at their interrelations, and not be a 'ghetto specialisation' on the South only.
Increasingly it has become global.

GLOBAL OR SOUTHERN?

An issue apparent in David Crocker's definition, and implicit in Denis
Goulet's, is whether development ethics has a global scope or refers to
'developing countries': the low-income countries of the South, and also
now many of the former communist countries of eastern Europe following their economic collapse in the 1990s and the revision downwards of
the figures for their former income levels. Should it cover all countries?
Even if it covered 'developing countries' only, it would consider three-
quarters of the world by population, plus their relations with rich countries. One can point though to the difficulties of drawing a line between
'developing' and 'developed' countries; and to the concern that current
development in the North is unsustainable, unsatisfying, and damaging.
Fundamentally, if we look at the root concerns of development ethics –
the insistence on not equating societal improvement to economic growth,
and on identifying and comparing value and strategy alternatives; the
concern for not ignoring costs and their varieties and distribution – they
apply with almost equal force for rich countries.

It makes sense therefore to see development ethics as a subject of
global scope. It still has a natural primary focus on issues in and affecting
the South, given the South's predominance in the world in terms both of
population and need, and its subordination in most other terms. The broadening of the scope of development ethics parallels the evolution of development studies itself (see e.g. Hettne 1995). It in part reflects increasing
worldwide perception of the limits to salvation through economic growth.
Debates on the ethical premises and choices in 'sustainable development'
are certainly branches of development ethics, and at the same time
promote its integration into a broad global ethics.

Nigel Dower (1988, 1992) has added a definition of development
ethics in which global scope is explicit, and which also tries to make clear
the relationship of this field in practical ethics to others, to establish what
it does not cover. In his view development ethics treats moral issues that

arise in partly controllable social change, at whatever social level, whether in economically rich or poor countries or in their mutual relations. He makes a case for thinking of it as a single field, which parallels traditional ethics' question: 'How ought one to live as an individual?' by asking in addition: 'How ought a society to exist and move into the future?' Elsewhere he and others add a similar question for world society, as another part of the broader field of world ethics which he has delineated (e.g. Dower 1998). Questions of boundary definition – where does development ethics end? – remain; but this is true for other areas of practical ethics such as business ethics, and is manageable when viewed in that practical perspective.

This chapter has given an introduction to the character, emergence and rationale, and scope and methods of development ethics. The central theme of Chapters 2 to 8 is 'What is development?' as a normative ideal and set of concerns and criteria. In the course of examining proposed answers we will go further with many of the issues which have been raised in this chapter – notably poverty and undeserved suffering; distribution of the costs of change; sickness and violence; and the significance of culture.

DISCUSSION THEMES

1. What ethical questions do you find important and/or interesting about economic/ social/political development?
2. Why do ethical questions arise about economic/social/political development?
3. What is ethics? – what sorts of questions does it consider?
4. What sorts of methods can be used in ethics?

READING SUGGESTIONS

Crocker (1991) reviews the types of question that have led to, and are treated in, the more formal and self-conscious work on development ethics that emerged in the 1970s and 1980s. Gasper (1994) asks: 'What is development ethics?', and illustrates some of the major questions and viewpoints found in it, with reference to issues around international development asistance. Chapter 1 of White & Tiongco (1997) gives an interesting discussion of core questions in a theological treatment of development. Dower (1998)'s two chapters 'Aid, trade and development' and 'The environment and sustainable development' provide structured overviews of differing ethical positions in those areas. Goulet (1971) and Berger (1974) remain worth reading. In a 1987 sequel, Berger argued that his calculi of political ethics showed the superior performance and prospects of capitalism over state socialism.

On methods in ethics, Gasper (1996a, 2000a) discusses three complementary stages of work in ethics, with special reference to development ethics: reactions to experience; systematisation of ideas; and adaptation in application. White & Tiongco's 'pastoral cycle' is similar – first experience, then analysis, then action and review; see also Hicks (2000). Nagel (1987) and Held (1990) are helpful short extracts about methods of thinking in ethics (including both reasoning and feeling). Some recommended introductions to ethics for general readers are Williams (1972) and Singer (1997, ed. 1994).

CHAPTER 2

THE MEANING OF 'DEVELOPMENT'

2.1 PURPOSES AND THEMES

What do people mean by the term 'development'? Many different things. Even a single person is likely to use the term in several ways, and across people we see further variation. 'Development' is a seductive term which has had connotations historically of the unfolding of a necessary path of progress. Its usage has often combined ideas of necessity, influenceable change and fundamental improvement. Taking different aspects of this historical package of ideas gives different definitions.

This chapter tries to provide a map of the forest of meanings of 'development', with special attention to normative meanings. It is not concerned to debate the contents of development policy, but to clarify the goals and values to which policy is oriented. We are also not seeking to identify the single 'proper' meaning of 'development', though the precise scope of development ethics might depend on how broadly development is construed. There is no such, precise, single meaning. Instead we can increase our sensitivity to the types and range of meanings.

First, we need to distinguish between 'positive' (i.e. neutral, non-evaluative) and evaluative meanings. We do this in the second section. With positive meanings people do not have to share ethical values in order to agree on applications of the concept – for example if development is defined as urbanisation or high monetary income per capita (though this second example is somewhat marginal, as we will see). With evaluative meanings – for example development defined as high quality of life – people usually must share ethical values, at least to a substantial degree, in order to agree on application.

Second, we should understand why positive and evaluative meanings often become intertwined. We typically mainly describe the things that we value; further, as we will see, the entanglement can have a motivational and vindicatory role. However, even though the positive-versus-evaluative distinction is imperfect, sometimes a matter of degree, it is important. Since the term 'development' can legitimately take either type of meaning, and is often used to have both types simultaneously, a series of dangers arises. The term can be used vaguely and inconsistently, and without awareness of the values adopted in particular evaluative usages of 'development'. If we are not aware that value choices are involved we do not remain neutral; instead we are likely to adopt hidden values. Certain types of social change (e.g. industrialisation or commercialisation) become defined as 'development' *and* automatically considered good ('progressive'), regardless of their actual effects and the possible alternatives to them in particular cases. So both our evaluation and choice of social change become undermined. Without a positive/evaluative contrast, key purposes of development ethics – to identify the values used and to consider alternative values and actions – would be undermined.

Casualness and potential for confusion are reflected in the very terms we inherit, since 'positive' in English means both 'non-evaluative' and 'favourable'. The confusion arises because measurement of the degree of fulfilment of some desired value can often be done in a neutral way. The measured performance can be 'positive', meaning 'above zero on the measurement scale', and 'favourable, desirable'; while the measurement process has been 'positive' in the third sense – non-evaluative, not depending on shared values concerning the merit of what is measured. While 'positive/normative' is the standard pair of terms for this last contrast, for our purposes we will often use the pair 'neutral/evaluative'. 'Evaluative' is a subset of 'normative' and concerns judgements of good/bad. ('Normative' also includes 'prescriptive', judgements of what should be done.)

Third, we should distinguish and understand the roles both of ahistorical conceptualisations of development, such as development as industrialisation or progress, and of historically specific conceptualisations, such as 'the transformation of the West/North since 1500 and its impact on the East/South'. Neither type is exclusively correct; both are helpful for those working in development studies and practice. In section 2.3 we look at some historically specific positive definitions. They prove to have normative aspects too, for the positive aspects which are focused on have often tacitly been selected for their assumed normative importance.

In section 2.4 we examine ahistorical evaluative definitions. This is probably the predominant branch, and is a central focus of development ethics. We will see a number of important contrasts within this class of definitions. The chapter's fourth issue concerns the contrast between achievement definitions and opportunity definitions, with a subsidiary question regarding whether the definitions focus on being or having. The fifth issue contrasts universalist and relativist definitions: are the criteria for development universal, or specific to a particular place and group and its values? (Relativity according to time takes us to other historically

neutral/evaluative

specific definitions.) One relativist evaluative definition is that 'development' means whatever a particular group prefers. In the past generation a major broadening has occurred in the aspects of life emphasised in universalistic evaluative definitions. These now extend far beyond the aspects covered by GNP per capita, for example to refer to peace, security and non-violence.

The last major issue concerns whether, although evaluative meanings of 'development' may differ, according for example to their different visions of 'the good life', there are still important common elements (actually shared, or logically and/or ethically required) across all these different views. Many authors argue that there are. Some do so by asserting as universally shared normative requirements the conditions for being able to act in pursuit of whatever one's other values are, rather than any uniformity in those other values. We might agree more on required opportunities and capacities than on required destinations. How adequate are such definitions that see development as providing the preconditions for unspecified ends?

2.2 AHISTORICAL DEFINITIONS OF 'DEVELOPMENT'

USAGES ACROSS THE DISCIPLINES

'Development' is a term ubiquitous in daily language. It can refer to the emergence or elaboration or evolution or improvement of almost anything: an idea, a paper, a project, a musical theme. It refers too to the unveiling and fulfilment of an inner potential, as of the images hidden within exposed photographic film; it is the opposite of envelopment.

In biology, 'development' combines these two aspects, elaboration and unveiling/ fruition, to suggest a drawing from inherent potentials to achieve preset ends. One sees university posts advertised for developmental biology ('for any aspect of animal development'), plant development, developmental genetics ('including molecular evolution of genomes, mutational processes') and so on. The biology usage matches the definition of development as 'a stage of growth or maturation or advancement' (*Oxford English Reference Dictionary*). It has had great influence in social science too.

The usage extends into psychology, with some modulation. Developmental psychology is a huge field concerned with the maturation of individual persons. A book such as Nancy Eisenberg's *Social Development* (ed. 1995) looks at socialisation of the individual, while Harke Bosma et al.'s *Identity and Development* (1994) considers how individuals' senses of identity emerge and change. We see university departments and centres of human development studies (the one at Massey University, for example, considers 'lifespan human development', infants and families, adolescence, adult learning, etc.), developmental disability studies and developmental language studies.

In a very different field, the University of Glamorgan has a Department of Property and Development Studies. 'Property development' is a transitive usage. Development here is thanks to the action of an outsider, not to the action of that which becomes developed. Property developers, like architects, sometimes feel, however, that their work unveils the potential of a site.

We clearly have a range of scales and agents in 'development'. Scale varies, from cells to organs, to individual persons, families and groups, to localities and sub-national regions, countries, the world, and beyond. From those human sciences which focus on systems at a higher level than the individual, a field of 'development studies' emerged during the past half century, looking at nations, localities, regions and the world. As it has come to reflect more on ethical priorities and choices, this field has increasingly returned to consider individuals too.

USAGES IN DEVELOPMENT STUDIES

We see the following four major types of usage of 'development' in development studies literature (cf. Gasper 1996a; Thomas 2000):

A. More neutral ('positive', non-evaluative) usages
  1. Development as fundamental or structural change
  2. Development as intervention, action
B. More evaluative usages
  1. Development as improvement, good change; or as the good outcome
  2. Development as the platform for improvement, that which enables or allows improvement.

The qualifier 'more' acknowledges that usages may not be pure cases. But differences in emphasis remain clear, and important. A writer can present some changes as fundamental, say changes in social structure, without offering or implying a judgement as to whether the change was good or bad.

A. More neutral usages

A1. First, 'development' may be seen as *change, especially fundamental/ structural/ 'qualitative' change.* We should note that 'change' can be interpreted as either the process of change or the outcome.

In the crudest usage, development is equated with economic growth, or, in outcome terms, GDP per capita. GDP stands for gross domestic product. It is a measure of the value of goods and services produced by a national economy over a year. To avoid double counting, only goods used for final consumption or investment are included, not those used up in producing the final goods. Gross national product (GNP) adds to GDP the income that accrues to domestic residents from investment abroad, and deducts the income earned in the domestic economy which is owned by people abroad (Bannock et al. 1992). GNP per capita is therefore the better measure of development as welfare (though still not a good one), while GDP per capita is a better measure of productive forces. ,

Peter Berger proposed that we need more than one term, in fact at least three. We should contrast economic growth with *modernisation*, seen as the major structural changes required or implied by long-term economic growth, including industrialisation, urbanisation, globalisation, and the transformation of relations of production. He reserved the term 'development' to mean such changes which we conclude are desirable. For many other writers, in contrast, (economic) development means (economic) growth plus technological modernisation.

An idea which has been enormously influential and which supported the conception of development as 'structural change' is that development occurs, indeed must occur, in a fixed series of stages. Major variants of this approach were found in Marxism and Walt W. Rostow's *The Stages of Economic Growth* (1960).

A2. Second, we have the transitive usage, 'we develop you': 'development' as *action, intervention, aimed at improvement*. Whether the intervention achieves improvement remains a separate question.

Roland Koch argues that the transitive concept of development typically involves a claim that we develop you because we understand appropriate ends and means better and sufficiently; we understand the necessary and beneficial logic of economic change and modernization, revealed by history and economics. Just as a genetic code determines much of an organism's unfolding, so the logic of economic advance is asserted to determine necessary ends and means (Koch 1993, cited in Lopes de Souza 1999). Marcelo Lopes de Souza contrasts this transitive concept with both the unconscious self-development of an organism and the reflexive self-development of conscious agents ('we develop ourselves'). Two claims in favour of self-development rather than 'you develop us' are that it is often more effective and inherently more desirable. Such claims lead us to normative usages. Some are directly evaluative, others are about instrumental roles.

B. More evaluative usages

B1. Third, 'development' can mean '*improvement, good change*'; or, in outcome form, 'an achieved improvement' or 'a good state or situation'.

Why should improvement be called 'development'? Thanks to the biological metaphor for societies. To underline the difference from the neutral usage (A1), prefixes like 'genuine' or 'real' are sometimes added here to 'development' (e.g. Slim 1995). Studies of development in biology and social psychology go on to cover the ageing, decline and death of organisms, and even, in palaeontology, extinction of species. Optimistic social science rejects these associations for advanced human groups and the species as a whole.

The scope of improvement usages varies. In perhaps declining order of scope, 'development' can be described as (1) all good change; (2) desirable economic growth and modernisation (Berger's usage); (3) fulfilment of *good* potentials, or maturation to allow that fulfilment (e.g. Segal 1986, cited in Crocker 1991); or, verging on a historically specific definition, (4) fulfilment of the potential to greatly increase material welfare and reduce suffering in the South – a potential which became dramatically visible at least from the late 1940s.

We see the 'good situation' usage of 'development' extended even to cases where there was no major change in the known past, as in arguments that some peoples' way of life is well developed even though they are far distant from the path of modern technology and economic organisation. The San peoples of the Kalahari in southern Africa used to sustain themselves with relatively few hours of work. Goodwin (1994, cited in Margulis 1994) relates how the Hunza in the far north of Pakistan enjoy extraordinary average levels of health, and shun, after bad experiences, use of chemicals on their lands and crops. Fallon (1999) generalises this picture of health to all isolated traditional peoples. If, however, we compare affluent modern populations not with small remote groups but with the mass of preindustrialised rural and urban populations, we see impressive gains in life expectancy and reduced morbidity, as well as in education and other indicators.

If 'development' means 'improvement' or 'a good state', then economic growth, technological modernisation and whatever else are only hypothesised means towards development. The hypothesis may become hidden and forgotten. Some authors suggest that because capitalist expansion benefits ruling groups, its model of economic growth becomes identified with development *in toto*: a proposed means becomes seen as the only appropriate end. The biological metaphor of a precoded potential to unfold also contributed to this idea of a single necessary path of improvement.

Improvement as judged by whom? Many authors declare: the people. 'Whatever in the mind of a people represents improvement, progress, an advance of collective welfare, may be viewed as development,' argue Valaskakis & Martin (1980: 89). Earlier they propose even more broadly that 'only the subject (whether an individual, an ethnic group or a nation)

→ Do Africans want change?

be the ultimate decider of what is and what not development' (ibid.: 89). Yet in many important cases these three deciders disagree. In other respects too this very open definition raises questions: concerning how the mind of a people has been formed, possible commonalities in the ends people choose, and possible universally required means for self-determination.

B2. Fourth, 'development' can be interpreted instrumentally, as *that which facilitates or enables improvement*. Denis Goulet adopted this fourth usage: development refers to those changes which are instrumental towards improvement (e.g. Goulet 1995). What is seen as development here is both value relative (it depends on what is considered progress) and theory relative (it depends on theories about what will lead to that).

Barth (1992) proposes that subjectively chosen definitions are more effective for furthering action and improvement. So if we adopt the instrumental usage then part of development may be to make one's own definition of development.

If something – perhaps women's education – automatically furthers improvement, there is a tendency to include it in the very definition of improvement. If it only provides the basis, the opportunity, for improvement, then we have three stages: (1) 'development', i.e. changes which create (2) opportunities for (3) improvement. Opportunities may or may not be taken.

Martin de Graaf's influential paper 'Catching Fish or Liberating Man' (1996) combined the third and fourth usages (B1, B2), evaluative and instrumental. He argued that development is about developing people – growth of capacity and capabilities – both for itself and because it is instrumentally crucial. John Maynard Keynes also spanned these two usages with his aphorism that 'economic development is the possibility of development' (quoted in Roy 1994). He reserved the term 'development' for improvement, which 'economic development' allows but does not guarantee.

One can encounter deep resistance to distinguishing meanings and turning 'development' into a family of concepts, each of which captures different aspects of complex situations and processes of change. Some people show a strong desire to believe that there is a single thing to be described, that all aspects must go together. Besides lack of conceptual sophistication, other forces contribute to this: the allure of the economic growth programme, with its vision of salvation through good feeds; and the wish to deny alternatives, in order to force societies into the bright future which supposedly they can achieve if prepared to undergo some pain. The term 'development' helps to span the aspects, motivate, and justify the pain. Similarly, for those predisposed instead to condemn, a single oversimplified target is far more convenient.

2.3 HISTORICALLY SPECIFIC CONCEPTIONS OF DEVELOPMENT: ON CHANGE, INTERVENTION AND PROGRESS

Some other definitions of development include specific historical reference. Table 2.1 contrasts them with the ahistorical sorts of meaning that we have just considered.

Lately a number of thinkers have declared that 'development' is a concept and practice that dates from the end of the Second World War – and which probably will not and should not survive long in the twenty-first century. It represents a specific era in which countries of the South and East tried to copy the Northern economic growth model which had emerged in the previous two centuries; an era thus already dominated by giant industrial economies but with a space provided by the decline of colonialism and an intensified conflict between the capitalist and socialist versions of the economic growth model. Many authors, such as those in *The Development Dictionary* (Sachs ed. 1992), refer to 'development' as the agenda laid down in US president Harry Truman's 1949 inauguration speech, to extend and intensify the longstanding Westernisation project, now minus the negative connotations of colonialism and with comprehensive global scope: 'Development's hidden agenda was nothing less than the Westernization of the world,' declares Sachs (1992: 3–4). Those who remember the Soviet Union and its major global influence for much of the twentieth century may highlight a North–South rather than West–East contrast here.

The theory that 'development' dates from the 1940s has become quite popular. It seems to reflect a perspective from Latin America. The Spanish and Portuguese colonies in Latin America attained independence in the early nineteenth century, almost a century and a half before most

Table 2.1 Ahistorical and historically specific definitions of development

DEFINITIONS OF DEVELOPMENT	*POSITIVE (VALUE-NEUTRAL)*	*EVALUATIVE*
AHISTORICAL	E.g. rise of GDP per capita; industrialisation	E.g. increase of universally specified priority capabilities
HISTORICALLY SPECIFIC	E.g. rise and expansion of Western European cultures from the 15th century; attempted spread of Northern growth models to the South since 1945	E.g. fulfilment of the stated preferences of group X at time Y (including preferences not reflected in GDP)

countries in Africa and Asia, indeed long before many of those had become colonies. In the late 1940s and early 1950s Latin America awoke to find itself, to its surprise and chagrin, now classified as 'under-developed' by the new United Nations and its dominant member the USA, alongside nearly all of Africa and Asia. Its poverty was now deemed a problem, seen as fertile ground for Communism. By the criteria of the newly created national economic accounting, Latin America was found wanting and backward compared to its affluent, thrusting northern neighbour. From this rude awakening, Latin America flung itself expec-tantly into the new world of national economic plans, capital–output ratios, 'growth poles' and the like, the world which some of its intellec-tuals later came to sceptically label 'developmentalism'.

Yet 'development' did not begin in the 1940s. Sun Yat-Sen, the founder of republican China, published a book entitled *International Development of China* in 1922. In other countries and earlier periods many worked on parallel themes. We are indebted to Cowen and Shenton (1996) for a massive history of the concept and practice of 'development' in the past two centuries. It shows all four types of concept from section 2.2 in extensive use from the early nineteenth century, although they present the concept of 'development' as primarily attached to the idea of intervention, in the schools of Henri de Saint-Simon (1760–1825) and Auguste Comte (1798–1857). Fundamental socio-economic change (our usage A1) was seen to involve great costs and destruction; it is profoundly normatively mixed. Scientifically guided intervention (A2) could channel this creative destruction towards improvement (B1), or at least to establishing the basis for improvement (B2). Marshall Berman's *All That Is Solid Melts into Air* similarly discusses the 'desire for development' shown by the protagonist in Johann Wolfgang von Goethe's drama *Faust* (1808–32). 'Goethe's Faust is the first, and still the best, tragedy of development' (Berman 1983: 39–40). Nor is planned earthly improve-ment a project that began in the eighteenth century (see e.g. Wallerstein 1991, for an overview from the late fifteenth century on), or one unique to the West. Let us take a longer-term picture than the Latin America-centred view.

We might discern, roughly speaking (and from a Northern develop-ment studies institute at the turn of the millennium), three ages or eras of development. The first spans 'developments' from 'the rise of man' to the emergence of modern states in Europe around the sixteenth century – notably the emergence and evolution of agriculture, cities, and civilisa-tions. The second consists of 'the rise of Europe' (and North America). The third is 'the global development era' from 1945 (or, some authors prefer, 1917).

The rise of Europe had perhaps two main phases. The earlier, from the sixteenth to the late eighteenth century, showed a modest but clear and highly significant acceleration of socio-economic advance, reflecting a strengthening of several driving forces: market systems, capitalist institutions and culture, global commerce and colonisation, and inter-state rivalry. A second phase, from the nineteenth to the mid-twentieth century, achieved further acceleration, based on the increasing ability to generate and apply science via technology in economic production and social management, and increased inter-state rivalry in the face of the emergence of the first industrial nation, Britain. A consequence was the rapid colonisation or quasi-colonisation of much of the rest of the world by European settlers and armies. Global spread of disease was one side effect:

> Cholera, perhaps previously endemic in the Indian subcontinent, spread outside it for the first time in 1817, probably carried by the personnel of the British Raj. It reached Europe in 1829, and then moved on to North America with Irish emigrants escaping the 1840s famine. That cholera was waterborne, and that resistance was far higher amongst healthy well-fed people, was demonstrated by John Snow, a London doctor, in the 1840s; and the bacillus responsible was isolated by the German biologist Robert Koch in Calcutta in 1883. (Radford 2000)

Much of social ethics, including liberalism and utilitarianism, emerged to advise on the ordering and rationalising of a commercialising, urbanising, industrialising society. Some theories, such as John Locke's doctrine of property, can be read as proposed justification for those who acquired the Americas and other 'countries of new settlement' against the wishes of the resident populations.

The third era extends from around the end of the Second World War. It involves intensive, conscious and coordinated interventions worldwide to pursue improvement, particularly via economic growth. The examples, and largely the methods, of Europe and America predominate, including until 1990 those of the Soviet Union. What distinguishes this phase is neither its intensive intervention nor a global scale, but its comprehensiveness, extending to all countries and involving an elaborate though economics-dominated body of doctrine. Conscious major state-led intervention for national economic advance dates at the latest from around the 1860s for Germany, Russia, Japan and many of the lands of new European settlement. Much of Latin America, Turkey, and elsewhere joined a generation or two later. Development was already global. The 1940s brought a set of factors that added universality and urgency: the beginning of decolonisation and the formation of the United Nations; the perception of a now vast, quantified gap between technological potentials and the levels of living in most of the world; and the pressure of competition between capitalist and Communist models, highlighted by the Communist capture of power in 1949 in the world's most populous country.

In the post-colonial states, 'development' meant both social improvements and 'catching up', to restore parity of power and esteem with those more advanced. National unity was built around the belief that these two objectives were complementary. In reality, argues Wallerstein (1991), choices between them were often necessary. Some ruling elites have prioritised 'catching up': including costly armaments, national airlines, and more sacrifices for the poor.

The 1990s may have opened a new sub-phase, given the defeat of Communism, gradual shifting of the world centre of gravity away from the North Atlantic, and increasing doubts concerning the feasibility and desirability (social, cultural, and environmental) of permanent modernist 'development'. Predominant concerns of development from the 1950s through to the 1980s included moving beyond colonialism, achieving post-colonial self-respect and independence through material advance, and aiming to match the ongoing enormous such advance seen from the 1940s in the North and West. By the 1990s and into the new century, the predominant concerns have perhaps evolved to trying to come to terms with globalisation – an integrated global economy, power system and cultural web; with polarisation, in and especially between societies, as some regions of the world struggle with new disease burdens and endemic conflict and inevitably then influence other parts; and with identifying and respecting or evading the limits to consumerism, the quest for answers through commodities.

Some authors employ a historical usage of 'development' but delimit it by also using a specific concept of development such as one of those noted earlier: economic growth, industrialisation, societal modernisation, Westernisation, state action, national strengthening, increase of positive freedom, increase of well-being, spiritual advance, or whatever. One can draw a matrix with such concepts as one dimension, and different temporal starting points as the other dimension – development as from the start of time, or from 1500/1492, or from 1945, and so on. Other relevant start dates are 1750 and the 1860s. Dozens of possible usages can then be distinguished and very many are found in practice.

2.4 ON IMPROVEMENT: ISSUES IN EVALUATIVE AHISTORICAL DEFINITION

What is improvement, what is a better life? Some definitions of development offer universal criteria; others instead argue or assume that improvement is whatever a society or community or individual concludes it to be. Intermediate or mixed positions are possible: some stances, for example, finesse the contrast by arguing that all societies happen to, or can, agree on certain values; or by arguing that development consists of providing preconditions for whatever form of better life decision-makers perceive, and that these preconditions have a large degree of universality and provide a range of opportunities which decision-makers can choose from. Thus three related issues deserve attention:

- the balance between universalism and relativism, with the choice between objectivism and subjectivism as an ancillary issue;
- the degree of commonality across positions;
- the now widespread use of instrumental definitions of development, in which development is seen as providing opportunity, choice, freedom; with an ancillary choice between opportunity to have or opportunity to be.

We can start with the choice between instrumental usages and end-state evaluative usages, in other words between definitions in terms of opportunity and of achievement (types B2 and B1 in section 2.2). We then look at the claims of GNP/GDP per capita as a normative measure of development. Its continuing attraction despite crippling defects partly lies in its ability to seem both a measure of opportunity and of achievement, both a universal measure and one sensitive to differing local values.

DEVELOPMENT AS OPPORTUNITY OR AS ACHIEVEMENT?

'Development' may refer to a desired end state, or to the precondition which permits what is desired. If the latter, then it easily links to neutral definitions of development as a type of fundamental change, say industrialisation. Instrumental definitions have long been popular, with development seen as providing opportunity to achieve what one wants, allowing choice between different goods and ways of life.

For several decades the United Nations, the most representative organisation in the world, has established and used definitions of development and related concepts. For a long time it used GDP per capita as the single measure, and indeed perhaps definition, of development. In the 1980s the UN Committee for Development Planning added non-GDP criteria for specifying the least developed countries. Three criteria were then used:

1a. a cut-off point for per capita GDP (US$473 in 1990), but with
1b. a higher cut-off point (US$ 567 in 1990) in case a country fulfilled both the other criteria;
2. a manufacturing share of 10 per cent or less in total GDP;
3. a literacy rate of 20 per cent or less.

A country would be declared least developed if it satisfied criteria 1b + 2 + 3, or 1a + 2. In 1990 a more complicated, broad-based definition was recommended. It was still an instrumental definition which sought to measure the economic basis for promoting human advance: 'Least developed countries shall be defined as those low-income countries that are suffering from long-term handicaps to development, in particular, low levels of human resources development and/or severe structural weak-nesses' (Simonis 1992: 4). The underlying concept of 'development' appeared to remain long-term growth of per-capita GDP.

From 1990 the work for UNDP on 'human development' arrived at an alternative concept, long familiar in various other development circles: 'development embraces not only access to goods and services, but also the opportunity to choose a fully satisfying, valuable and valued way of living together, the flourishing of human existence in all its forms and as a whole' (World Commission on Culture and Development 1995: 15). 'Human development can be expressed as a process of enlarging people's choices' (Human Development Report 1996: 49). Economic development and 'human development' thus became concepts which were emphasised by different sections in the UN. In the same way as John Maynard Keynes had done, 'economic development' is seen as providing the opportunity for 'development' in broader terms, but not as guaranteeing it; and this broader 'human development' itself consists in individual persons having a wide range of valuable opportunities, which they might or might not use well.

Let us examine some examples. The then Minister of Local Govern-ment, Rural and Urban Development in Zimbabwe, John Nkomo, offered an opportunity-for-being definition of development: 'a process of change in social structures, physical infrastructure, technology and skills, culture and moral and spiritual values which creates conditions and an environment for a happier and more contented humanity' (1995: 3). This combines a neutral description-of-change component, namely the acquisi-tion and having of infrastructure etc., with a specification of the desired outcome (happier and more contented people) for which the specified changes are considered instrumental, that is, provide the opportunity.

A document of the Baha'i religion provides a more extended example. It proposes that (1) economic advance is only a means, and that what it allows, (2) fulfilment of basic needs for housing, health and so on, is also only a means, towards (3) 'extending the reach of human abilities' so as to provide 'foundations for (4) a new social order that can (5) cultivate the limitless potentialities latent in human consciousness' (Baha'i Inter-national Community 1999: 18; enumeration added).

The conception of development as enlargement of people's choices comes from Amartya Sen and originally from the Nobel Prize-winning

Caribbean economist Arthur Lewis (1915–91). For Lewis development meant widening the 'range of human choices' Lewis 1955; cited in HDR 1996: 46). Valuable options are what matter, not simply having more options: one might prefer a situation in which one has little or no choice, except the opportunity to achieve what one wants most, over a situation in which one has a surfeit of choices, distractions and temptations, even if that wide range includes one's most desired option. (Elster (1984), explores this scenario, starting from the case of Ulysses and the Sirens.) The UNDP's *Human Development Reports* (HDRs) thus stress 'people's capabilities to lead the lives they value'. This can be read as a liberal position which trusts that people's values are reasonable or which sees values as beyond reason. Sen, however, adds that the relevant choices are those between things which people have *reason* to value.

Choice is stressed in this conception of development for it takes choosing as quintessentially human. Robert Nozick (1938–2002), the prominent American libertarian philosopher, argued in 'The Experience Machine' (1974b) that people want not only pleasure, but the knowledge that they are acting independently, in direct contact with reality. He proposed, perhaps optimistically, that people would not opt to spend their lives connected to a machine which simulates for them, with a complete feeling of reality, whichever pleasing or exciting situations they wish. This sort of perspective can be shared across otherwise large ideological divides. Anisur Rahman, for example, a radical Bangladeshi development economist, similarly contrasts 'consumerist' and 'creativist' (or 'activist') views of development (Rahman 1992).

The popularity of precondition/opportunity definitions such as Sen's 'capability' language, partly comes from problems with state-of-satisfaction definitions; levels of felt satisfaction are so relative to personality and expectations. However, other types of outcome definition are possible (including in terms of 'functionings', in Sen's language), and many people want the concept of development to have a direct concern with valuable being, not only with the capability for valuable being. For example:

> Development is a process transforming structures – particularly those of production-consumption and major institutions – so that 'basic human needs are satisfied for an increasing number of individuals at an increasingly high level' (M. Markovic), within the framework of meaning provided by culture and the outer limits provided by nature. (Galtung 1980: 105)

This definition again includes reference to instrumentally useful changes, but now requires that they bring greater satisfaction of basic human needs, not merely provide the opportunity for that.

In Table 2.2, provided that the havings and beings referred to are desirable, cases 1 to 4 might form a sequence of ascending importance: an

Table 2.2 Development as opportunity or outcome and as having or being

TYPES OF DEFINITION	*OPPORTUNITY*	*OUTCOME*
STATE OF HAVING	1: Opportunity to have	2: A having outcome
STATE OF BEING	3: Opportunity to be	4: A being outcome

opportunity to have (case 1) may be less valuable than an outcome of actually having (case 2). Having will often provide an opportunity to be (case 3), which is still less valuable than the being outcome (case 4).

In practice, having-outcome concepts are often used as indicators for opportunity concepts (e.g. GNP per capita is used as an indicator of people's range of options), which in turn are used as indicators for the being-outcome concepts (e.g. happiness). A low-level outcome concept like GNP per capita thus unfortunately becomes taken as an indicator for a high-level outcome concept like happiness.

Beyond the definition in terms of choice, the HDRs have extended the human development concept far beyond the aspects covered in their Human Development Index (HDI), which are limited to those for which data can be obtained for all countries. The concept now encompasses:

1. empowerment, seen in the expansion of capabilities, plus participation;
2. equity in distribution of basic capabilities and opportunities, so that everybody has at least a certain minimum; choices must be not only for the rich;
3. sustainability, of 'people's opportunities to freely exercise their basic capabilities';
4. community membership, belonging;
5. security, notably in people's daily lives (HDR 1996: 55–6).

The additions recognise that human life is too complex to be captured by one slogan about choice or capabilities (although the HDRs sometimes still use it). The UNDP also now includes both 'fulfilment and capability' in its definition of 'development' (HDR 2000: 17).

THE GROSSNESS OF GROSS NATIONAL/DOMESTIC PRODUCT

We saw that GNP per capita is a somewhat better measure of welfare than its sibling GDP per capita. It is still highly unsatisfactory. These concepts were never designed as measures of well-being; instead they measure monetised economic activity. As normative measures they have massive failings, even granted that they measure opportunities rather than achievement of well-being: for they include much which should be excluded for normative purposes, exclude much which should be included, and weight inequitably whatever is included. Despite decades of criticism (e.g.

Mishan 1967) their use as welfare measures continues on a large scale. Even innovators in the economics profession such as Amartya Sen and Partha Dasgupta still in their 1990s work took GNP/GDP per capita as a component of well-being measurement, since it is a measure calculated for all territories. They supplemented rather than avoided it. In what follows we will speak of GDP, the more widely available measure, but the comments all apply to GNP also.

Much of GDP measures lack of or loss of well-being: it includes many things which are costs rather than benefits, like commuter travel, or which merely counteract other costs caused by economic growth itself ('defensive expenditures'), like waste disposal and counteracting the effects of environmental pollution. Defensive costs grow far faster than GDP in rich countries (Ekins & Max-Neef eds 1992: 254). For example, economic growth sometimes contributes to stress, illness and conflict, all of which are unmeasured in GDP and which need not necessarily feed back to reduce it. But a number of the responses to the problems – increased expenditure on medicines and on medical, welfare, police and legal services – will add to GDP. Conflict-induced (and sometimes conflict-inducing) military and security expenditures often form a major boost to GDP. Thus net economic performance can easily be portrayed as improving while net societal performance declines (as shown by e.g. Daly & Cobb 1989).

A second wrong inclusion for a normative measure is that GDP includes investment, not only consumption. Dasgupta's 2001 treatise on well-being recognises that we should use final consumption per capita instead of GDP per capita for that part of present well-being related to the measured economy. Even there, economists' figures for final consumption include for example armaments production (and GDP further includes the costs of later decommissioning).

Major exclusions are, first, that GDP ignores non-monetised aspects of or contributors to well-being, such as household work, leisure, freedom (UNDP 1996: 56-7), good health, interesting work and pleasant surroundings, and aspects of ill-being such as uncountered pollution. Second, it ignores inter-personal distribution, and instead weights costs and benefits according to the purchasing power of the recipient. Luxuries of the rich receive great weight; the goals of the moneyless receive none, and frequently remain unfulfilled. Thirdly, GDP is a gross, not a net, measure, and ignores the use of stocks of capital. In normative discussion one should at least refer to net product. Even current measures of NDP (net domestic product) still ignore non-commoditised forms of capital, notably environmental capital (Dasgupta 2001).

Given these massive failings, one alternative is to try to modify GNP/GDP for each of the above deficiencies (see e.g. Daly & Cobb 1989). In converting a measure of monetised economic activity into a measure of sustainable capacity or of welfare it must lose the original role. Herman Daly and John Cobb recognised this and called their measure instead an index of sustainable economic welfare. It showed declines for the USA from 1976 to the late 1980s, quite contrary to the figures of GDP per capita.

Another option is to prepare a different synthetic indicator of societal welfare. The Physical Quality of Life Index, for example, combines statistics on infant mortality, literacy and life expectancy; and the UNDP's Human Development Index combines adjusted income, literacy, schooling, and life expectancy. These measures too bring interesting results, quite often different from the picture given by GDP/GNP per capita.

Since there is no adequate single synthesis, the HDRs amongst others mainly use a disaggregated approach. An adequate set of indicators will cover: social (e.g. health), ethical (e.g. distribution and human rights) and ecological as well as economic issues; the household economy as well as the monetary economy; and stocks as well as flows (Ekins & Max-Neef 1992).

UNIVERSALISM AND RELATIVISM

In one respect GDP/GNP per capita is an objectivist measure: it includes no clause of the form 'development/improvement is whatever a group of people think it is'. The same measure is deemed valid worldwide. Under the surface, it is subjectivist in a different way. While the measure is mandated worldwide, what it measures in each currency area reflects in considerable part what people in that area consider important. If the area is abundant in something which its people have no wish for, it will not be produced and will not contribute to measured national product – unless people in another area desire it, people in the first area see something they would wish to obtain with the sales revenue, and the product can be exchanged at a mutually attractive price. Proceeds from its sale can then be used for what the people of the first area do want.

From a historical perspective, unfortunately, this scenario is naïve. Powerful groups abroad have frequently invaded or otherwise enforced access to resources which they desired, irrespective of whether the owners wished to trade; for example in the military-backed opening of the markets of China and Japan in the mid-nineteenth century. The more an area is integrated into the world economy, the more the valuation of its resources will reflect not only local preferences but the preferences of those around the world with money. The clause tacitly becomes 'development/improvement is whatever people around the world with money and saleable resources, backed up by political and military power, think it is'.

Other qualifications apply to the proposition that the universal 'objective' measure GDP per capita rests on the subjective wishes of residents: the wishes of rich people are (dis)proportionately more registered than those of poor people; the wishes of those without purchasing power are not registered; and only those wishes which can be and have been recorded in money terms are included, thus ignoring much of life.

The popularity of the GDP per capita measure for a task – measuring human well-being – for which it was not devised and is in fundamental ways unsuited, derives partly from its combination of the two appeals: as a universal and 'objective' measure which yet derives from people's sub-jective wishes. Table 2.3 shows this in relation to other types of measure.

The UNDP's human development measures in the 1990s represent a move to more objectivism. The HDI incorporates mean literacy, mean years of schooling, and mean life expectancy, as well as per-capita GDP adjusted for purchasing power. A standardised universal measure allows worldwide and longitudinal comparisons. At the same time, the Human Development Report Office encourages countries, provinces and districts to modify some of the other indices, or add further indices, so as to reflect matters which they feel are of particular importance to them. Increased objectivism in the central measures is accompanied by encouragement of local variation in the definition of some other measures.

Universalist definitions of development (or poverty or well-being) apply the same measure to all times and places. This does not mean the values implied in the definition are shared in all times and places. The Development Ethnology Workgroup (AGEE) of the German Ethnology Society wished to 'dissociate ourselves from the commonly held concepts of development, which define the approach to and goal of development according to the standards of our [Northern] society. The term development

Table 2.3 Types of well-being measure

MEASURES OF WELL-BEING	UNIVERSALIST MEASURES: *applied to all times and places*	RELATIVIST MEASURES *chosen per time and place*
MEASURES OF NON-FEELING FUNCTIONINGS ('*objectivist*')	E.g. life expectancy	E.g. body weight – if chosen in a place as a measure of well-being
MEASURES OF FEELINGS-BASED CATEGORIES ('*subjectivist*')	E.g. GDP per capita (albeit a very poor measure of well-being)	E.g. felt fulfilment of duty or divine will – if chosen in a place as a measure of well-being

is retained [by us] but given a new meaning ... We regard development as an improvement in the situation of the affected groups in accordance with their own criteria, while necessarily taking into account global priorities'. An emphatically relativist definition of development is propounded, but in the next clause it is subordinated to universal values. 'Our fundamental position, which is based on a relativistic concept of cultural diversity, is thus subordinate to these global priorities: ... preserving the environment, the satisfaction of basic needs, and the safeguarding of universal human rights and liberties.' (AGEE, undated). Issues of internal differentiation and disputes over goals are evaded by AGEE's definition of 'affected groups' – 'groups of people with a common life context and common goals' – but cannot be evaded by ethnographers in practice. We look further at this tension in Chapter 8.

The authors of *The Development Dictionary* (Sachs ed. 1992) were more thoroughgoing relativists, at least at first glance. They attacked the concept of 'development' on the grounds that it proffers a universal concept of social improvement. Normative usage of the term is allegedly incompatible with the reality of 'diverse and non-comparable ways of human existence' (ibid.: 1992: 3). Gustavo Esteva considered endogenous development a contradiction in terms, for 'endogenous' implies coming out of a specific culture and its values, whereas 'development' implies some universal measure of improvement – rather than diverse culture-specific measures – and 'the oneness, homogeneity, and linear evolution of the world' (Esteva 1992: 12). Arce (2000) notes that some see a homogenising definition of development as part of attempts by metropolitan countries to control. Perhaps others see heterogeneous, diverse definitions of development as part of attempts to divide and rule.

As we saw, comparability may not in fact presume sheer homogeneity. Japanese culture and values are different from American, yet some comparison of their degrees of 'development', each measured partly in terms of their own values, is possible, and done in national income measures, governmental and alternative. Further, Esteva and his colleagues themselves go on to make greater comparisons, of the value of different ways of life. They do not merely say that, for example, American values and Z-ian values differ, or that Z-ians appear more developed in terms of their own values than Americans are in terms of theirs; they go further and strongly criticise American values (Gasper 1996a).

What if American or Z-ian values are changed in the very process which they are supposed to evaluate? Illich's claim (1992: 93) that 'most people become poorer as GNP grows' is untrue for low-income countries according to the available measures but could be more plausible if we use a definition of poverty based instead on preexisting cultural norms which become replaced. Amartya Sen (1988) notes that such 'value endogeneity' – not only the 'value heterogeneity' which Esteva highlights – sets limits to how much agreement we can reach on rankings of degree of development. He points out, however, that sometimes although a process alters values it is judged an improvement in terms of both the antecedent and the subsequent values. Similarly, concerning value heterogeneity, while the conventional focus on real income per capita implicitly assumed 'a fairly large intersection [i.e. area of consensus, across different times and places, e.g. Japan and America] of valuations related to objects of development, … it is by no means absurd to think that the actual extent of agreement is indeed quite large' (ibid.: 20–1). Let us look at this question of degrees of commonality.

⤙ COMMONALITY? ⤙

Michael Edwards defines 'development' in part as an increased opportunity for valuable being: 'the reduction of material want and the enhancement of people's ability to live a life they consider good across the broadest range possible in a population' (1999: 4). The definition is normative – indeed, he underlines that development is 'good change' – and subjectivist, as specification of valuable being is left to each group or individual. But, he continues, people agree on a lot. While interpretations and relative priorities vary between cultures and ideologies, the following appear to be universal aspirations:

- to be free from poverty and violence and the servitude these bring in their wake;
- to be loved and enjoy a sense of belonging;
- to feel more in control and less vulnerable to the vagaries of unaccountable power;
- and to be subjects of their own destiny rather than objects of the intentions of others. (Ibid.)

Good change increases the fulfilment of these aspirations.

Denis Goulet (1995) argues similarly, using different labels. For him 'development' refers to economic growth and modernisation, and is a means towards 'the good life'. Ideas of the good life vary between cultures. However, he argues, they always include attention to life sustenance, esteem, and freedom. He comes close to adding identity and meaning to his list of proposed universals. Both enter Manfred Max-Neef's picture (1989) of fundamental needs.

Many authors argue that there is an important degree of agreement across persons, cultures and periods in conceptions of good change and good lives. Some try to test or strengthen the claim of commonality through comparison of lists. If we take lists from, for example, Goulet (1995), Edwards (1996), Finnis (1987) and UNDP (1996), we find major

Table 2.4 Lists of proposed universal values

GOULET Ideas of the good life always include these aspects:	EDWARDS Development (good change) provides the possibilities for:	FINNIS Basic goods / values / aspects of well-being	UNDP Dimensions of human development
Life sustenance	Life & health sustenance Material sufficiency	Life Knowledge Play Aesthetic experience	Sustainability Security Equity
Esteem Freedom (Identity & meaning)	Esteem Freedom from [various] Participation Meaning	Friendship Exercising self-determination 'Religion'	Community membership Empowerment/ capability Participation

similarities, as in Table 2.4. However, we also see differences.

Alkire (2002), Clark (2002) and Qizilbash (2002) place such comparisons on a solid basis by looking at a wide range of lists and at principles of comparison. Sabina Alkire seeks to group similar factors, and to eliminate any which are clearly only means not ends. She then does find, across a large number of lists, a notable degree of congruence. Hans Küng (1997) undertakes a comparable exercise, more informally, with the same result. One can then essay a synthesised list.

One can ask whether these are coincidental commonalities amongst subjectivisms, or whether one can identify a universal pattern, a necessary commonality. Alkire proposes that John Finnis, a prominent legal philosopher, has given us a non-*ad hoc* methodology for construction of a list. Finnis seeks to identify the set of irreducible motives, those answers to 'why should I do this?' which do not lead to a further 'why?'. Although this descriptive exercise might not take us to a list of morally validated values – basic motives could include some which are destructive, of oneself or others – it can help in checking and organising ideas. Similarly for Amartya Sen, development means that people are able to have a fulfilled life, and fulfilment refers to personally and culturally specific aspects; but the ability rests necessarily on universal bases like longevity, health, and ability to function as a citizen. We will look at these issues further in Chapters 6 to 8, in connection with ideas of basic needs, 'Human Development' and cultural diversity.

2.5 CONCLUSION

We see that the concept of 'development' has many meanings and diverse aspects. It reflects and has influenced and helped to motivate centuries of changes and attempted changes. We can understand why its metaphor of the unveiling of a necessary path of improvement attracts: it reassures, justifies and commits people and societies on voyages which are marked in reality by great costs and cognitive and value uncertainties. For the purposes of development ethics, however, it is essential to dissect this language. To understand and make better value choices we need some more clarity on values.

The chapter's first two objectives, tackled in section 2.2, were to increase sensitivity to the distinction between neutral (non-evaluative) and evaluative meanings of 'development'; and to show forces and dangers involved in the elision of that distinction. The dangers include concealment of values, suppression of attention to actual effects of change, surreptitious furtherance of the values and interests of privileged groups, inattention to possible alternative paths, and prejudging any evaluation of the desirability of economic growth in particular cases. When an instance of economic growth appears intolerable, it can be dismissed as not 'real development'; so 'development' automatically gets good evaluations. Since the predominant operationalisation of 'development' in practice remains GDP growth, the result is that GDP growth can remain largely insulated from criticism.

Evaluative definitions of development have broadened in scope during the past generation (see e.g. Qizilbash 1996). In the 1970s Dudley Seers highlighted the growing belief that no concept and plans of 'development' should ignore income distribution and employment (e.g. Seers 1977). Broader definitions of 'development' slowly crept into UN deliberations. In the 1990s they swept forward via the UNDP and especially the Human Development Reports, in which the scope of 'Human Development' widened even year by year.

Later chapters continue with these questions. Chapter 3 looks at the economistic bias of previous developmentalism, and what has been meant by the terms 'effectiveness' and 'efficiency'. Like 'development' they acquire a status as supposedly so obviously important that they become beyond criticism, so that we often fail to examine how they are used and as a result acquiesce in concealed and questionable values. Chapters 4 and 5 examine further some of the omitted costs and neglected values: Chapter 4 looks at equity and how the costs of development are distributed; Chapter 5 looks at a later but now major emergent area in the widening of the concept of development: peace and security, and their converse, conflict and violence.

The third objective of the chapter was to see the relevance but insufficiency of historical definitions of development (section 2.3). A historical perspective is essential. Indeed the field of development studies can be characterised as an attempt at integrated understanding of fundamental historical changes and of responses to the challenges that arise, notably amongst the neediest areas and groups (Hettne 1995). No single historical definition ('development dates from xxxx') is adequate, certainly not the recently popular 'made in 1949' notion; but each of the start dates cited (such as 3500 BC, 1492, 1750, 1860 and 1945/1949) alludes to the opening of a significant phase. Historical definitions must combine with criteria for what is qualitatively fundamental change.

The chapter's remaining objectives were to introduce key issues and choices in normative ahistorical definition (section 2.4): how far is 'development' culturally relative? how adequate are evaluative definitions of development which focus on opportunity and/or choice? how far can we find common elements – shared or required – across the different evaluative meanings of 'development'? The issues involved will be investigated further in Chapters 6 to 8.

DISCUSSION THEMES

1. Identify several different meanings of 'development' that you consider important; including: (a) some neutral descriptive ('positive') meanings, i.e. interpretations of 'development' purely as a scientific term for use in describing, and/or explaining, without evaluating; (b) some normative meanings, i.e. interpretations of 'development' which see it as desirable social change, progress, etc. What do you mean by 'development', and why?
2. From normative meanings of 'development', select (or construct) one (*or* more) which you feel favourably about; and present arguments in its support.
3. For a selected country, analyse and compare the conceptions of development held by the State, business enterprises, intellectuals, communities, and individuals (and any other groups that you choose to add).
4. How much commonality do you see in the various proposed lists of universal values discussed in Alkire (2002) or Qizilbash (2002)?

READING SUGGESTIONS

Useful discussions of meanings of 'development' are found in Sen (1988), Crocker (1991: 465–7), Ingham (1993), and Goulet (1995, especially Ch. 4). Ingham for example outlines a series of debates on whether development should be understood as industrialisation or modernisation or democratisation or human development. Cowen & Shenton (1996) is a pathbreaking but opaque study of ideas of 'development' in the century and a half before the concept was, according to recent misstatements, invented in the 1940s; Cowen &

Shenton (1995) is a more readable statement. Thomas (2000) shows the dangers of reducing the meaning of 'development' to intervention, especially intervention in crisis-ridden countries. Ekins & Max-Neef (1992, Ch. 8) gives an excellent introductory coverage of indicators of development.

CHAPTER 3

'EFFICIENCY AND EFFECTIVENESS': MAINSTREAM DEVELOPMENT EVALUATION IN THEORY AND PRACTICE

3.1 INTRODUCTION: MAINSTREAM VALUE POSITIONS AND ALTERNATIVES

> People who are mystified if you ask them what 'good' or 'bad' means, appear to know what 'evaluation' means ... (Richards 1985: 1)

We look in this chapter at what mainstream development policy has meant by 'effectiveness' and 'efficiency'. This responds to the need argued in Chapter 1 to bring out and assess the value assumptions and value choices in development policies and practice. Chapter 2 has shown some of the choices in normative definitions of development, and the problems in taking the category of GDP/GNP as having normative importance, let alone as the key measure of development. This chapter examines the assumptions, normative and explanatory, which have lain behind that longstanding mainstream definition of development as centred on economic growth.

One mainstream type of evaluation measures *effectiveness*, the degree of achievement of objectives. There we need to ask which types of effects are stressed, which are left out, and which other features are reflected or neglected. Section 3.2 looks at meanings given to 'effectiveness' in development policy, in particular in international development cooperation. One finds a frequent gap between the criteria of importance used by the supposed beneficiaries of the policies and the criteria used by the policy planners and evaluators (see e.g. Narayan et al. 2000). Many of the latter groups have long been preoccupied with economic production, on the premise that market-type calculations give a synthetic measure of relevant costs and benefits. The underlying assumption concerning which values should be measured is liberal – that people should get more of whatever they want – but with markets taken as a satisfactory means of operationalising and measuring fulfilment of wants. A case study by Roland Hoksbergen will illustrate the tacit adoption of these assumptions in evaluations of development aid, sometimes in opposition to the principles which are publicly declared.

Choices are often controversial and painful. Many models and approaches tend to hide their values, and so hide whom they serve. Section 3.2 looks too at this issue of whose viewpoint is adopted in evaluation. Managerial approaches to effectiveness presume that managers, leaders or experts always set the objectives. This downgrades issues of democracy, participation and transparency. Market-based approaches, in business and as also standard in economics, take for granted an interpretation of consumer sovereignty which weights people's wishes according to how wealthy they are.

A second mainstream form of evaluation is economic cost–benefit analysis, which seeks to go further and measure *efficiency*: looking at not only how far objectives have been achieved, but at the balance or proportion between those benefits and the costs. It does this by using market valuations or modifying them where considered necessary, but still with the style of valuation found in markets, to measure and compare costs and benefits in money terms. Where markets are missing, or fail (due to externalities or monopoly, for example), economic cost–benefit analysis provides additional or adjusted prices, to allow a calculation of the 'net social worth' of a product or activity. The same questions arise about which aspects are included and which excluded.

Whereas the understanding of 'effectiveness' has broadened in the past generation to reflect a wider range of values, a bias to economic output and growth has remained ensconced in the economics interpretation of the trump concept, 'efficiency'. In practice it has referred to maximisation of net output as measured in monetary terms, and thus only to those things which can be monetised and only according to people's ability to pay. We look at these issues in section 3.3. Talk of efficiency or effectiveness which excludes equity objectives, other end-state objectives besides fulfilment of desires for commodities, and procedural objectives of participation and propriety, is very incomplete and likely to be misleading.

Section 3.4 shows how an interpretation of 'economic efficiency' depends also on the ideas adopted about the interrelations between monetisable activities and their social and natural contexts, and about how far the methods of calculation of a private businessman should be used for deciding on societal priorities and sustainable development. Emphases on interrelations, combined with objections to sole reliance on business-style rationality, have led to the emergence of broader normative conceptions of development: 'human development', 'sustainable development', 'sustainable human development'.

Section 3.5 looks at how, having identified different values employed in evaluation, we can try to understand and compare them, as parts of systems of thought or world-views. We consider the assumptions behind the predominant approach derived from mainstream economics, including the principle of consumer sovereignty – that the objectives to be served are those which consumers are willing (and able) to pay for – and see which issues of equity, need, and human development those assumptions might downgrade.

3.2   EFFECTIVENESS TOWARDS WHAT AND FOR WHOM?

EFFECTIVENESS TOWARDS WHAT?

Emma Crewe and Elizabeth Harrison describe a thriving programme in Sri Lanka in the late 1980s and early 1990s to design and produce fuel-efficient stoves. 'By 1990 230,000 rural households had a new Sarvodaya stove and 28 per cent of Colombo households had a portable equivalent. By 1993 40,000 stoves were being sold per year' (1998: 13). But the programme's external funders withdrew. The programme was thriving because the stoves saved women's time. The funders apparently considered this relatively unimportant. Their preset programme objective was reduction of woodfuel use. This matched a preoccupation with deforestation and a fear of resulting agricultural and climatic decline. In contrast, the unpaid time of women was deemed an abundant resource. Saving such time was considered to have little or no effect on national economic development.

This sort of prioritisation amongst effects has been common. Transport economics, for example, has typically evaluated projects in terms of their effects on monetised activities: by comparing investment costs with benefits seen as the reduction in traffic operating costs plus the monetary value added by new resource mobilisation. The time savings of actors engaged in business are converted into money terms, according to their rates of pay. The time savings of people not travelling on business are typically ignored in studies of low-income countries, again because such people are deemed not to promote economic production. Those travelling to visit their family, or to reach a hospital, have been considered to be using an abundant or at least economically insignificant resource, their own time; so this has conventionally been ignored in economic cost–benefit analysis – unless the time saving is reflected in payment of higher prices for tickets.

We see that evaluation of effectiveness is not a mechanical or neutral exercise. Choices have to be made, consciously or tacitly, about which aspects of an experience are important, and about their weights. To make such choices consciously one must first be aware of the range of effects. This would require asking a range of people, in order to obtain a wide perspective (see e.g. Dietz & Pfund 1988). Kurien (1981) notes how wide the range of impacts of foreign-supported hospitals in Kerala (India) appeared to local people. Hospitals had health impacts, but in addition they were part of the creation, expansion and competition of churches, involving a proliferation, indeed an oversupply, of health infrastructure; they could encourage external dependence and habits of importation and imitation; they were more accessible to better-off people; they could bring opportunities for corruption and for external leverage; and they were also part of a war for influence against a strong Communist movement.

One issue concerns programme managers' preoccupation with performance in terms of publicly declared preset objectives. They are held accountable by that criterion. This gives a danger of 'tunnel vision', looking only at intended effects, even though those could be less significant than unintended ones (Richards 1985; Gasper 2000b). White and Tiongco (1997: 115) describe a hand tubewell programme in Bangladesh, intended by the promoting NGO for irrigation of vegetables. Villagers preferred to use the water at home and moved the wells away from the fields. The NGO saw this as a deviation rather than as a considered improvement and began to issue pipes, which could not be relocated. The villagers' interest in the programme declined. The NGO concluded it was a failure.

A deeper issue concerns why some types of objectives are preset and why others become marginalised or ignored. The allocation of objectives into these sets is not random; there has long been strong implicit priority in most development policy to economic production. Roland Hoksbergen reviewed a large sample of USAID evaluation (i.e. *ex post* review) studies from the 1970s and 1980s. To take one representative example, he found the following features in a major set of USAID rural roads evaluations which spanned many low-income countries:

- individualism: the assumption that the key objective is to increase individuals' incomes and, more generally, individuals' preference-fulfilment;
- market-orientation: the presumption that the spread of markets is positive, and should be given weight in its own right; what is perhaps only a means became taken also as an end;
- in contrast, other means (e.g. community participation) were not accorded independent value;
- priority to quantifiable impacts.

These choices, and the corresponding omission or downgrading of other values, were rarely explicit and argued. Thus although other objectives have received increasing emphasis in recent years, some of the bias remains, embedded in certain methods or in the habitual assumptions which guide how they are used.

The mainstream preoccupation with economic growth has often gone further. Debate on the evaluation of development aid has for decades centred, and frequently remains centred, sometimes even exclusively, on whether aid increases economic growth; and on if not, why not, and if so, under what conditions (see e.g. Mosley 1987; Dollar & Pritchett 1998). The debate has eventually moved beyond seeking a generalisation for all countries, to distinguishing between the effects on growth in different situations and under different policy regimes. This still ignores other possible desirable effects.

Suppose foreign aid did not increase investment in recipient countries, but instead competed with the local private sector for scarce key resources, thus raising their price, and did allow recipient governments to increase consumption expenditures and reduce attempts to mobilise local resources for investment. Tim Allen and Diana Weinhold (2000) for example, are concerned not only when foreign aid (in this case, debt relief) could release domestic resources for military or prestige expenditure, but even when it is released for non-investment consumption. They find that countries which have received debt relief have 'generally equal (or lower) inflation and higher shares of government spending on capital' (ibid.: 869); but 'we find no evidence that [they] have increased either the quantity or the share of spending on education' (ibid.: 869). They refer only to a few years of government spending on education, in an era of forced reductions and stringency in public budgets and of externally promoted shifts of education funding towards families and the private sector. They do not treat the possibility of tying debt cancellation to agreed increases in education and health spending, and supporting the financial allocations by the other necessary inputs, including ideas, personnel and networks.

Some of such discussion questionably places expenditures on health, education, and social security as purely consumption expenditures. Yet 'at the margin[,] consumption of basic needs amounts to investment' (Dasgupta 1993: 248). Spending on the enrichment of what is in human heads is sometimes the greatest investment, even for economic growth, let alone for quality of life and human development. Ironically, 'capital' originally meant 'head' (as in *per capita*) or 'chief'. Nowadays monetary investment and its nurture is often the chief force in societies. Further, even if the contributions of social sector expenditures to economic development are recognised, health and education in particular are typically good in their own right, and indeed should rank as 'merit goods': goods whose human priority exceeds the value placed on them by market calculations.

Even if foreign aid had no effect on economic growth or human development expenditures, it would have allowed consumption to increase (at least of leisure time) in some wretchedly poor countries. Welfare gains – especially in very poor countries – matter, not only economic growth gains; indeed the latter have no independent weight but only matter in so far as they contribute to welfare (as we will discuss in Chapter 7 on the 'human development' approach). The issue of whose consumption has increased must of course be addressed: is it that of the lowest-income groups, low-income groups, elites, or a kleptocracy?

In the case of health expenditure, examples of extraordinary benefits, past or prospective, from some aided programmes have been highlighted in recent years in a rediscovery of the priority of health (e.g. Sachs et al. 2001). We saw that some of this rediscovery uses only the language of economic growth, as opposed to an allegedly 'purely emotional pitch' of talking about poor people's remediable suffering. In growth language, the low-cost restoration of the sight of many elderly people in poor countries by cataract removal would be treated as of little significance. Other parts of the new wave of concern for health are nourished by a more humane vision, a direct concern for human dignity and human rights. Economic growth still dominates much discussion of aid, but less than before the agenda-shifting adoption through 1990s UN and OECD conferences of targets for halving absolute poverty and human development deficits by 2015. Alkire (2002: 27) adds, though, that while early 1990s World Bank policy documents began to talk of not only consumption but education, health, nutrition and environment as of independent importance, still 'relationships, aesthetic arrangements, religion, participation, culture, meaningful work or play were not registered as intrinsically important'.

EFFECTIVENESS FOR WHOM?

The 'logical framework approach' became in the 1990s a near-universal format for externally funded public sector and NGO development projects and programmes. It obliges and constrains the statement of objectives in various ways: they must be stated as a logically connected hierarchy, typically of four or five levels, and normally with only a single objective at each of the top one or two levels. Its heavy emphasis on preset intentions brings the danger that we have seen of neglect of unintended effects. Similarly its insistence on a single, supposedly consensual, set of criteria – 'the project's objectives' – can obscure the issues of who supports and selects these objectives (Gasper 2000b).

Fuller versions of the approach do open with 'stakeholder analysis': identifying the range of affected groups and their various perspectives on the problem area, and specification of whose concerns will be used to guide the project design. Crewe and Harrison (1998: 86) show how in a woodstove project in Kenya, the Kenyan NGO focused on fuelwood use,

Table 3.1 A first look at standpoints in global ethics

WHAT RANGE OF EFFECTS SHOULD BE CONSIDERED?		Are there global-scale responsibilities?	
		Yes	*No*
Are national boundaries ethically important?	*Yes*	1. E.g.: Consider effects in all countries but with less weight for effects not in one's own country	2. E.g.: Consider only effects in one's own country 2*. Consider also effects on foreigners if these contribute to domestic interests
	No	3. E.g.: Consider effects wherever they occur, without differential weights according to national location	4. E.g.: Consider only effects for oneself and one's friends 4*. Consider equally effects worldwide, but only those that affect one's money profits: the market stance

the British NGO on incomes of the rural poor, the British funding agency on the number of stoves used, and the local stove producers on their financial profits. But stakeholder analysis is politically sensitive and frequently omitted (Gasper 1997b). As Crewe and Harrison stress, 'one person's failure can be another person's success' (1998: 1).

Sister to this issue of 'whose goals?' is the question of 'which affected parties should be considered?'. Only those who provide resources? Or all local residents, or all national residents? Or anyone affected, wherever in the world? And animals? Also other life and, as apparently some deep ecologists believe, even the inanimate world?

Let us compare views on paying attention to programme effects on persons elsewhere in the world. Table 3.1 shows that this question is not the same as 'are national boundaries ethically important?'. Some people consider national boundaries ethically insignificant but also reject any general concern for others' welfare, locally or worldwide, whether on grounds of benevolence or duty. This quite widespread position (no. 4 in the table) is still a global ethic in the sense that it is a consistently applied viewpoint on the distribution of duties (none, it asserts), and possibly backed by a theory (for example, Nietzschean).

A variant of this quasi-Nietzschean position is the ideology of the unfettered global market (4* in the table). This is arguably the most influential global ethic. It too rejects national boundaries as ethically significant and it further ignores any claims from those without purchasing power. However, it pays attention to the revealed demands, backed by money, of people anywhere in the world. The pure private businessman counts monetary benefits worldwide, as recorded on markets, in so far as they affect his profits. The concern is only for his profits, but the scope is global, responsive to the desires of anyone who can pay. Further, business prudence may induce acceptance of a transnational responsibility to respect contracts and respect customer interests. National boundaries are at most of secondary significance, for knowing which laws to follow where, and in so far as the businessman has some personal loyalty to a country.

Economic cost–benefit analysis by a government can diverge from using market prices, but it shares the structure of business calculations. Where it more significantly diverges is in that it is meant to include all economic effects on residents or citizens of the country concerned. An indirect concern for benefits outside the country enters via the explicit concern for the benefits of domestic suppliers when they are paid by foreigners. The analysis takes position 2* if foreigners are given no weight independent of their role as business partners, and a type of position 1 if they are given some but lesser weight, as often in 'foreign assistance'. Nationalist foreign policy also pays no independent attention to benefits abroad, but gives them instrumental attention as part of alliance-building, and hence again illustrates position 2*. Less market-oriented administrative decision-making may adopt a narrower version of position 2, excluding benefits outside the country concerned as being not part of the remit of its government; but the enlightened self-interest variant (2*) is perhaps more common.

Thus judgements of effectiveness and efficiency depend on who is included within the evaluative field of vision and with what weight, and on whose field of vision it is.

3.3   EFFICIENCY IN TERMS OF WHICH VALUES?

The term 'efficiency [is] a concept that has meaning only in the context of an agreed set of objectives', explains the World Bank's 1983 *World Development Report* (p. 41). Such objectives can include objectives about inter-personal distribution, typically reflecting one or other interpretation of equity. Yet, two pages later the same *World Development Report* was speaking of 'occasions when the goals of efficiency and distribution conflict', as if the agreed set of objectives does not include (equitable) distribution. Indeed, historically and still to a great extent, the dominant interpretation of 'efficiency' has typically included only the objective of measured economic production/consumption. We should at most call this interpretation 'economic efficiency', and not honour it with the label of efficiency in general. But the 'efficiency' label has enormous legitimising power and functions as a trump card in the modern vocabulary. No one can declare themselves against it. If a policy option is deemed inefficient, that usually sinks it. So contenders try to capture the label, to serve their particular set of objectives. This is what business interests and mainstream economists have successfully done for a long time. We need to ask: 'Efficient by which values?'

Mainstream economists have focused on growth of aggregate production and national income. Business and other sectional interests may focus on sectional gains but advocate these behind the language of 'efficiency'. For example, the land reforms that accompanied decolonisation in Kenya in the 1960s were guided and limited by a prejudgement that large farms are more economically efficient. Later evaluation of results found that smallholdings and densely settled cooperatives had been more economic than lightly settled large holdings (MacArthur 1976). Not infrequently, the policies behind an 'efficiency' label have been less economic as well as less equitable, and 'efficient' only for elites.

This section highlights the confusion of economic production with efficiency for society in general. It and later parts of the chapter then examine dangers common with even a delimited notion of 'economic efficiency':

- unargued acceptance of existing distributions of monetary power;
- overestimation of our ability to calculate economic impacts when economy, society and environment overlap and profoundly influence each other;
- overreach in the claims made from the notion of economic efficiency, based on a view of the world in which the economic or business approach to making choices is considered rational for all or nearly all of life; and
- misplaced presumption that monetised values automatically represent human priorities.

WHAT IS EFFICIENT DEPENDS ON WHAT ONE'S VALUES ARE

The confusion in the 1983 *World Development Report* reflected an ocean of misusage. 'Efficiency versus equity' has been a ubiquitous phrase in economics literature. But efficiency concerns the relationship between valuable results and the valuable means that have been used to achieve them. Judgements of degree of efficiency (and of 'efficiency' in the sense of maximum degree of efficiency) depend then on which objectives and values one uses – amongst which equity is likely to be one, in any public discourse – and on their relative weights. So there are different interpretations of 'efficiency', according to the specification of the objectives being considered (Sen 1975; Shubik 1978; Richards 1985; Le Grand 1991).

The confusion in use of terms partly reflects the problem of clarifying the levels and scope of the objectives which are taken into account. Figure 3.1 distinguishes:

- a series of four levels of activity and objectives (as in the 'logical framework' formulation in programme planning): input(s), output(s), the purpose which justifies the output(s), and the broader goal to which the purpose contributes;
- four concepts of performance: effectiveness, technical efficiency, economic efficiency, and overall efficiency.

One could make further distinctions in both respects, and we mention a few later, but the figure presents the major issues. (It extends the analysis given in Carley 1980.)

Some of the terms used in the figure can be described as follows:

1. *Effectiveness* means the (degree of) achievement of a higher level of objective: outputs, purpose, or goal. Thus there is a family of effectiveness measures. None is sufficient as a measure of performance, for they do not consider the cost of the inputs used.

2. *Technical efficiency* means productivity, the ratio of output to input. ('Productive efficiency' is sometimes the label used; Brown (2000: 66) uses 'service efficiency'.) The term 'efficiency' originated here, in nineteenth-century engineering calculations, for example of how much energy a machine delivered compared to the energy used as input (Simon 1976). Technical efficiency too is not enough as a performance measure, for it considers the amounts of the inputs and outputs but not their value to the decision-maker.

2*. Once there are multiple inputs, then assessment of performance requires some way of aggregating them, to judge the overall resource use. Sarvodaya stoves allow more productive use of women's time, but perhaps not of wood; evaluation of the stoves will depend on which input is valued more. Frequently inputs are aggregated using market prices or other assigned prices, and then compared with the non-monetised level of achievement of the key output (or purpose or goal). This is a measure of *cost-effectiveness*. For example, one can compare the money costs of different ways of achieving a given level of health improvement. Cost-effectiveness too does not suffice to say whether the input use is justified by the output, i.e. whether the value of the output outweighs the value of the input. It only allows us to compare the relative returns of different routes to the same destination.

3. *Economic efficiency* surpasses all these measures. One applies prices to both outputs and inputs to obtain aggregate measures of their value which can be compared, to judge whether the activity as a whole is justified.

We should also incorporate other objectives when we talk of efficiency, such as equity, participation and appropriate procedure. Tony Killick (1981) is unusual in that his concept of economic efficiency also covers performance in terms of equity objectives. He insists that 'economic efficiency' must reflect all the criteria considered by economists, including

Figure 3.1 Relationships of concepts of efficiency, effectiveness, equity and quality of life

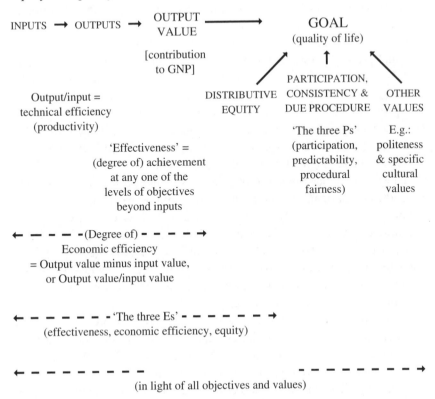

equity in distribution. Stuart Nagel (1984) notes that *economics* has at best still only looked at '*the three Es*': effectiveness, (economic) efficiency, and equity. He argues that we must also look at '*the three Ps*', which political science emphasises for policy choices:

- Participation, as a goal in its own right, not only as a useful means;
- Predictability or consistency (this might help economic efficiency, but is also important on grounds of fairness; price stability is an example);
- Procedural fairness (which may involve such criteria as: first come, first served; queueing; one person, one vote; majority rule; lottery; having to prove an accused person guilty; fair opportunity).

We can add Politeness: treating people in all ways with proper respect. 'Poverty is humiliation, the sense of being dependent and of being forced to accept rudeness, insults and indifference when we seek help' (a poor woman in Latvia, cited in Narayan 2000).

Other objectives too can be added, such as independence, or the creation of knowledge. Nowadays one might add the heading of environmental impacts, in so far as they too cannot be adequately captured by economic measures. It is hard to see how all these objectives and the Ps could sensibly be measured on a market and included in some measure of national product. Treating them separately might also make it less likely that they will be ignored. So, objectives like participation should not be treated in the format of economic calculation, but instead should set limits on it. Should we still use the term 'efficiency' at all when we move so far beyond economics measurement? The reason to do so is to underline that economics measurement does not capture all our important objectives, and not to cede the prestigious 'efficiency' label.

These broad headings for objectives (economic efficiency, equity, procedural–political, other) each contain many particular objectives. Equity objectives usually cover several different aspects of equity, for example (see Chapter 4). There are varied political objectives, each with many aspects. Unless the relative importance of the objectives within each heading, and of the broad headings themselves, is agreed, there will be much room for disagreement on 'overall efficiency' even if we agree on which are the relevant headings.

Given these types of objective which do not correspond to commodity production, 'economic efficiency' as used by most economists – maximisation of net product over time, calculated in terms of scarcity prices and with discounting of future results as appropriate – is not the same as overall efficiency. Could one salvage a claim for commodity production as the definitive criterion for efficiency, by arguing that economic capacity is central because it is transformable into anything else whereas other values (like 'spare' time with family or friends, or a sighted old age) are not? No, for economic values are not so central; we cannot get all other values through them, nor are they the sole factor with claims to centrality. Economic development itself is critically dependent on human capital, social capital and culture, and on socio-political stability, all of which rely on much more than commodity inputs.

Before we examine further the limits of attempts to have a separate category of economic efficiency, let us assume that a self-contained sphere called the economy does exist, and consider what exactly economic efficiency could mean in it. (The following sub-section can be omitted by readers who are less interested in precise exposition of the economics usages and of the values behind them.)

TACIT VARIANTS OF ECONOMIC EFFICIENCY: PARETIAN AND UTILITARIAN

The discussion of economic efficiency in economics textbooks can be confusing, even when the unqualified term 'efficiency' is not used to describe performance in terms of just a restricted subset of objectives. Students are told that (full) economic efficiency means (1) that no one can be made better off without someone else being made worse off: the 'Pareto optimality' criterion (Bannock et al. 1992). The criterion's meaning depends on which concept of benefit is used: the outcome of free choice, or fulfilment of preferences (*ex ante* or retrospective), or satisfaction, or some other. Students are also often told that economic efficiency means (2) maximisation of utility or of net benefit. These two criteria are often incorrectly fused (e.g. Brown 2000: 62). The second meaning is narrower. The first, Pareto optimality, only ensures that there are no unused moves in which someone would gain and no one lose; it does not ensure maximum utility. One can often raise overall utility by moving away from a 'Pareto optimum', for example moving away from a market equilibrium in which some destitute people starve, by raising taxes for humanitarian relief at the expense of other groups.

Both meanings differ from the general meaning which we used above: (3) maximum degree of attainment of one's objectives (Le Grand 1991). For we have more objectives than maximisation of utility or net benefit, and those objectives typically include views on distribution which legitimate certain changes that make some people worse off, such as taxation to prevent starvation or to fund reduction of infant mortality in poor families.

The 'Pareto optimality' concept can less tendentiously be entitled '*Pareto efficiency*' (Stiglitz & Driffill 2000), since numerous arrangements in an economy fulfil that condition, and it seems absurd to say all are optimal. The criterion means that there is no waste, in one sense, but that does not justify use of the term 'optimal', which means the best that one can attain.

One reason behind the odd label 'Pareto optimality' is that if one believes that inter-personal comparisons are meaningless or impossible, then one cannot say whether a redistribution from one person to another will bring an improvement, and hence cannot say that one Pareto-efficient point is better than another. All such points are then dubbed optimal. Many leading mainstream economists declared that inter-personal comparisons of advantage were arbitrary value choices (e.g. Robbins 1938; Friedman 1953), beyond the competence of economics, which therefore should only with scientific objectivity seek such 'Pareto optima'.

A second reason is that, according to welfare economics, every possible Pareto-efficient arrangement could (given certain assumptions) emerge as the equilibrium in a competitive market. Which arrangement emerges depends on the initial allocation of property rights and resources. In that sense then, every Pareto-efficient point could be an optimum – *if* one approved the corresponding initial allocation.

Attainment of economic efficiency in the sense of maximisation of net benefit implies that neither increasing nor decreasing the level of output would be advantageous; the marginal cost of production equals the marginal benefit from consumption. An ideal market is supposed to achieve this as follows: suppliers adjust their level of production so as to equate their marginal cost to the price; buyers adjust their level of purchase so as to equate their marginal benefit to the price; and the price adjusts so as to eliminate any excess of supply or demand (see e.g. Le Grand et al. 1992; DeMartino 2000). At market equilibrium the amount that suppliers willingly supply at the current price equals the amount that purchasers want to buy, so that there is no pressure for the price to change. An ideal market is thus supposed to move through mutually agreed steps to an equilibrium which maximises net benefit because marginal cost = price = marginal benefit across the market.

Whether this happens depends on the nature of prices and the fulfil-ment of a standard list of conditions, such as absence of monopoly power, the availability of full information to capable decision-makers, and absence of external effects, as described in any competent microeconomics textbook. Failure to fulfil any of these conditions means that the equation of marginal (societal) cost to marginal (societal) benefit fails. In the case of monopoly power, producers are able to keep their sale price above the marginal cost of production, because competition does not force it down; external effects in either production or consumption mean some costs and benefits are not measured by the market prices; in the case of poorly informed or incapable decision-makers, market prices will again poorly reflect costs and benefits; and so on. Dasgupta (1993, section 10.5) shows for example how underpricing of environmental resources in poor coun-tries leads to underpricing of their primary produce exports: a subsidy from some of the poorest groups in the world to some of the richest.

Economic policy analysis usually goes far beyond identification of only Pareto efficiency. More influential but unstated is the ethic of *utilitarianism*, which is that we should maximise a measure of total welfare/utility. It too marches under the banner of efficiency: 'Efficiency-related objectives are concerned with maximising, over time, the total welfare accruing to the economy as a whole,' stated a standard textbook on industrial development (Kirkpatrick et al. 1984: 192). This utilitarian perspective is seen in economic cost–benefit analysis of projects, and underlies much wider areas of mainstream economics treatment of choices in policy and legislation. The marginalisation of distributive objectives, as lying outside the scope of 'efficiency', may reflect business values. The utilitarian criterion of maximum societal net benefit becomes operationalised for mainstream economists through actual- or quasi-market calculations. Economic efficiency often becomes interpreted to mean the maximisation of GDP over time (as calculated in terms of scarcity prices and appropriately discounted). Discussion of 'efficiency versus equity' then arises, in terms of the supposed trade-offs between maximisation of an aggregate of net societal benefit and its desirable inter-personal distribution.

Paretian welfare economics is presented as value neutral. It looks only for *Pareto improvements*: changes which benefit at least one person and harm nobody. The criterion is likely to be invoked against calls for greater taxation of the wealthy. The moral premise adopted is that the existing legalised distribution of rights and resources must be accepted; if a polity has not changed it, that is taken to mean the polity endorses it. In practice, economics mostly proceeds with a different criterion. It looks for *potential Pareto improvements*: changes which *would* still benefit at least one person *and* harm nobody, provided that those people initially harmed had been fully compensated. Such changes are judged to be actual improvements *even if* no compensation is actually paid – and even when the net gain involves the rich benefiting and the poor losing. This converts a surface Paretianism into an actual utilitarianism. It relies on either of the following questionable premises:

- If a polity has not arranged compensation then it must consider that the change does not merit it; for example, a right of polluters to pollute may be accepted, or accepting personal losses in the cause of net societal gain may be part of an implicit social contract.
- Issues of distribution should be left for consideration in another arena, using other policy tools – the 'I leave this to my (absent) colleague' stance (Alexander 1967).

This style of justification, in which anything that exists is taken to have been agreed, links sometimes to a scepticism as to whether any further improvements are possible: for if they were possible would they not have been made already (see e.g. McCloskey 1996)? The real is rational, and optimal. If everyone believed this principle it would be self-refuting, because no one would ever have changed anything. It reads absurdly too in an ever-evolving world.

Markets themselves ignore the Pareto-improvement criterion. The move to a market equilibrium includes infliction of monetary losses on various people: for example, the entry of new suppliers in response to an attractive margin of price over production cost will reduce the price, to the detriment of existing suppliers. But at the equilibrium point no Pareto improvements are possible. Net benefit is maximised, as measured in terms of prices which reflect the present distribution of income and assets, the distribution of power, information, opportunities and tastes, and market structure. If those factors change, then the calculation of which allocation is economically efficient would change.

We can now see how 'economic efficiency' and the related terms are used differently in different ideological perspectives:

- In a pure utilitarian perspective, there are no independent distributive objectives. Social optimality and the maximisation of aggregate welfare are deemed identical.
- A pure market perspective can recognise distributive objectives but deem the existing distribution of rights and resources to be just and all goals to be adequately catered to by the market. The market equilibrium is then seen as both economically efficient and socially optimal.
- In a qualified market perspective, well-functioning markets are deemed to provide economic efficiency (both Pareto-efficient outcomes and maximised net product); but social optimality is seen as dependent on values concerning inter-personal distribution, on which opinions will differ.
- In an enriched utilitarian perspective, well-functioning markets may achieve economic efficiency, but there are many goals which are non-economic and/or beyond markets; 'social efficiency' is therefore a more encompassing concept than economic efficiency. 'Social optimality' also reflects appropriate inter-personal distribution of these economic *and* non-economic costs and benefits, and may be called 'overall efficiency' or 'total efficiency' (e.g. Johnston & Kilby 1975).

CONCEPTS OF EFFICIENCY AND PRACTICES OF VICTIMISATION

Efficiency language is a patchwork of different concepts and terms, open to misuse and abuse. Paretianism is importantly different from utilitarianism, though we often see them invoked by the same person at different times. Policy ethics can clarify concepts and their underlying values by thinking in terms of levels and the relations between them, and by combining insights from economics and other subjects.

We can conclude first that efficiency is a relational concept: 'efficiency' is only efficiency in terms of certain values or certain beliefs concerning what is valuable. Different values can lead to different conclusions about what is efficient. Shubik (1978) and Le Grand (1991) explain in detail how efficiency is often misunderstood and how an 'equity–efficiency trade-off' makes no sense when efficiency means ability to attain one's independently valued objectives. So, second, any talk of efficiency which excludes equity objectives, many other non-commodity end-state objectives and procedural objectives is very limited. It will mislead unless it makes clear which objectives it has taken into account. Economic efficiency must not be confused with a broader societal efficiency or optimality.

In politics, clarification of value differences is rarely sought. Political positions seek to present themselves as good for all groups. But in the professional practice of much of mainstream economics too, value concealment and/or value confusion exist besides its formal rigour, and serve the political programme of those with wealth. We tend to see Paretianism invoked to rule out redistribution away from the rich, yet utilitarianism invoked to excuse redistribution away from the poor (as when displacing them to make way for physical infrastructure which serves the better off). John Whitelegg in a review of the first four years of the journal *Environment and Development Economics* condemned its neglect in practice of the interests of the poor and of all but a small monetisable proportion of environmental impacts.

> In West Bengal and in Calcutta ... there is an accelerating process of environmental deterioration that imposes itself on the very poor and is linked to rapid economic development ... The decision-makers are very well informed of the consequences of their decisions ... the whole life-support system of Calcutta is under threat from a process that meets all the criteria laid down by financial institutions and international development agencies ... If a rickshaw puller in Calcutta ... is poorer, sicker, more insecure or more repressed as a result of economic change, that change is more accurately described as a redistribution of power and wealth in favour of the rich than as 'development' ... Who is valuing what when flyovers are deemed to be the solution to Calcutta's transport problems when only a tiny percentage of the population have access to cars and no one is interested in the conditions under which people, walk, cycle or use the trams? The decisions, as always, will be cloaked in the respectability of a CBA [economic cost–benefit analysis] or similar assessment, but the outcome is already known. (Whitelegg 1999)

Michael Cernea, the leading authority on forced resettlement ('involuntary displacement'), reports that it affects approximately ten million people per year, for the sake of dams, factories, ports, highways, airports, new housing. In a large proportion of cases, including in the largest developing countries – India, Brazil and perhaps China – displacement has been handled 'in a disastrous way' (Cernea 1999: 5). 'While development theories proclaim the goal of poverty reduction, development-caused displacements have generally resulted in the contrary – the impoverishment of those directly affected ... Financial costs ... are measured carefully, while the ... social costs ... are covered up and overlooked in practice' (ibid.: 4–5): 'landlessness, joblessness, homelessness, marginalisation, food insecurity, increased morbidity and mortality, loss of common property assets, and social disarticulation' (ibid.: 18). These costs are imposed on poorer groups by exploiting their 'political power-lessness ... and their lack of access to information' (ibid.: 7).

In India most displacement has happened 'without rehabilitation, but with abject and chronic impoverishment following it' (ibid.: 4). The exclusion is due not only to oversights or devotion to the principle of potential Pareto improvement. If large categories of cost were identified and not ignored, in many cases this would turn a calculation of aggregate benefit into a picture of net damage (see e.g. Alvares & Billorey 1988). As of 1998, India was still using an 1894 Land Acquisition Act – designed for moving individuals in order to permit construction of societally important facilities – to displace and destroy whole communities. There was no national legal framework to define the rights of those at risk and the duties of the state and investors to identify costs and provide compen-sation and rehabilitation. National officials declared that resettlement was a sub-national responsibility; sub-national officials declared that land acquisition was ruled by national legislation which ignored such issues. Sub-national legislation, where it exists, is often blocked, not ratified or not applied (Cernea 1999: 21–2). Commitments made in international loan agreements are ignored (ibid.: 14). Cernea does not doubt the value of much of the infrastructural investment; for example: 'In the past 15 years, the share of households with access to clean water has risen by 50 per cent, bringing dramatic improvements in health and the quality of life' (ibid.: 24). But there is no justification for not identifying, mitigating, and sharing the costs of change, rather than victimising the weak.

3.4 SETTING ECONOMIC EFFICIENCY IN SOCIAL AND ENVIRONMENTAL CONTEXT

By clarifying that there are important values which economic efficiency does not cover, we already somewhat downgrade its importance. We see next that some of those values have a prior claim, because economic life in the long run rests on respecting them or because they have a deeper normative significance.

LIMITATIONS OF A SEPARATE CONCEPT OF ECONOMIC EFFICIENCY

One's view of what will be economically efficient depends on one's theory of economic development. Producing the goods in which one immediately has a (comparative) advantage due to one's current resource endowments might not bring efficiency over the long-run. For that, one should take into account which lines of production have the most impact in generating growth of skills, technical advance, and so on. Such issues are the stock-in-trade of development policy debates. But even more important interconnections have lain outside the field of vision of mainstream economics.

Economic activity has effects on things such as political stability, environmental degradation and decisions on family size, which are both important in themselves and not measured or measurable by prices, and which then feed back and affect economic activity. Great concentrations of wealth not only register on an equity scale but can corrupt institutions and undermine future activity. What is economically efficient depends therefore on these extra-economic impacts, which are hard to predict and open to much disagreement. Economists' claims to know what is efficient in economic development display a spurious precision, and are sometimes totally misleading. A 2002 report in *The Economist* expounded once more the supposed economic efficiency of slavery in the pre-1860s American South, as if the costs of the following civil war were a totally unconnected matter. 'The most obvious facts are the most easily forgotten … no increase in material wealth will compensate [men] for arrangements which insult their self-respect and impair their freedom,' remarked R. H. Tawney.

Economic stresses contribute to social combustibility and political conflict, even collapse. In Chapter 5 on violence we look at examples: economic liberalisation in Sri Lanka since the late 1970s, and harsh economic adjustment in Yugoslavia in the late 1980s and Rwanda in the early 1990s, directly prior to their implosions. Similarly, a significant correlation is seen between aggressive forms of religious fundamentalism and economic patterns which leave large numbers of young males unemployed or insecure, and feeling socially excluded and devalued.

These 'side-effects' are not measured in economic calculations, but increasingly feed back to the global metropoli which have fostered and enforced such economic policy regimes in the South (see e.g. Sassen 2001). The decline in health systems in large parts of the South has fed the spread of tuberculosis, malaria and other disease, internationally as well as within nations. Unemployment in the South fuels illegal migration and exportation, not least in drugs, to the North. Many flights from the Caribbean to Europe now contain a high proportion of unemployed passengers who risk their lives as drug couriers, carrying their cargo in small plastic bags which they swallow before check-in and plan to excrete after arrival.

Figure 3.2 locates 'the economy' in the context of other human and natural processes. The sphere of monetised activity, plus some other

Figure 3.2 The economy in context

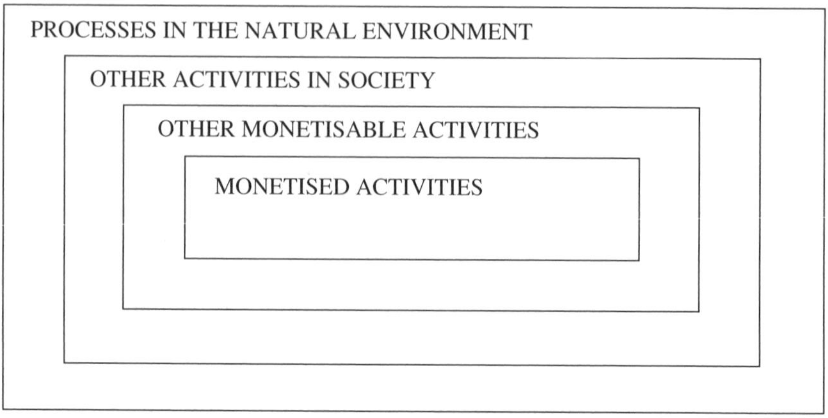

PROCESSES IN THE NATURAL ENVIRONMENT

OTHER ACTIVITIES IN SOCIETY

OTHER MONETISABLE ACTIVITIES

MONETISED ACTIVITIES

monetisable activities, constitute the economy as measured by economic statisticians. It affects and is affected by the natural environment, and by (the rest of) society, which contains both other monetisable and non-monetisable activities. Economics as an academic discipline and profess-ional sub-culture has assumed that 'the economy' is largely neutral with respect to its social and natural environment: that the economy does not have major impacts on aspects of these environments which in turn have major influence on the economy itself (Gasper 2001a); or at least that any such impacts are in the form of very slow-moving or relatively infrequent 'parameter shifts'. These assumptions do not hold true in many important cases (Swedberg 1991; Dasgupta 1993; Norgaard 1994).

In recent years, evaluation of business performance has been influenced by the notion of 'the triple bottom line': social and environmental as well as financial. (Here 'social' refers also to economic impacts which do not financially affect the organisation itself.) The notion is a major advance, in a language meaningful to businesspeople. Its limitations are the suggestions that social and environmental impacts are as measurable as the financial results, and that the three are disconnected (Zadek 2001). The sort of visualisation in Figure 3.2 can better suggest the connections. It includes not only the grey and changeable boundaries between mone-tised and other monetisable activities (e.g. some things are put in money terms by economic statisticians even though nobody buys or sells them), but also those between monetisable and other social activities and entities, and between the social and the natural/physical. It conveys the dependence of the more interior, more monetised spheres on the 'services' of the more exterior spheres; the inadequacy of performance measures for interior spheres which ignore their impacts on more exterior ones; and the dangers that arise if the two-way connections are not given central attention, as monetisation and associated attitudes – instrumentalist, individualistic, hedonistic – spread wider.

Discussion is complicated because many economists oscillate between different meanings of 'social'. First, 'social' in economics often refers to the summation of effects on individuals in the market, as in the concepts 'marginal social cost' or 'marginal social benefit' (e.g. Le Grand et al. 1992, Ch. 1), even when there are no effects external to the market. 'Societal' is a clearer label for this. One sees that sometimes economists refer to 'social efficiency' in this sense, summing the effects through the market on all individuals. But in our terms this is at most 'economic efficiency'.

Four other usages of 'social' each make a different contrast with the world of the market. Sometimes 'social' is used to mean, secondly, what is residual to, not in, the market. This matches the view of sociology as being focused on the environment for markets, an interpretation that was forced on it as a later arrival on the disciplinary scene than economics (Swedberg 1991).

Sometimes, thirdly, 'social' is instead used to mean non-monetisable, while 'economic' covers monetisable effects, whether marketised or not: as in the contrast made between the 'production benefits' and 'social benefits' of education (Le Grand et al. 1992, Ch. 3). Production benefits are where education raises skills that can be used directly in production for market; while by 'social benefits' Le Grand et al. this time refer to socialisation of the young. In addition 'intrinsic benefits' refers to the direct satisfactions from greater learning.

Fourthly, 'social' can refer to the combination of monetised and other effects, including environmental damage, as in the famous formulation of 'the problem of social cost' by Ronald Coase. Here the term 'social efficiency' refers to maximising net valued benefits, without reference to their inter-personal distribution.

Lastly, matching the interpretation of sociology as instead a comprehensive social science that integrates many fields, 'social' sometimes refers to the summation of all our concerns (market and non-market), including those for inter-personal distribution and environment. We saw that we can use for this concept instead the terms 'overall efficiency' or 'total efficiency'. Only if markets reflected everything important in life would this concept merge with the fourth and the first.

Powerful groups can use these complications and ambiguities to their own advantage.

ECONOMIC EFFICIENCY CONFINED TO A DELIMITED ROLE
WITHIN A HUMAN AND PHYSICAL CONTEXT

Daniel Rush Finn points out that the boundaries of the sphere of market-ised activities change over time. Some things that were previously outside the market become commodities, perhaps legalised, perhaps not – for example, rights to pollute; and some that were previously marketised, for example slave labour, become (more or less) removed from the market. He illustrates both types of movement in Figure 3.3. The dotted lines represent two cases of earlier market boundaries which have changed: in one case the sphere of markets expanded, in the other case it shrank.

Figure 3.3 Changing market boundaries

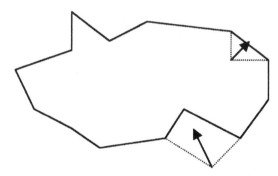

Source: Finn 1997

Some 'other monetisable activities' (see Figure 3.2) should never be monetised: they should be 'no-go areas' for markets (Figure 3.4). In other words, some exchanges should be 'blocked' (Walzer 1983; Rustin 1995). For example, the services of the judiciary and the police force should not be for sale: one should not be able to buy a prosecution or a legal verdict, nor the vote of a legislator. Likewise life should not be a commodity: one should not be able to buy the services of an assassin and thus the life of another person. Peter Brown (2000: 94) adds that sometimes life is consciously allocated, as by medical and military personnel, but in principle not on a market basis: babies for adoption should not be sold. In systems of free-market health care, however, life-saving treatment is allocated according to purchasing power.

The prohibitions on commoditisation are on grounds of moral repug-nance, and in several cases also in view of the preconditions for a market itself to function adequately – that is, for the story that the market pro-duces efficient outcomes to retain plausibility. If one can hire an assassin to eliminate a business opponent, competition may be crushed. Also trust

Figure 3.4 Limits to permissible extension of market boundaries

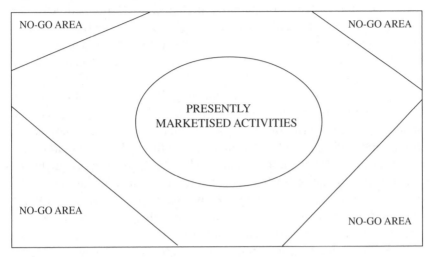

disappears and costs soar, for security services and mutual monitoring; many transactions become unworkable. If jobs can be bought, then competence and confidence and legitimacy are undermined. In some cases, commoditisation of a good might undermine society in general, for example when certain forms of objectification of persons and sale of oneself or others are involved. Even in systems of private education, places and diplomas are not to be sold to the highest bidder. For markets to simply survive, let alone perform relatively well, market valuation and market trading must not extend into many areas of life (see e.g. Miller & Walzer eds 1995).

Brown holds similarly that 'fiduciary goods' must be given priority: 'those things necessary for the protection of human rights and the bio-sphere' (2000: 81). 'Fiduciary' means 'held as a trust, on behalf of others'. He writes of 'ultimate order efficiency', the criterion used to design parameters for the economy rather than to calculate advantage within the economy. He defines this criterion as one whereby 'we treat all life with respect, and justify differential treatment' (ibid.: 65). He notes how in contrast the utilitarian criterion of economic efficiency, using the potential compensation principle, allows intolerable injustice.

> [It] moves the power of eminent domain – the power to take property with compensation in pursuit of the public good – from the public sector to the private sector. [It] permits the taking of someone else's lungs for private purposes of disposing of air pollution … [provided the market measure of benefit exceeds the measure of cost]. Moreover there is no assurance that the injured person actually be paid. (Ibid.: 81)

In practice there is no assurance either that the injury will even be identified and costed. Comparably, in the case of protection to the biosphere it can be argued that some things should not be tradeable: that any serious environmental damage should instead be cleared up as part of an activity, not merely paid for, let alone condoned because of the activity's benefits.

For Brown, Finn and similar authors (e.g. Walzer 1983; van Staveren 2001), a picture of distinct spheres of life is both a good description and an appropriate prescription. The market calculation of a businessman is not an appropriate or sufficient method in other spheres, including for much of the determination of public choices. This contrasts with the perspective of many mainstream economists, in which the further we can extend market valuation and calculation the better, since the market is seen as a unique combination of ethical liberalism, systematic calculation, and relative administrative simplicity.

The application to public policy analysis of an economic worldview derived from private financial calculations can generate severe distortions:

1. Inclusion of only paid-for benefits, as we saw in the case of travellers in low-income countries outside of paid work hours.
2. Ignoring all unpaid inputs as costs, which leads to blindness to the work and lives of women in the home.
3. The treatment of all paid inputs as costs. Viewed in a societal-decision context this leads to exaggeration of labour costs, by ignoring the positive personal value of much paid work. Part of such work could be seen as a benefit, or at least as involving a transfer payment, not as a cost to society.
4. The practice of discounting future costs and benefits, at rates more or less closely linked to real market interest rates, generates massive bias against caring about longer-run effects and future generations. It treats a problem of distributive justice between generations as if it were a technical calculation by a single selfish businessman seeking to maximise profit by comparison of his options over time in a growing economy. It thus totally misrepresents the social content of the choices involved (Brown 2000: 82–3). It involves at best a gamble, as in the case of global warming, that damage inflicted on future generations will be counteracted by technical fixes which have not yet been devised. Alternatively it is a statement of indifference: 'What did the future ever do for me?'
5. Some of the direct distortions generate responses which bring further distortions through deliberate manipulation. Discounting at market or near-market interest rates downgrades benefits overall more than costs, since the measured costs are more concentrated in the start-up period. It then generates a counteracting tendency, to try to maintain the estimated attractiveness of activities by ignoring as many costs as possible. The built-in exaggeration of real labour cost would similarly encourage a compensating tendency to deny or underestimate many other costs and to exaggerate or fabricate many benefits. Numerous methods are used for such 'cost control' and creative accounting of benefits (see e.g. Gasper 1987).

MEANS AND ENDS

So far we have assumed that economic results have to be supplemented by consideration of other costs and benefits, as contributors to overall quality of life. However, questions remain concerning how far the things measured by economics have independent significance. Income and wealth have no such significance. We are concerned rather with how having them affects the way people live or can live: in other words with a series of criteria – happiness, health, contentment, creative expression, and so on – which are closer to the social and psychological, and for which income and wealth are unacceptably poor proxies. Zadek (2001: 114) proposes, extending the spirit of Keynes to an ecologically conscious era, that 'the economic is best thought of as being about means rather than ends ... economic activity is ... the process through which humans create social and environmental outcomes'.

The so-called Easterlin paradox, formulated by the American economist Richard Easterlin, states that people's declared state of happiness does not on average increase as their personal income rises over time. (For recent restatements see Easterlin 1997, ed. 2002.) For example, there is little or no increase in average satisfaction in rich countries despite major rises in real GNP per capita. One possible explanation is that GNP is such a misleading welfare indicator. However, the paradox remains, even though less intense, once we use more adequate measures of real income. Another possible explanation is that happiness is relative to the degree of fulfilment of expectations, and that expectations go on rising. New wants and felt needs emerge as old ones are fulfilled. This fits economists' principle of the insatiability of want: particular wants may become satiated but new ones appear. It fits too Abraham Maslow's hypothesis of a hierarchy of needs, some of which are felt earlier ('prepotent') while others become felt more strongly when the prepotent ones are satisfied. But Maslow's later levels of need are not commodity focused, so his hypothesis is inconsistent with unending demand for commodities, except by a particular route. If higher needs – for creativity, self-extension and self-transcendence – have not been addressed, they become partly displaced and expressed in distorted form in the continuing pursuit of wealth and commodities, which provide temporary thrills but not enduring satisfaction, leading thus to a never-ending quest for new thrills.

Others dispute Easterlin's empirical claim, and refer for example to increased leisure and early retirement by many in rich countries (Costa 1997). But they absorb his basic evaluative point: income is not the real measure of improvement; we must look at more fundamental aspects. The lives of their dreams which the economically successful in rich countries attain when they retire sometimes look remarkably close to the whole lives of at least some simple-living people in their countries and elsewhere: less hurry, less stress, more time for their families and friends, more time to think and explore.

3.5 UNDERSTANDING VALUE SYSTEMS

The main objective of this chapter has been to clarify the value choices involved in judgements of effectiveness and efficiency, even more than to evaluate and advocate particular choices. Insight into the choices can be deepened by not only identifying the values that have been used, but examining systematically their ideological grounding and trying to understand their rationales. This section suggests some ways in which it can be done.

COMPARISON OF VALUE POSITIONS IN DEVELOPMENT EVALUATION

Values typically come not as random combinations but organised in systems, though not always tidily and consistently. These systems are moral and social philosophies, ethics, world views. One can examine how each system fits together internally and possibly more or less fits (or used to fit) a particular context; and then compare systems and look at where they agree or complement each other, and where they fundamentally conflict.

After his extrication of the tacit values in USAID development programme evaluations, which we saw in section 3.2, Roland Hoksbergen diagnosed their underlying world- and life-view. To illustrate that there are alternative perspectives, he did the same exercise for two more development approaches. One he called humanist: its focus is on extending human freedom through raising consciousness more than through raising consumption (Haque et al. 1977). The other came from an American Protestant voluntary development agency, Church World Service (CWS). Hoksbergen remarked that for USAID 'the evaluation methods are clear, while the world- and life-view is obscure. With CWS, it is just the opposite' (1986: 296). In each case. however, he draws out a picture from their publications and practice. I have constructed Table 3.2 from his comments. We see each evaluation approach as a reflection of an approach to development, with foundations in particular views of people, society and value priorities.

Let us extend Hoksbergen's picture of the system of ideas in economics-derived development evaluation, and bring together its various assumptions that we encountered in this chapter. (The next sub-section can be omitted in a first reading.)

Table 3.2 Applying Hoksbergen's method for comparison of development evaluation approaches

(Exercise: to complete this table)	MAINSTREAM WESTERN ECONOMIC (e.g. 1980s USAID)	HUMANIST (Haque et al. 1977)	RADICAL CHRISTIAN (Church World Service in 1980s)	ANOTHER VIEW, IDENTIFIED BY YOU
VIEW OF PEOPLE	Self-interested, rational maximisers	Malleable social creatures, who both adapt to and create their social environment	Created by God in his image; yet responsible for the fall into sin	
VIEW OF SOCIETY	A collection of individuals who compete in conditions of scarcity	Part of a process of historical evolution that moves progressively towards higher stages of order	Created perfect by God, flawed by man. God works to redeem his fallen world, through good people	
KEY VALUE JUDGEMENTS	The purpose of human life is for individuals to pursue happiness as they themselves define it (Hoksbergen 1986: 284). Individuals should get as much as possible of what they want (ibid.: 285)	The purpose of life is the enhancement of both individual and collective personality. The goal of development work is to promote that enhancement	Life problems are products of sin. The purpose of human life is to participate in God's purpose, obey him, restore God's community	
EVALUATION APPROACH – views on e.g.: 1. market prices 2. output values v. process values 3. quantification	1. Competitive markets are ideal systems of valuation 2. Consumption is the valuable end by which alone options should be evaluated 3. Quantification is more objective, and what is quantified is more important.	1. Focus on raising consciousness, to understand how life can be changed and improved 2. Material goods are important foci in so far as they allow creative potential to unfold 3. Self-evaluation is central	Not (then) well worked out, but included: 1. Focus on growth of local self-reliance and capabilities 2. Focus on quality of process, not material outputs 3. Joint insider–outsider evaluation	

THE STRUCTURE OF MARKET-DERIVED ARGUMENTS

We will first specify the overall structure of an argument to accept market profitability as the criterion for allocating resources, before examining and refining the details, especially the normative presuppositions. Similar arguments would arise in defence of GDP as an adequate measure of societal welfare. Table 3.3 uses a tabular format by R. V. George as a more user-friendly version of Stephen Toulmin's famous diagrammatic format for specifying argument structure (Toulmin 1958; Gasper & George 1998; Gasper 2000c). It directs our attention also to available counter-arguments to a claim, and to implied possible replies to them.

Note that the ideas and values of free-market advocates go beyond the theory of market success, to assess also the significance of market failures and to include political arguments. Nor is market ideology identical with

Table 3.3 The structure of an argument that we should accept market profitability for deciding resource allocation

I PROPOSE THAT [CLAIM]	GIVEN THAT [DATA]	AND GIVEN THE RULE/PRINCIPLE [WARRANT] THAT	UNLESS [REBUTTAL]
This activity is worth doing	It is profitable, as calculated using market prices and the market rate of interest	1. Markets are Pareto efficient; they effectively help consumers to get what they want and can pay for 2. Only workable, not perfect, competition is required, and present; and external effects (unmeasured by markets) are exaggerated, or favourable, or apply equally to all activity options 3. Consumers should get what they want and can pay for 4. Existing incomes and property rights are just	1. The calculations are wrong (e.g. the projections are too optimistic, or used a wrong formulation of the without-the-activity case) 2. The market ignores many important costs and benefits 3. Other requirements for Pareto-efficiency are not met in this case 4. The rate of interest used, or the process of discount-ing, is unacceptable 5. National citizens should receive priority over foreign consumers 6. What people want in this case is immoral 7. The market unjustifiably ignores those who cannot pay 8. Vital process values (e.g. due consultation, majority rule) have been ignored

the entire practice of capitalist systems, which for example has included recurrent recourse to force.

We saw that major assumptions behind claims for the Pareto efficiency of a market equilibrium include: there are no important 'external effects', unmeasured by markets; consumers (and producers) are competent and rational; no important information is lacking; no important power is held by any single buyer or seller; and there is no illicit interference with the market operations (such as by hiring criminals to damage a competitor's workshop): markets and selfishness do not extend into all behaviour. Market advocates typically load upon market critics the burden of proof concerning the first four requirements: the critics must show that the degree of divergence from the assumptions is important, e.g. that competition is not sufficient. Market advocates are sometimes unaware of a further assumption: the absence of major feedbacks to markets from their impacts on the social and natural environments – for example, if people diverge from market rules and rebel when they find outcomes intolerably inequitable.

This leads us to identify moral assumptions behind the more ambitious claim that a market equilibrium is socially desirable and not merely Pareto efficient. We can group these assumptions under three heads.

1. Assumptions that no important values have been omitted or differentially affected: those things not valued by the market are not important (e.g., sometimes, non-production time, or processes of deliberation) or not affected by these choices; or economic capacity is considered the key to everything else. Economic output is given direct normative significance or is treated as an excellent proxy for the real ends to which it should be a means. We saw earlier that these assumptions are often invalid.

2. The assumption of justice both in the distribution of assets and opportunities and in the processes which led to the equilibrium. This assumption too rests on often unacceptable premises: that if a distribution has not been changed, that means it has been endorsed; and that if compensation for damage is not given, it means none was considered to be due by the appropriate authorities, say because gains and losses will perhaps balance out later or because accepting losses is part of a citizen's duty. Cost-effectiveness analysis (CEA) is a tool against the bias to the rich which is built into market and market-based valuation. We can for example compare health expenditures in terms of their human value rather than market value, by the quality-adjusted years of extra life they produce per funding unit; take for instance a high-tech capital-city heart centre which benefits relatively few people versus a cheaper programme that maintains many rural

health centres and benefits a huge number of people. CEA shows the inequity of investing in the former, though in money-led medical systems it can do nothing about it. In Chapter 4 we consider criteria of equity, and cases where markets do not fulfil them. In Chapter 5 we look at the particular but huge case of human-rights violations from violence, and consider security as an important component of development and how economic calculations sometimes jeopardise it.

3. The assumption of acceptability of the preferences of the market agents. It is held then that consumers should be sovereign, given a further premise that markets have not invaded any no-go areas (Figure 3.4 above). The label, consumer rather than citizen sovereignty, is exact, for it applies only to those with purchasing power. The next subsection examines the principle more closely.

'CONSUMER SOVEREIGNTY'

Mainstream economics uses some simple starting points; it believes they are the best possible. First is that agents have more wants than they can attain, so that they feel scarcity; in fact, for practical purposes, wants are assumed to be endless. Second, third and fourth are that agents are self-interested, rational, and the best judges of their own well-being. These four assumptions are indeed usually good starting points, rather than starting by assuming that agents are completely fulfilled, altruistic, irrational, and not well placed to evaluate their own situation. They are not equally good as finishing points. Sometimes good arguments exist for not accepting them.

Under apartheid in South Africa, casinos were confined to the remote black 'homelands' and neighbouring countries. After the political settlement in 1993 leading to majority rule in 1994, some private corporations launched a large-scale programme of new casinos in or near major population centres, including near the 'high density' low-income black urban areas. Casinos take special measures to capture the lower-incomes market, such as lower prices on some days and providing special buses to transport the gamblers. A series of reports during 2001 cited cases of compulsive gamblers of all ages and both sexes, losing large sums repeatedly, sometimes reduced to sleeping in the casinos, and bringing harm to themselves and their families. The government minister responsible publicly expressed grave concern.

An assumption that agents are the best judges of their own well-being is less questionable for businesspeople and corporations, given the resources they have for analysis. Debate focuses more on consumers. The phrase 'consumer sovereignty' is sometimes read descriptively, to mean that consumers are sovereign, in that producers are induced via profit-seeking and competition to provide what consumers want. Sometimes it is read normatively, to mean that consumers should be sovereign, their wishes should prevail concerning what is good for them. The normative claim can rest on three different bases: that consumers do make good choices; that the alternative stance is worse – to use someone else's judgements and estimates of what is good for a person and how good it is; or quite differently, that people have the right to make their own choices and mistakes.

Consumers will not make good choices automatically and unconditionally. Our wants are not simple; for example some are wants to not have other wants (such as the desire to smoke or a compulsion to gamble). Establishing a mature balance between wants involves skills. Choice is also unlikely to bring satisfaction if taken on the basis of weak information. Markets often do not provide consumers with full and reliable information, for it is hard to exclude people from information and therefore to ensure payment for it, so its market supply is weakened. Instead, in a commerce-dominated society, one of the main types of information that adults get will be images that say the good life is obtained through high consumption of commodities; there is too little counteracting public information (Rhoads 1985). Casinos in southern Africa, faced with mounting criticism of their hard-sell campaign, now assign a few staff to talk with apparent problem gamblers, and display posters to reduce illusions about the chances in gambling. But information and decisions concern more than data; images, self-images, habits, capacities and willpower enter too.

The issue of consumer sovereignty goes beyond whether choices are good for the chooser. Other people are affected. Some wants may thus be unacceptable, notably wants that bring harm to others, including even wants to harm others. Mainstream economists have unfortunately often taken a don't-want-to-know, even nihilist, approach to ethics and discussions of values, in which they confuse acceptance of all wants with a value-neutral stance.

We cannot automatically draw policy conclusions for state control or prohibition from showing cases where wants diverge from needs. Other values also come in, of freedom; and state control might not help. In South Africa, the government fears that without legal outlets, illegal gambling will thrive, but with less control and with no government share in the proceeds as taxation. The policy implications to provide better information and promote consumer skills are, however, very clear.

3.6   CONCLUSION: BEYOND ECONOMISM

We began this chapter with Howard Richards's complaint that evaluators often fail to think about values. The comment applies even to exogenous values, the explicit criteria used in evaluation; and more so for endogenous values, those embedded within the evaluation approach itself (Carley 1980). The chapter has tried to contribute to what Carley recommends: more explicitness about value judgements made; formal debate between different views; and morally aware analysts.

We looked specifically at the ethics implicit in twentieth-century mainstream discussions of development, in the languages of 'effectiveness' and especially 'efficiency' used in economics and by most government and inter-governmental development agencies and consultancy companies. We saw that the conception of efficiency in mainstream economics omits inter-personal equity. The two are typically seen as competitive. Economic cost–benefit analysis (CBA) adjusts for market 'imperfections', but does not compensate those who are adversely affected by changes. Except in the very rarely used variant which weights benefits and costs according to the wealth of who is affected, it has no independent interest in inter-personal distribution. It uses the idea of 'potential compensation' and an assumption of citizens' duty to bear costs during initiatives which are calculated to be of overall national benefit. Cost-effectiveness analysis can counteract part of CBA's bias. It still has a bias to what is measurable, but is not restricted to the monetary.

Underlying the narrowness of these languages is a perspective that has been called *economism* (see e.g. Ekins & Max-Neef eds 1992; Teivainen 2002). It has various possible expressions, which are interconnected but not necessarily all adopted together:

- the idea that the economy is a separate sphere, interrelated with the rest of society only peripherally and periodically rather than fundamentally and continually, and hence able to be adequately analysed and planned for in separation;
- the alternative but related idea that the economic sphere is primary, that society is only or at least primarily an economy, a system for the provision of saleable goods; thus countries are increasingly referred to only as economies (e.g. 'the transitional economies') and the world itself as 'the world economy';
- the further connected idea that people are primarily 'economic men', driven by wants for the sorts of goods considered in economics; they are not fundamentally driven by other concerns, for rights, justice or other meanings;

- the idea that most or even all of life should be understood, valued and managed in terms of economic calculation;
- specifically the idea that societal development can satisfactorily be measured by GNP or some modification thereof, as the primary or only indicator; while some authors in Ekins & Max-Neef (eds 1992) call this 'developmentalism', we should not cede the term 'development' to an economistic interpretation;
- the proposal that the economy should be managed according to its own supposed inherent technical requirements and without political 'interference' (Teivainen 2002).

Common to all the usages is a style of taking models or procedures which are valid for specific limited purposes in economic analysis and extending them to cover the analysis or evaluation of much more of life, with little or no use of other ideas. Some economists do think they cover nearly all of life, not just a limited part. For they see life in the terms sketched by Roland Hoksbergen: that the world consists of, firstly, individuals, who have wants that lead to scarcity and necessitate choices, which they make so as to maximise their utility; and, secondly, of markets and quasi-markets, a series of arenas for which economists' tools of analysis are thought to very largely suffice. Narrow bounds of vision also reflect narrow bounds of accepted responsibility, which in turn reflect overnarrow theories of how people are interconnected, of the duties arising (if any), and of the responses available. The pure businessman can ignore his effects on other businessmen because they are seen as equally self-interested, capable competitors, responsible for themselves.

Economism – the hypertrophy and overreliance on narrow economic ideas – is, however, not identical to strongly pro-market stances. Pro-market stances can be based on over-narrow pictures of relevant effects and values, such as we criticised in this chapter, but certainly not all are (see e.g. Berger 1987, Das 2002); and types of narrow economistic thinking were prominent in state socialism too.

Once economism is entrenched in public life it is hard to dislodge. Divergences from it typically 'cannot be afforded', when evaluated by the very set of inadequate measures and narrow values which are in dispute but also in power. Peter Brown, in his sister volume in this series, rightly concludes that economics is too important to be left to conventional economists alone, and that parts of mainstream economics require considerable reconstruction.

1. Select a particular project, programme or policy, or an evaluation study. What are the values that you find being used? How would you describe them in general terms? Try to identify the 'world-view' implied by that project/programme/policy/evaluation. Should any other values be considered?
2. Complete Table 3.2.
3. What does 'efficiency' mean: (a) as used in economics textbooks and (b) in everyday uses, for instance in policy documents, speeches and newspaper editorials? Investigate some examples of each type.
4. A student asked: 'I know there is no perfect right or wrong, but why does Hoksbergen criticise economic cost–benefit evaluation so much? What is wrong with looking at costs and benefits if resources are scarce? I was thinking about examples from health-care planning, comparing the health benefits from different types of health expenditure.' What are Hoksbergen's criticisms and what are your comments? Is 'looking at costs and benefits if resources are scarce' a sufficient description of economics' cost–benefit analysis?
5. Prepare a table similar to Table 3.3, to analyse the structure of an argument that we should accept the results of an economic cost–benefit analysis for allocating resources. 'This activity is worth doing, given that it is profitable, as calculated using adjusted prices and an adjusted rate of interest as set by public authorities; and given the principles that … ; unless …' Try to specify the principles assumed, in the third column, and the potential rebuttals/counter-arguments to the claim, in the fourth column. Some will be the same or similar to those in Table 3.3, and some will be different.
6. Evaluate the large-scale introduction of casinos in South Africa, including near to low-income areas.

On value choices in evaluating development programmes, see Crewe & Harrison (1998) on the ethnography of aid, Hoksbergen's (1986) probing of underlying world- and life-views, and White & Tiongco's (1997) comparison of four such views (in Ch. 3 and Appendix A). For a more detailed method for comparing evaluation approaches, with reference also to theories of programme operation, knowledge, and research practice, see Shadish et al. (1991). For analysing the values and assumptions behind policy positions, see Fischer (1980). DeMartino (2000) gives an illuminating exposition and critique for a general audience of the mainstream economics world-view. O'Neill (1996) is enlightening on which forms of interaction between people imply mutual responsibilities.

On concepts of efficiency, the following are helpful. For a general readership: Carley (1980), Nagel (1984, Ch. 5) and Richards (1985, Ch. 4). For those with some economics background, see Killick (1981, Chs 1 & 2), Shubik (1978) and especially Le Grand (1991, Ch. 3), which explains in detail how efficiency is often misunderstood and how an 'equity–efficiency trade-off' makes no sense when efficiency means ability to attain one's independently valued objectives.

Discussion of explanatory variants of 'economism' – views which consider economic factors and economic motivations as overwhelmingly the most important, and direct, causes of human behaviour and social change – goes back at least to Lenin, Gramsci and other critics of 'vulgar Marxism'. In this chapter we focused on normative variants, which hold that societies should be managed overwhelmingly according to economic calculations, for example according to the criterion of maximizing production/GNP. For critical assessments of normative economism see Richard Norgaard (e.g. 1994) and Wolfgang Sachs (1999); and authors like John Cobb and Hazel Henderson. Teivainen (2002) examines the form of economism that defines 'economic' issues as apolitical and to be kept outside politics. He illustrates its role in Latin American economic reform programmes, especially in Peru, and its impact in reducing the power of political democracy.

On the relationships between economic activities and their natural and social environments, and between economic and other objectives, see Ekins & Max-Neef (eds 1992) and Norgaard (1994). Dasgupta (1993) identifies goods which are destroyed if marketed, and others unsuited to market allocation (sections 6.3 & 6.4); and provides valuable examples of the mutual interaction of institutional, environmental, and economic conditions (Ch. 10). Le Carré (2001) gives a disturbing picture of how the money power of giant pharmaceutical corporations can corrupt institutions and flout human rights in pursuit of profit, from Kenya to Europe to North America. Ekins & Max-Neef (eds 1992) and Söderbaum (2000) give surveys of required reconstructions and transformations in mainstream economics.

CHAPTER 4

'EQUITY': WHO BEARS COSTS AND WHO REAPS BENEFITS?

4.1 SACRIFICING THE WEAK

The opening chapter introduced development ethics' concern with identifying and responding to preventable and undeserved suffering that typically is inescapable for its victims, and with the distribution of the major costs as well as large benefits that economic development can bring. The costs of change have often been inflicted upon the weak, as we saw for giant dams, famine, international debt and structural adjustment.

This chapter looks first at wider evidence on inequity. Secondly, it clarifies and assesses concepts of 'equity'. Section 4.2 identifies and illustrates a series of concepts. Section 4.3 provides a fuller, theory-based, list. It shows how these various criteria of equity and appropriate distribution are employed, including in combination, in political discourse on debt and rights to land. Section 4.4 introduces explanations for the presence of multiple criteria, such as socio-political conflicts, opportunism, diverse situations and the insufficiency of any one criterion or approach; and discusses their elements of complementarity. We will mention but not pursue a third area, issues in implementation of concepts of equity, with reference to who has what responsibilities. These three stages of discussion – evidence; concepts and theory; policy choice and implementation – broadly match the three stages of work in ethics which we identified earlier (section 1.2).

In some cases the allocation of costs to those who do not share in the benefits is unconscious: the costs and the marginalised are barely perceived. Two to three million people died 'off-screen' in India during 1943–45 while the colonial British government mobilised resources for the war with Japan and Germany, including through inflationary expenditure. Rice prices soared in the Bengal Presidency, the area closest to the battlefronts, due also to compulsory procurement of part of the crop for military personnel and prioritised groups, hoarding in expectation of further price rises, and government restrictions on the movement of food. In parts of Bengal, low-income groups like labourers, fishermen and artisans who relied on purchase or exchange to obtain rice could no longer obtain their subsistence requirements (Sen 1981). In utter contrast, in wartime Britain during the same years a coalition government of national unity mobilised all resources for the war effort while ensuring that all citizens had access to adequate diets. British life expectancy rose far more in the 1940s than during either the previous two peacetime decades or any of the decades that followed (Drèze & Sen 1989).

In the 1980s the USA funded a vast expansion of military expenditure not by raising domestic taxes but largely by attracting funds from abroad through high interest rates. This affected interest rates and availability of funds throughout the world. The debt burden faced by low- and middle-income countries increased enormously, while in many cases powerful groups siphoned huge amounts illegally to the North. Numerous countries in the South entered macro-economic crisis, which led them to severely cut public and total expenditures on health and education.

In another type of case, allocation of costs to those who do not benefit is entirely conscious. In 'I want it, I take it' cases no justification in terms of general principles is given. But in most cases, past and present, some principle of justification is proposed – during millennia of slavery, in colonial expropriation of lands from previous occupants, and in twentieth-century sacrifice of the interests of those displaced to build dams for the benefit of others who are already more prosperous.

Many Spaniards declared their acquisition of the Americas by force to be justified because the native peoples had abhorrent practices such as human sacrifice which transgressed divine law (Parekh 1997). This was officially rejected by the Spanish king and the Pope as grounds for enslavement but remained a *de facto* defence given for conquest. The seminal seventeenth-century English liberal philosopher John Locke also rejected such reasoning, but defended the colonisation of North America on other grounds (Arneil 1996). His arguments grew out of those of the English colonisers, that fruitful use of land conveys both the right to the fruits *and* right to the land, 'provided enough and as good be left for others'. 'God gave the World to Men in Common; but … it cannot be supposed he meant it should always remain common and uncultivated. He gave it to the use of the Industrious and Rational, (and Labour was to be his Title to it).' (Locke 1690, para. 34, cited in Arneil 1996). Land uncultivated by the native Americans, even land that was lived on, hunted on or had been enclosed, could fairly be appropriated by Europeans provided that they cultivated it (Arneil 1996: 73). This was God's wish, for He had instructed man 'to be fruitful and multiply'. Thanks to an international system of commerce the Europeans were interested, and endorsed by Locke, in appropriating large areas. This was deemed to be good for the Amerindians too, who would gain from the example of Industrious Rationality.

Some authors have weakened Locke's proviso that 'enough and as good be left for others', asking instead whether the excluded became worse off than before, and claiming that they were (and would have continued) so poor otherwise that their new situation was no worse or even better: 'the baseline is so low' (Nozick 1974a discussed in Gasper 1986). Peter Brown holds instead that Locke's proposals were an attempt to operationalise a notion of trusteeship, in which 'the ultimate rationale for private appropriation of the commons is that it serve the common good' (2000: 91). He stresses that Locke's system included, besides the famous proviso, natural-law obligations to promote the subsistence of all.

In an intermediate set of cases, the suffering of the already disadvantaged is perceived but not seen as anyone's responsibility. The Great Irish Famine of the mid- and late 1840s is notorious for the deaths of probably a million people in a land then part of the wealthiest country of that time, only a short sea journey from its mainland, and for the continuing export of food while people starved. Apparently twice as much food entered Ireland as left during those years (I follow in this account Tóibín 1998), but much food still left while huge numbers starved to death or to the point where they succumbed to epidemic outbreaks, not least around the belated relief feeding points. The opportunity was seized to 'clear' much of the Irish countryside, to replace peasant with capitalist agriculture.

Rural people were dependent on a dominant staple crop of potatoes. When that failed for years repeatedly, due to disease, they had no purchasing power and no other realisable rights to ensure their survival. In Amartya Sen's language they lacked effective 'entitlements', legitimated and effective claims, to food. The price of oatmeal increased ten-fold in 1845–6, fanned by speculative hoarding by local traders and farmers, both Catholic and Protestant. Eventually, in the exceptionally cold winter of 1846–7 poor relief was provided but deliberately in the form of sheer subsistence rations in return for work. Many were too weak to fulfil the requirement of work or were killed by it. The public works system was then discontinued but not replaced by direct food relief until several months later. By mid-1847 three million people were receiving government food relief, provided as loans to be repaid later from local taxes. The government declared the famine over, but deaths continued far above normal levels for the next three years. Around a million of a population of eight million emigrated during 1845–50, in addition to the million who died. Perhaps another million left during the next decade or two.

The Great Famine was used to restructure the Irish countryside, a project foreseen and supported by the Liberal government of Russell and Palmerston. Legislation to give tenants more rights was prevented. In

1847, as the famine reached its peak, Sir William Gregory, a prominent Anglo-Irish landowner, added a clause to the Irish Poor Law which was endorsed by the British–Irish Parliament in London, including by most of the Irish MPs. It prohibited poor relief to any family which held more than a quarter of an acre (1 hectare) of land. Starving tenants were forced to give up their holdings, and landlords became able to shift to more profitable livestock farming. 'The country grew economically in the second half of the 19th century on the strength of the land clearances.' (Tóibín 1998: 23) That many in Ireland, Catholics as well as Protestants, prospered from the famine and its aftermath, contributed to an extraordinary lack of historical research later. The matter was too sensitive. Simple pictures of British barbarism, or Irish fecklessness and sloth, ruled instead. A leading British official involved in responding (or not) to the famine – Charles Trevelyan, Assistant Secretary to the Treasury – declared at the time that God in His 'Supreme Wisdom has educed permanent good out of transient evil', by forcing the Irish to reform their supposedly indolent ways (cited ibid.).

In the preceding chapter we found that mainstream economics' priority category of efficiency quietly omits inter-personal equity. Equity is left for separate 'non-efficiency' policies, or left out altogether. Utilitarianism is willing to sacrifice individuals for a greater good: it has no independent concern with equity or equality. If these help towards the greater good, that is fine; when they do not, then 'we must break eggs to make an omelette'. The typical stance in economics is in fact quasi-utilitarian: its calculations of benefit and cost are in money terms rather than in terms of utility as persons' satisfactions or strains, and so are biased towards people with greater purchasing power. People with no money are ignored.

Surely all societies are forced to sacrifice individuals sometimes? Why might one say that utilitarianism, and especially economics' quasi-utilitarianism, are unjust? What can we mean by an equitable distribution of benefits and costs between people – anything more than that we like that distribution, just as we may like a type of wine? Dictionaries define 'equity' as: justice according to natural law or right, meaning regardless of what official laws say (Webster's); freedom from bias or favouritism (Webster's); impartiality or fairness in acts or (implicitly) in outcomes (Collins). This does not yet help us much, for very different interpretations exist of natural law or right, bias and fairness. 'Equity' is a potent term, like 'efficiency', so we encounter multiple claimants to the throne, and frequent lack of precise and consistent usage.

Economics literature includes valuable discussions of ways of trying to promote equity via taxation, subsidies, laws, investment, and so on; of the perverse effects possible when the measures affect people's incentives and perhaps lead behaviour in an unintended and undesirable direction; and of who actually receives the resources that are redistributed. In Britain in the 1980s, for every pound spent on rail subsidies for the poorest fifth of the population, almost ten pounds went on subsidising the rail travel of the richest fifth. Rail travel subsidies are an indiscriminate way of trying to help poorer people, as the greatest beneficiaries are more affluent commuters who reside in distant suburbs or charming rural locales. Similarly for every pound of government funds to support university education for the poorest fifth of the population, five pounds went to support it for the richest fifth; and so on, in various sectors (Goodin et al. 1987). 'Britain's middle classes, after all, did not set up their welfare state just because they felt sorry for the poor. They did so to provide social insurance for themselves in a world [that had been] traumatised by [economic] depression and war' (*The Economist*, 17 October 1987).

Is this capture of benefits by middle (and upper) classes unfair? The subsidies were determined by an elected government, benefited all who qualified for, say, university education, and were perhaps to general advantage: for example, if the affluent did not commute by train they would drive, causing many problems. But the economics and other literatures commonly do not make clear what they mean by equity or fairness. They sometimes assumes it means equality, and at other times mix together different ideas. Let us see the ideas involved.

4.2 ASPECTS OF EQUITY

CRITERIA OF DISTRIBUTIVE EQUITY

We talk often of equity. For example, many definitions of the purpose of regional planning are in terms of establishing spatial equity or, more simply, reduction of inter-regional differentials. Yet the term 'equity' tends to be used loosely. The three italicised categories below are incorrectly treated as interchangeable.

> Our development is concerned with the *distribution of the benefits* of development. In other words, *the degree of inequality* (which encompasses inequality between individuals or social groups and inequality between areas) is regarded as an important criterion for measuring development and the reduction of inequalities is considered to be one of the most important goals of development. *This concern with equity* is well expressed in [the phrase] Growth with Equity. (Chikowore 1988a: 3; emphases added)

But more *equity* need not imply more *equality*; for instance some individuals or regions might be thought to have earned more or need more. And other aspects than the distribution of benefits concern us too, including the nature of the distribution processes.

This section presents a number of concepts of equity. It illustrates their relevance to criteria in Zimbabwe for selecting people for resettlement, rules for access to grazing, and the issue of positive discrimination. Zimbabwe, ruled by European settlers from 1890 to 1979/80, is selected because tensions there around distributive justice have been extremely high. Inequalities in wealth and income have been great in several over-lapping dimensions: (a) between whites and blacks, (b) between the lands allotted to them under the white settler regime pre-1980; (c) between professionals, manual workers and peasants; (d) between urban and rural; (e) between those with good land, cattle, and non-agricultural incomes, and other people in rural areas; and (f) between those with privileged access to other scarce resources (like new cars, foreign currency and travel) and the remainder of the population.

One preliminary clarification concerns 'equity regarding what?'. Distributive equity concerns the inter-personal (or inter-group) allocation of costs and benefits. Sometimes the term is used more narrowly, to concern only the distribution of benefits, and a second term, contributive justice, is used regarding how contributions of inputs are shared; but here the term will refer to both inputs and outcomes. More distinct from distributive equity is procedural equity: fairness in the procedures that are used. Again, however, there is overlap. When President Julius Nyerere reviewed the first decade of his *ujamaa* socialism in Tanzania, he covered facets of all three:

> There are three aspects to the development of greater equality within a nation. One is differentials in personal incomes. The second is different degrees of access to public services, and the extent to which taxation-supported activities serve the interests of the people as a whole rather than those of a small minority. And the third is participation in decision-making. (Nyerere 1977: 48)

All affect equality of opportunities for a good life. There is also equality before the law. Since people's locations and skills differ so much, their situations appear different according to which of these aspects we consider.

Each of the aspects requires further subdivision. Michael Walzer (1983) distinguishes 'spheres of justice', each of which he says has its own appro-priate criteria of equity and fair procedure. His 'spheres' include: assurance of basic subsistence; markets for conveniences; and allocation of group membership, responsible jobs, education, affection, recognition and political power.

Another preliminary clarification is to ask: 'Equity amongst whom?' We noted in the last chapter different standpoints on how far to extend the geographical boundaries of evaluation; and often discussions concern equity not between individuals but between classes, regions, genders, races, nations. Greater equality between regions or races or nations does not necessarily increase equality between persons.

Here we concentrate first on the equity concepts themselves. We will focus on distributive equity/justice, with reference included to procedural aspects. William Blanchard assembles a list of different norms or criteria of equity, interpreted as fairness (Blanchard 1986):

A. Equality
B. Need
C. Effort expended
D. Money invested
E. Results
F. Ascription
G. Fair procedure
(H. Demand & preference)

View A is the simplest interpretation. Equity is seen as meaning *equality*; inequality is seen as inequitable. We need to ask why (section 4.5 will look at some responses); and again, equality of what? Equality in some dimensions is not equitable. Equalising average distances for both the rich and the poor from public facilities such as parks would neglect that the rich have more transport possibilities, (bigger) gardens, more other entertainment, and live in lower-density areas.

View B holds that fairness implies distribution to whomever is most in *need*, not simply to whomever is present. Needs are not equal: for example, the old and the sick need more. A classic socialist ideal of distributive justice is 'to each according to his needs', at any rate for the stage of 'full communism'. This is often paired with the contributive principle of 'from each according to his abilities'. We require criteria to prioritise 'needs'. Rich areas might 'need' extra policing, but not as a priority claim on government resources. An area's need for further parks might be judged in terms not just of its shortage of parks but its overall deprivation. Even so, there is no point in providing a park that would not be used, even if 'needed'. In Chapter 6 we will consider priority criteria and who prioritises.

The third and fourth views (C, D) concern not one's current state but instead what one has *done*: how much one has contributed in terms of *money* or *effort* (which can be measured by quantity or quality); in other words 'to each according to his contribution'. The conventional Marxist ideal during earlier stages of socialism was 'to each according to his work'. Using this criterion, President Mugabe warned workers of 'Lenin's saying: "Those who don't work neither shall they eat"' (Mugabe 1987: 10).

The fifth view (E) concerns not what one has done but what one *will do*. Here resources can fairly go to people who will (we expect) make best use of them and produce the best results. Some people feel that this criterion takes us beyond the scope of 'equity', and matches rather the production maximisation concern of 'economic efficiency'. Arguably the term 'fairness' might still cover it, if we feel it is fair to give land to those people who will make it flourish, not degrade it. 'Overall efficiency', we may recall from Chapter 3, pays attention to both production and equitable inter-personal distribution.

Blanchard's sixth type of norm (F) returns to who one is, but now with restrictions concerning who has the right to benefit: on grounds of *ascriptive* status, e.g. sex, age, caste, race or nationality. These are grounds which an individual can do nothing about, at least in the short run. For example a city council may consider it fair to only allocate housing to people who are already registered as residents, even if other people need housing more or would maintain it better.

The seventh type of norm (G) holds that an allocation is fair if it is produced by *procedures* that are accepted as fair. Some of the possible procedures are an unbiased lottery, inheritance, a first-come-first-served rule, or fulfilment of freely made agreements. In practice:

> Whether in Russia or Bolivia or India, poor people say that they often do not get paid when they complete a job and have no recourse to justice ... They complain of loan officers who deduct 20–50 per cent of loans as 'processing fees', policemen who are oppressors rather than protectors, and justice that is available only to the rich. (Narayan 2000: 4)

Lastly, but perhaps going beyond the bounds of equity or fairness, there is the norm that distribution should be to the people who show that they most *want* the good (H). *(Expressed) demand* might be measured by degree of use, if there are existing facilities; by levels of requests or complaints, although this gives a bias to educated people; or by the money that people are willing to pay, but this prioritises the wants of the rich. *Willingness to pay is,* however, seen as an equity concept by many people – on the grounds that if the user does not pay, then who will and why should they? – unless bad income distribution or major externalities and risk are present. Unexpressed preferences can be investigated through public hearings, panels and surveys.

These norms or criteria sometimes overlap or are hard to distinguish; yet the list helps us to think more clearly about equity. Let us take two cases in Zimbabwe – selection for resettlement and access to grazing lands – and the general issue of positive discrimination.

AN APPLICATION TO THE REGULATION OF GRAZING IN ZIMBABWE

How should access to communally held grazing lands be distributed, given both the very unequal ownership of cattle and the dangers of overgrazing? Norman Reynolds (1987) tried out different possibilities on a group of farmers.

> 1. 'We had a fascinating discussion with five large farmers ... they could not carry the community with them [on grazing management], it was each man for himself ... We asked if they thought it unfair that they enjoyed their birthright while others could not. This caused some hesitation. It was an unfair question one responded. They had the right to graze, the others simply had no cattle. It was not their doing.'

These farmers' response fits Blanchard's norm G: open-access grazing is thought to be a fair procedure, so they deem its outcomes fair, even when very unequal. This view seems to be accepted too by many of those who have no cattle; they dream of a time when they will have animals to share the grazing.

> 2. 'All right, we agreed, but if you accept that there is a need to set a carrying capacity, how would you allocate the rights to graze. They ... had no answer ... [They] were suspicious of [each adult having equal grazing rights] ... because most of the rights could not be exercised [since most people have few or no cattle].'

The farmers reject the simplest variant of norm A, the norm of equality, allocation to each community member of an equal amount of grazing land or rights to graze the same number of cattle.

> 3. 'What if people could exchange their rights for a price fixed locally, say $10 per livestock unit ...? [Most] were not happy. Why pay to others, why increase the cost of running cattle?'

The proposal was to supplement equal rights with norm H, allocation according to demand and ability to pay. The aim was to overcome the objection that many rights could not be exercised, by allowing those who cannot or do not wish to exercise their rights to rent them to others who would want extra rights. But this would leave the large cattle-holders directly worse off than under the system of open access. What might induce them to accept such a cost?

> 4. 'What if the community agreed to tax themselves, say 50 per cent of the going price of a grazing unit would go into a fund to improve the grazing[?] The rich would be compensating those who could not exercise their grazing rights and providing the cash upon which the poor would pay the same ... tax.'

This final proposal adds norm E, i.e. a concern with effective use, to norms A, G and H which had already entered the discussion.

Suddenly there was interest from all five farmers. They saw management, efficiency, investment and equity as possible. (All quotes for this case are from Reynolds 1987: 22–3.)

Jan Tinbergen's theorem in policy studies says that we need at least one policy tool for every policy objective. Here for the three objectives of equitable distribution, production (implying land should not be left idle) and conservation, three tools are suggested: equal grazing allocations, plus a system of renting, plus a tax for improving grazing.

Such combinations of norms are common. Canaan Banana, the former president of Zimbabwe, extolled the needs criterion: 'Man's right, indisputable right to means to life ... "to each one according to his need"... One cannot think of a better order for the Zimbabweans ...' (1987: 6). On another occasion, asked about his purchase of a large house in the low-density suburb of Mount Pleasant a few years after independence, he added the criterion of amount contributed:

I try to save, but each time you get money, say, you go to the beerhall. After ten or twenty years I have saved reasonably enough for a house, then you come and say, 'You are a capitalist!'... [Not] everybody who is poor has been exploited. They might have exploited themselves. (Banana 1988: 5)

AN APPLICATION TO SELECTION FOR RESETTLEMENT IN ZIMBABWE

The original criteria used for rural resettlement after Zimbabwean majority rule in 1980 were broadly these:

1. Age: adults not more than 50/55 years
2. Citizenship: Zimbabwean
3. Family status: head of household, with dependents
4. Health: good
5. Income: low
6. Landholding: little or none
7. Agreement to (a) not have any formal sector employment, and (b) not hold land outside the resettlement area
8. First come, first served: the queueing principle

Criteria 1 to 4 can be seen as ascriptive (Blanchard's norm F). They were used in an initial screening-out of some applicants, to make the selection process more manageable. Each ascriptive criterion is a rough-and-ready indicator for a more substantive criterion. It is usually considered fair for example that a government discriminates in favour of its own citizens in such cases: because citizens are members of a group that operates under shared procedures for contributions, opportunities and receipts, and are presumed more likely to have made relevant contributions in the past. The age and health criteria, and perhaps that of family status, could be proxies for ability to use the land well and produce desired results (Blanchard's norm E). In all cases the proxies are not very accurate indicators; but they are easy to apply and hence good for screening. The screening was not very restrictive, with one exception: the exclusion of women applicants who had husbands working elsewhere. The absentee husband was presumed to be the head of household, and the household was excluded by criterion 7a, prohibition of outside employment.

The more restrictive, and hence major, criteria used were numbers 5, 6 and 7, which like number 3 are need criteria (norm B). Criterion 6 – having no or insufficient land – initially also covered many who had been displaced to 'protected villages' or went to other countries during the liberation war. Criterion 7a – having no other employment – might also be a proxy for concern with production results, if one believes that this requires full-time farmers. There is much evidence, however, that farming success is related to having outside sources of income. Criterion 8, the queueing principle, comes into play if screening still leaves many more candidates than there are current resettlement places, as was the case.

So need was the main criterion, subject to some ascriptive conditions; plus, of course, the criterion of willingness to move, which fits Blanchard's demand norm (H). The criterion of equality did not figure directly, but its implications correlated fairly well in this case with those of the principle of need; in addition, those selected were supposed to be given resources of equal potential. Actual selection did not always match the official criteria:

> [The President] said there had been instances where people who had jobs and had no pressing need for land were resettled at the expense of productive farmers. This mostly occurred where the beneficiaries were related to the officials who identified people eligible for resettlement. (*The Herald* newspaper, 27 March 1990)

And it was largely impossible to enforce criterion 6; at most, people as a result passed their previous landholding to a relative.

Besides the original official criteria, other criteria came forward in public discussion:

    9. Ability to use the land well
    10. Service record in the liberation war
    11. Historical claims of people in a particular area
    12. Strength of desire to settle the land

The criterion of ability to use the land well was advanced by the small-scale commercial farmers and 'Master Farmers' (i.e. those with a formal farming qualification), and by some Parliamentarians. Fears were voiced that extension of average Communal Area farming into resettlement areas was bringing misuse and degradation. Norm E was used here: a concern with future results, with an assumption that a Master Farmer certificate is a good proxy for farming ability. The Zimbabwe government gradually moved towards emphasising this criterion. From around 1983, criterion 6 (having little or no land) declined, from being almost a necessary and sufficient condition, to being just one consideration; and Master Farmers were no longer excluded from resettlement. By 1988 Enos Chikowore, the Minister of Local Government, Rural and Urban Development, said: 'Rural district councils should identify the *potential* individual settlers on the degree of individual family need, then *select*, giving preference to those with either a proven track record in farming, or keenness and potential ability' (1988b: 5; emphases added). Since many were needy, the key consideration became productivity. An extraordinary further twist was added by Minister Victoria Chitepo: 'The Government will not consider for resettlement those communal farmers who have intentionally neglected or misused their natural resources in order to be resettled in better land'! (1988: 2). Some peasants became blamed for overpopulation and were to be excluded on grounds of their poor quantity or quality of effort.

Rather than looking to future results or present needs, some criteria refer to the past: either the immediate past of the liberation war, or back to earlier generations and the question of which community was displaced by the European settlers from a particular piece of land. Looking at people's war records fits norm C (effort expended). It does not seem to have been used much for resettlement to family farms. The criterion of historical claim to a particular piece of land is used by many rural people, and is based on norm G (fair procedure). The claim is that the land was previously rightfully inherited and held by a particular local community, then unrightfully seized from them, and should rightfully be returned. This was rejected by the government, for the local people were not necessarily those most in need. The government sought to impose national-level norms over local norms. In addition, referring to past occupation would open up many questions: what if the previous owners had themselves displaced another group by force? do claims from the past have to be discounted in weight according to how long ago they refer to?

The final criterion, no. 12, matched norm H (demand): the intensity of desire to settle the land, as shown by actually taking possession of it, i.e. by 'squatting'. This is a present-oriented criterion, like need. Strong demand might also be a good proxy for future results. In principle, the government always rejected squatting. Squatters are again not necessarily those most in need or best able to use the land. Some 'squatters' were not poor and landless, but instead those with the urge, resources and skills to expand: for example, those with cattle that sought extra grazing and could provide draught power. This would be a positive qualification in terms of a results criterion, but not in terms of the neediness norm (if we consider needs of people more than needs of cattle). In practice, many squatters managed to acquire land (Gasper 1990). Some political leaders, as opposed to civil servants, supported squatters; and it was not politically acceptable to remove all or most of the squatters, especially after they had begun to invest. But after endorsing many of the initial squatters, the government wished to control further land allocation. The Minister of Rural Development declared 'total war on squatters', saying they 'were a menace and wanted to destroy and plunder the country's resources' (Chikowore 1987).

By 1990 the criterion of expected future results had become dominant. The new Minister of Agriculture declared:

> Land will not be given to anyone who wants it. We made mistakes in the past by giving land to people who, in turn, leased it to others, who were only interested in cutting down trees for firewood. We will give land ... only to those who have proven knowledge and ability of how to use the land ... those who have the desire, commitment, knowledge, ability and wish to use the land. (Mangwende 1990)

Overall, the Zimbabwean government originally gave priority to the present-oriented criterion of need, and in practice some weight too to manifest demand. It did not give priority to past-oriented criteria. Over time it increasingly stressed future-oriented criteria of ability to use the land. All this changed dramatically in the late 1990s. The ascriptive criterion of support for the ruling party became overriding.

POSITIVE DISCRIMINATION?

The different pulls of past, present and future are thus one key theme in disputes about what is fair. Consider the arguments in Africa over whether to offer special inducements to expatriate nationals to return. As of the late 1980s, around half of Ghana's graduate manpower was abroad, for example. They would not give up what they enjoyed there in order to return unless compensated in some way. The required inducements might be an effective investment in terms of future return on national resources. Yet the people who would directly benefit would be those who, it could be argued, firstly deserved less because they had shown less loyalty in the past, and secondly needed less reward in the present because they were already better off (and had been so for many years) than their compatriots who stayed at home. Most of those who had stayed in Ghana were strongly opposed to offering inducements, even if foreign aid were available to pay for them.

In the Ghana case people debated positive discrimination towards those who were already advantaged. Usually positive discrimination is supposed to be for those who are less advantaged. Amongst the arguments put forward as to why African-Americans should be subject to lower college admission standards, we can again distinguish arguments that refer to past, present and future.

In terms of the present (or, strictly, the near future): 'the Faculty Senate at Berkeley has argued that certain ethnic backgrounds should themselves be taken as qualifications for admissions, since such diversity encourages "a more dynamic intellectual environment and a richer undergraduate performance"' (Hacker 1989: 63). Another present-oriented argument is that certain ethnic groups are on average poorer and more needy; in practice, however, positive discrimination policies rarely apply those criteria to individual admissions, and typically benefit disproportionately people from wealthy and middle-class families within the prioritised groups.

Next, in terms of the past: 'a further argument is that blacks, in particular, are entitled to special consideration, in order to compensate for having been held back by enslavement and discrimination [in previous and current generations. Similarly, military] veterans, who lost time serving their country, have points added to their civil service scores' (ibid.). One version of the argument is that Afro-Americans would have done better in their school education if not for previous discrimination. Another version is that people need to be compensated in some way or other for past discrimination as a whole, and that education is the area where they wish to receive support.

'A third view takes a practical turn, arguing that for its own well-being the nation needs blacks in a wider range of positions.' (Ibid.) This is a concern for future results. So in contrast to the Ghana case, here the past, present and future considerations may point in the same direction.

Similar types of argument can apply to former freedom fighters in various countries. Firstly, they unfairly lacked past opportunities because they were away to fight. This argument fits a criterion of fair procedures, under the special case of compensating for unfairness. The second argument is that former fighters deserve to be rewarded for their actual fighting. Rewards could include money or special opportunities (i.e. reverse discrimination), but not the grant of educational qualifications.

4.3 A DEEPER ANALYSIS OF CONCEPTS

We can now distinguish distributive criteria and understand them as past-, present-, or future-oriented. This section goes deeper. We follow the framework provided in Sen (1984), with additions and modifications. Its logical structure helps us to see more possibilities and more connections.

SEN'S FRAMEWORK FOR UNDERSTANDING DIFFERENT DISTRIBUTIVE CRITERIA

Amartya Sen analyses ten important types of criteria of appropriate distribution. He uses as a guide his identification of the components of the utilitarian ethics which underlies most economic policy analysis.

Utilitarianism holds that policy should aim to maximise the sum of all individuals' utilities. The meaning of 'utility' often remains conveniently ambiguous, as satisfaction or preference fulfilment or merely free choice. These need not be the same, but the standard economics assumption is that people always choose what they prefer *ex ante* and still prefer it *ex post*. The 'revealed preference' assumption declares that if something was chosen, that shows it was preferred. Preference fulfilment matches Blanchard's norm H.

Utilitarianism consists of three logically separable claims (Sen 1982):

> 1. *Consequentialism*: one should assess options and actions by their consequences/effects/results (only); i.e. we should look to the future rather than the past.
>
> This looks similar to Blanchard's norm E, that one should look at results; but note that it covers immediate results as well as those in the longer term, and it concerns any type of result, e.g. need fulfilment. While I have discussed need as a present-oriented criterion, one can also consider fulfilment of needs in the future. Since there is no sharp line dividing 'present' and 'future' – we face gradations of short-, medium-, and long-term futures – I will from now contrast only future- and past-oriented criteria.
>
> 2. *Utility base:* the results that one should consider are utility effects; all relevant results can be measured in terms of a common denominator, namely utility, as experienced by individuals.
>
> Sen uses here the label 'welfarism' for the claim that a society's situation should be judged only by the welfare of its individual members, seen as the set of their utilities. His label is problematic, since 'welfare' can be understood in many ways other than utility, and since 'welfarism' has different meanings in everyday language, associated with welfare states. 'Utility base' is a better label.
>
> 3. *Sum-ranking*: one should rank options and actions by the (net) sum-total of valued effects they produce in society.

Utilitarianism has been a major strand in ethics, in policy economics (e.g. in cost–benefit analysis; MacIntyre 1977) and in planning (Eversley 1973, Sillince 1986). Its prominence reflects its relative clarity and broad scope, which make it a good starting point in discussion. Objections can be raised to each of its elements, and we can then see how other criteria of distribution reject some or all of them. Table 4.1 indicates areas of agreement and disagreement. (Some entries are placed in brackets where a theory might in principle adopt either of the options or there are other complications. The letters after most theories indicate the criteria to which they most closely correspond in Blanchard's list.)

Table 4.1 Components analysis of norms of appropriate distribution

DISTRIBUTIVE NORMS COMPARED IN TERMS OF THE COMPONENTS OF UTILITARIANISM	CONSEQUENTIALISM (look only to the future, at effects)	UTILITY BASE (look only at satisfaction effects or fulfilment of choices or of preferences)	SUM RANKING (rank situations by the sum total of the valued effects)
1. UTILITARIANISM [E] *Results*	Yes	Yes	Yes
1a. ECONOMIC COST–BENEFIT ANALYSIS	Yes	Yes (measured by willingness to pay WTP)	Yes
2. PARETO CRITERION	Yes	Yes	No
3. RELATIONAL PRINCIPLES	Yes	Yes/No	No
3a. EQUALITY-WEIGHTED COST–BENEFIT ANALYSIS	Yes	Not in terms of WTP / Yes in terms of different weights	Not in terms of WTP / Yes in terms of different weights
4. RAWLS	No	No	No
5. NEEDS [B]	Yes	No	Yes/No
6. OTHER RESULTS [E]	Yes	No	Yes/(No)
7. CONSTRAINTS SET BY OTHER RIGHTS	No	No	(Yes)/No
8. DESERTS; LABOUR RIGHTS [C]	No	(No)	(No)
9. HISTORICAL RIGHTS [D, G] *Money invested & Results*	No	No	(No)
10. AGENT-SPECIFIC DUTIES [F]	Yes/No	(No)	(No)

The analysis is more systematic than Blanchard's and leads us to see more criteria. Sum-ranking implies no direct concern with distribution. Utilitarianism has only a possible indirect concern, for example if one believes that moving to a more equal distribution will transfer goods from people who obtain lower marginal utility from them to people who will have higher marginal utility. But if unequal distribution leads to greater total utility then it would be supported. We saw that utilitarianism is in principle willing to sacrifice individuals for the greater good. At the extreme, a man might be 'cannibalised' for the spare parts needed to save many others or a great man; a human guinea pig may be subjected, without being asked, to tests that could yield important knowledge; conscripts can be sent to their death in war; and one generation can be sacrificed for the greater benefit of future generations. If it is clear that a particular sacrifice does not increase total utility, perhaps due to various indirect negative effects, then utilitarians will not advocate it; but they are ready to consider sacrificing individuals.

Utilitarianism has the great merits in principle of considering everyone who experiences utility, in a systematic evidence-based fashion. We observed though that its main operationalisations in practice, versions of economic policy analysis such as cost–benefit analysis, in fact exclude everyone without money and typically weight other people according to their wealth. This variant is so extreme, and so important, that we highlight it separately (1a). It might be called 'money-tarianism'.

Many theories reject sum-ranking. The most minimal departure from utilitarianism is the *Pareto criterion* in economics (no. 2 in the table), which avoids summing the utility gains and losses of different people. All it can therefore say is that a move in which at least one person gains and no one loses is an improvement, with a corresponding claim about retrogressions. But in real policy moves there are virtually always some people who lose as others gain. And the criterion of only potential improvement of this kind is typically operationalised in money-tarian form, as seen in Chapter 3.

Some other criteria which reject sum ranking are more helpful. One set are *relational or comparative principles* (no. 3), so called because they give independent weight to some aspect(s) of the pattern of inter-personal distribution. The simplest example is the equality principle: equal results are best. Another example is the maximin principle: that we should choose the option which does best for the person (or group) at the bottom. This principle supports inequality as long as it means the poorest get more than they otherwise would.

The maximin principle is popularly associated with the American philosopher John Rawls. It actually forms only one part of his proposed principles of justice (Rawls 1972). Rawls' *theory* (no. 4 in the table) further differs from utilitarianism in its 'currency' for comparisons. Rawls is centrally concerned with the distribution of 'primary goods', including rights, liberties and opportunities, and the requirements for self-respect, not just with utilities. Sen extends this concern, to avoid bias against people for whom such requirements are more costly (e.g. those who are less talented, or who need more; Sen 1984). He emphasises the attainment of valued functionings, like a long healthy life, and capabilities, the freedom to achieve those valued functionings. Both authors reject the utility-base assumption. Sen considers utility/satisfaction an unreliable and incomplete measure of well-being or advantage, since people's preferences and satisfactions typically adapt to their circumstances. The deprived may not frustrate themselves by preferences they cannot fulfil; the privileged may focus on unfulfilled wants. In both cases their felt satisfaction may give a misleading measure of their welfare. Sen's approach will be discussed further in Chapter 7.

Principles of *need* (no. 5; the same as Blanchard's norm B) similarly reject a utility denominator. They posit that some people have greater needs than others and should receive more resources, regardless of whether this produces more satisfaction than the alternative uses. If we expect that young people are more effective satisfaction-generators than are old people, principles of utility would direct resources more towards the young, principles of need relatively more towards the old. Needs are different from wants; one can say that children need education, or that populations at risk need inoculation, even if they don't want it. In health sectors, discussions of equity focus on need fulfilment and equality of access. We investigate this criterion more in Chapter 6.

Next, there are positions (no. 6 in the table) which are consequentialist, concerned with maximising the attainment of approved outcomes, but which do not take utility or need-fulfilment as the objectives. Many *other results* are advocated: for example, to increase knowledge or capability or freedom or participation or national greatness or prestige – for their own sake, not because they advance utility or another objective. Mixed positions are possible. Values like freedom or democracy can also appear as setting constraints on the pursuit of other objectives (no. 7). Rights based on considerations like freedom here set limits (absolute or non-absolute) on what can be done to achieve other goods. Rights might in turn rest on considerations of basic need (Li 1996).

Positions 8 and 9 concern other asserted *rights* presented as independent claims to benefits. Both positions reject consequentialism and instead look to the past. Position 8 covers claims that people *deserve* something because of their previous contributions; hence the word 'deserts'. Contributions could be judged in terms of effort or money (Blanchard's norms C and D), or skill and effectiveness, or loyalty and commitment, and so on. Where people are considered as deserving of something just because of what they are – male or white or a holder of a party card – we come instead to Blanchard's ascriptive heading. Basic human rights arise in respect of being a human being, not – consider children – on the basis of past contributions.

In position 9 people are *entitled* to things that they obtained in the past through *fair procedures*, regardless of whether or not they deserve or have earned them. They may simply have been lucky, or have inherited goods from people (usually their own family) who were in turn entitled to them. In this position it is held that a person has a right to give her goods to whomsoever she chooses; and that the beneficiary of a fair transaction has the same right. The libertarian philosopher Robert Nozick expounded an extreme but influential version in which this principle of entitlement had absolute priority, above for example the needs of the starving. This is one interpretation of Blanchard's norm G of fair procedure.

Position 10 holds that one has a *duty* to give priority to certain other people to whom one is responsible, even if those are not the people most in need or most deserving or best able to benefit. The duty could stem from a general relationship, e.g. to one's children or parents or fellow nationals, or from a specific commitment, say if one has made a promise. Some people claim in support that if one lacks a strong commitment to one's family then one is unlikely to be committed to anything else outside oneself. However this position is a further step away from the universalism seen in utilitarianism or needs theories. The (extended) family has an ascriptive/agent-specific morality that preferentially includes family members and not others.

The list we have drawn from Sen is more structured and insightful than Blanchard's. In addition it looks not just at equity or fairness, but also at other criteria for appropriate distribution. There is no consensus on the exact scope of these terms. People hold differing theories of what equity and social justice mean, and wish to gain the legitimacy that goes with the terms by putting forward definitions that match their interests.

One does not have to look far to find these principles in public use, as we will now see. The difficulty on the contrary is that we find so many of them in simultaneous use, without an overall framework. Section 4.4 will consider possible responses.

LAND, RETURNS AND THE FRUITS OF EFFORT

In discussions of the land question in Zimbabwe, we find reference to all the criteria. Interestingly, Robert Mugabe drew, via Julius Nyerere, on parts of the same Lockean philosophy used by the European settlers in North America and southern Africa.

> These God-made or nature-made phenomena are ours together ... I find my views on this subject in very interesting coincidence with those of Mwalimu Julius Nyerere who says ... 'land is simply God's gift to his living creation. There is no human effort involved ...' [DG: This is the context for application of a pure equality criterion. Nyerere seems to apply it to all living creation, not only humankind.]
>
> Nyerere then proceeds to state that whenever a man 'uses his intellect, his health and his ability to make anything, that thing becomes his property' ... Indeed when an individual expends his own labour and energy in exploiting any natural resource at his disposal, *provided* others are also entitled alongside him to similar exploitation of that resource, then the product of his labour must morally be his, and he is *fully entitled* to use such product to his own benefit or in *any* other manner of his choice. On the basis of this moral reckoning ... workers are certainly entitled to the fruits of their labour. (Mugabe 1984; emphases added)

This is the criterion of returns to effort. The property rights which it is held to establish – subject to a proviso of equal opportunity for others (including both those now and later?) – include full entitlement to use as the owner sees fit. Yet President Mugabe went on to advocate 'socialism [that] subordinates the interests of the individual to the common or general interests of society'. One implication could be that he considered that the proviso of equal opportunity is typically not fulfilled, once resources have been occupied by a few.

One can add several other limitations of the claim to full entitlement to 'the fruits of one's labour'. In particular, when we talk not of Robinson Crusoe but of a complex social division of labour, where each contribution can be vital, the social product is not objectively divisible between the various inputs according to their contributions.

The white settlers in Rhodesia claimed, in good Lockean style, that they had brought into use natural resources that were in surplus or insignificantly used. But they seized the best land, which by definition is scarce; they explicitly removed others' legal entitlement to use that land, and coerced their labour in order to develop it; and in time all land became scarce. Their entry clearly did not satisfy Locke's proviso.

Settlers also defended their acquisition on procedural, utilitarian, or deserts grounds. The procedural claim – that the Rudd Concession in the 1880s was a binding agreement, with the responsible authority, which transferred land ownership rights – is false (see e.g. Riddell 1987). Even if it were not, many people would dispute that any authority had the right to transfer its people's birthright. Disputing that courts should be allowed to decide on compensation for land acquired for resettlement, President Mugabe declared similarly: 'I cannot be dragged into court, I, Robert Gabriel Mugabe, with ancestral roots that go back generations and generations, by a settler who only came here 90 years ago' (Mugabe 1991). A complication is that in only very few cases was the land still held by the descendants of the original white settlers. Most owners had bought their farms. However, while the Government upheld 'the right to acquire, hold and dispose of property', it felt it must balance this against other claims: 'it could not, with a decent conscience, allow ... the rich landowners to hold government to ransom at the expense of the landless' (Minister Emmerson Mnangagwa, *Financial Gazette*, 14 December 1990).

The utilitarian claim, that settler colonisation led to far greater economic development than would have happened otherwise, can satisfy only utilitarians, even in so far as it were true, and then only for a limited period: for the arrival of the liberation war itself made clear that the presence of a settler regime was slowing development. After 1980 the utilitarian defences of commercial farms were pushed back, as peasant farming at first blossomed; but they possibly remained valid in some cases, including for the biggest export product, Virginia tobacco.

One also encounters a defence on deserts grounds: not of the original settler acquisition but of the current property rights in law, or at least of a right to compensation. This is the argument that the main value of the land is not inherent but has been produced by investments, and that the rights to these and their products are vested in the current owner. Such investments were mostly made, however, with labour whose cheapness reflected the settlers' discriminatory policy regime. The land grab under Mugabe's government from the late 1990s represented a downgrading of all such nuanced estimates, and a switch to prioritise one sub-set of historical concerns, the injustice of the land seizures by whites from the 1890s through to the 1960s.

WHOSE ARE THE INTERNATIONAL DEBTS?

In the 1980s the newly independent Zimbabwe was able to cope with its foreign debts. 'When the foreign exchange cake is presented, we, naturally, and in all fairness, feel bound to invite our creditors to join us in partaking of the cake' (Mugabe 1987: 7). This fits a procedural norm of accepting duties which one has incurred under procedures which one accepted (position 9 in Table 4.1). Repayment is made not simply on grounds of prudence (future-orientation) but because one has obligations from the past.

In the 1990s, however, Zimbabwe moved into the sort of economic straits which many African and Latin American countries had faced for some time and which had led to questioning the premises of the international debt-collection regime. In the 1980s and 1990s international financial institutions, directed by Northern governments, imposed economic adjustment measures on the low-income countries of the South, which gave strong priority to repayment of foreign debt over domestic expenditure, even on health and education. The argument that, on grounds of need, the poor could not be required to repay, or repay on this scale, was overridden by assertion of the primacy of contracts and their necessity for long-run improvement for all. A typical late-1980s statement of concern adopted those criteria, albeit in qualified form: 'It is necessary to avoid payment defaults which could destabilise the international financial system ... respect for the contract by both parties sustains the essential trust factor ... The duties of commercial banks towards their depositors are essential and must be fulfilled ... However, creditors cannot demand contract fulfilment by any and all means, especially if the debtor is in a situation of extreme need' (Pontifical Justice & Peace Council 1987).

A stronger objection disputed the historical legitimacy of the system. The Cuban ambassador to Tanzania said of Third World debt: 'The debt is simply immoral and cannot be repaid. It cannot be repaid because the people of the Third World have paid it already' (*The Herald*, Harare, 8 May 1987). His argument can be read in various ways: first, that the Third World had paid enough during colonialism and neo-colonialism (see e.g. Davis 2001); second, that it had paid enough on current loans but was swamped by 1980s rises in interest rates; and relatedly, that the procedures it had become involved in were not fair, in respect of the operation of financial markets and the other markets and forces which together lead countries to acquire loans.

These sorts of objections to the debt-generation and collection system made little headway for a decade. Only more precise historical examination, feeding into massive campaigning efforts such as Jubilee 2000, and the arrival of some more enlightened Northern governments, allowed steps forward on debt relief at the end of the 1990s. Joe Hanlon (2000) and others have shown the unique and deplorable specifics of the squeeze-out-the-debt regime applied to struggling countries in the South during the past generation. Hanlon's account deserves detailed summary.

- In the past two centuries there have been several major financial cycles, each consisting of four phases: (1) growth and credit extension, (2) accelerated and over-extension of credit, (3) crisis and defaults, (4) debt restructuring and write-offs. Periodic write-offs are the normal other side of the coin to profit-making. But uniquely in the late twentieth century the major lenders and their governments 'have worked in a much more co-ordinated way to prevent default by individual countries, and to bring collective pressure on debtors' (ibid.: 881). This has operated in particular through the International Monetary Fund (IMF), created in 1944, whose approval has in practice been necessary for access to funds from rich countries. The system has ensured that private investors and lenders, who reap the full benefits of good judgement and good luck, are cushioned against misjudgements. They are therefore encouraged in loan-pushing, as happened on a large scale in the 1970s and early 1980s to recycle oil exporters' surpluses. 'Moral hazard can only be avoided if lending institutions are now forced to accept their responsibility for past bad lending' (ibid.: 898).
- The major present-day creditors, who rigorously supervised the ever-growing mountain of debt and repayment since 1980, were themselves forgiven debtors or defaulters in the past. Since they defaulted in the 1930s, Britain and France have never repaid to America debts of over $25 billion incurred during and after the First World War. Many American state governments never repaid foreign loans on which they defaulted in the 1840s, and which the US government

repudiated in 1930. Germany was excused most of its pre-war debt in 1953. No conditions were set on how the amounts forgiven could be spent, unlike in the current debt-reduction scheme for the South.

- Repayment terms applied in the Third World debt crisis since 1982 have been far harsher than those applied after 1945 to Germany, a richer country, which received 'the unprecedented [concession in 1953] that repayments would only be made out of German trade surpluses – if the allies wanted debt repaid, they had to [first] buy German goods' (ibid.: 885). In contrast, IMF–World Bank practice, assiduously supported by Germany, has been to estimate 'how much money could be squeezed out of a poor country' in repayments (ibid.: 886): 20–25 per cent of export earnings was the *reduced* ceiling specified in 1996 for the highly indebted poor countries (HIPCs), many of them devastated by the AIDS pandemic. It was further reduced to 15 per cent in 1999 – compared to the maximum of 3.5 per cent applied to Germany from 1953. The discrepancy is even greater in terms of percentages of GDP: an average over 4 per cent for the HIPCs, compared to 0.4 per cent for Germany.

- The Universal Declaration of Human Rights, officially accepted by the creditor nations, states that 'Everyone has the right to a standard of living adequate for the health and wellbeing of himself and his family … [and] the right to education'. The latter right is re-affirmed in the creditor nations' 1996 DAC (the OECD Development Assistance Committee) targets, which also include a halving of extreme poverty by 2015, massive improvements in health, and more. In domestic law, human rights take priority over debt: 'If a company goes bankrupt, no one would expect the children of the owners or employees of the company to drop out of school to go to work to pay the company's debts' (ibid.: 889). Yet the equivalent and more have been expected and to a large degree enforced by the 'advanced nations' throughout the 1980s and 1990s. Hanlon estimates that about a quarter of the debt should be written off on this ground: to allow spending to ensure basic human rights.

- Much of the debt (Hanlon estimates another quarter) was originally extended, or guaranteed, during the Cold War to countries of which it was known that a considerable proportion would be wasted or disappear in corruption by kleptocratic but 'friendly' rulers who were often aided and abetted from the creditor countries. 'The $2.1 billion Bataan nuclear power station [in the Philippines] was built on an earthquake fault and never used. [President] Marcos is said to have received $80 million in commissions from builder Westinghouse. Filipinos will continue to pay for this corrupt project until 2018' (ibid.: 897). The principle of repudiation of 'odious debts' is established in international law. It allows rejection of debts incurred by illegitimate rulers and not used to benefit the people of the country. The partner of the principle of proper procedure is the principle of repudiation of the results of unjust procedures.

4.4 ASSESSING THE DIFFERENT INTERPRETATIONS

Four insights take us beyond simply noting the variety of criteria. First, all the interpretations of equity are about equality of something (Sen 1984). Second, we can understand this underlying primacy of a general criterion of equality as a recognition of human dignity. But third, there is no one essence of equality. The plurality of significant types of equality reflects the plurality of aspects of life and available types of information. Fourthly, the disputes over their respective importance reflects, again, different perspectives on the nature of persons and societies.

We find so many criteria in use partly due to lack of sophistication, so that different and conflicting criteria are used without awareness; sometimes as a product of opportunism; but also as a symptom of social transition, during which various forms of social organisation coexist; and finally, as a reflection of inevitable pluralism in our life and concerns, and of the limits of any one set of concepts.

EQUALITY OF WHAT? WHY EQUALITY?

The word 'equity' implies treating equivalent cases equally; but which range of cases do we cover, and equally in what respects? Equal benefits to people with unequal needs will not produce equal well-being, for instance. We can assess or propose equality at input level, at activities level, at results level, and at impact levels, and we get different answers according to which of these levels we refer to.

Amartya Sen underlines, however, that in all cases the criteria concern equality of something: whether incomes, welfare, reward in proportion to deserts, formal access or real access to goods, or receipt in proportion to need or desire or payment. Even utilitarianism, although lacking any independent concern for outcome equality, puts equal weight on a unit of utility of any community member. The disagreements are about in which particular respect people should be treated equally.

Why should equality have any significance? Greater equality of income could conceivably increase total utility or need fulfilment, for example by direct or indirect effects on health, skills, peace and so on. It might similarly be conducive to some other desired objectives, like participation. But are there any reasons to value equality in its own right, not just as a possible means towards other objectives? Equality does not even seem attainable for some goods, notably so-called positional goods like social status or physical location. We can't all be equidistant from all facilities (so we need instead threshold criteria of maximum acceptable distances).

For some of the writers who face the question, the answer appears to be no, equality should not be valued in itself. In *Anti-Dühring*, Friedrich Engels held that: 'any demand for equality that goes beyond [the abolition of classes] necessarily passes into absurdity'. One line of positive response (noted in Miller 1982) is that equality of material conditions could be so intimately connected with certain objectives, such as dignity or equality of opportunity, as to be viewed as an objective in itself. But equality of conditions is, strictly speaking, here still a means to other ends.

A more adequate response exists. Equality should be the starting point in discussions on distribution as an acknowledgement of the dignity and humanity of each person. In the absence of sufficient information that establishes that people should be treated differently – due to different needs, deserts, rights, skills or whatever – the presumption is that they should be treated equally. And information is indeed often unreliable or unclear, partly because it is supplied by those with vested interests in the decisions that are to be made. So our presumption in favour of equality survives as more than just a starting point. Inequality is not necessarily inequitable, but any inequality has to be specifically justified, whereas equality does not. Second, all interpretations of equity are about equality of *something* (e.g. equal treatment in terms of the rules, equal chance to be involved in making the rules, equal fulfilment of basic needs, or whatever). Equality respects the equal humanity of all.

The above argument establishes a general case for equality of material conditions too, in its own right. We need reasons for divergence from it; and all such reasons that are acceptable must use equality-of-something language. Thus Rawls's theory justifies those material inequalities which benefit the worst off and arise out of a system of equal liberty for all. The material-equality objective will be far from overriding given the several other relevant dimensions, equality in which will not imply equality of material conditions. Consistent with this, feelings about material inequality seem to vary greatly according to the case, the society and the era. Only by tacitly presuming that egalitarianism must put *overriding* weight on material equality could Deepak Lal (1976) allege that egalitarians in development policy must support the Khmer Rouge in Kampuchea (Cambodia) and their quick way to equality: killing the educated. Kampuchea highlights the difference between reducing poverty and reducing inequality. The Khmer Rouge were good only at the latter. The extreme libertarian view of Robert Nozick which Lal expounded is refutable, for having a similar sort of monomania. It claims *absolute* rights for holdings which are obtained through fair procedures – for example, a right to reject any taxation on income which has not been obtained by theft. This absolutism leads it to absurd and inconsistent conclusions (Brown 2000; Gasper 1986).

SELECTING FROM OR INTERRELATING THE PRINCIPLES

We can refute extreme versions of a principle, but all the principles mentioned earlier have claims in some situations. The plurality of frames of reference reflects the many aspects of life even in one society. We are interested, for instance, in both past and future. The different weightings of the various principles reflect different circumstances and cultures. Robert Nozick's type of wildly unbalanced libertarianism was an assertion of the already privileged, in a form more characteristic of the USA than most countries. Since America has hegemony as well as exceptionalism, however, one must follow its debates with utmost care.

As there are many plausible distributive criteria, we need to balance or choose between them when making policy choices. For example, we might consider it just for people to inherit goods, yet see some of the results thereof, including the basis for future interaction, as unfair, so that we would consider it appropriate to partly override or limit (by inheritance taxes) those rights for the sake of a greater social good. We could try to do the balancing or choice intuitively, or in terms of a unifying general theory which derives the different criteria as special cases of deeper principles and/or shows how they fit different settings. Philosophical analysis is important because intuitive balancing of the criteria can become muddled, and is certainly done differently by different people. Certain theories try to derive all or most of the other commonly seen criteria by deduction from a single set of principles. For example, utilitarianism, some theories of human needs and Rawls's theory all attempt this. Thus utilitarians often try to rationalise other norms as being special cases or working approximations of their theory, by presenting them as feasible practical guides to utility maximisation in specific situations.

But the information we can obtain on any one of the criteria – needs or deserts or utilities or whatever – is inevitably imperfect; so we will need to use many criteria (Sen 1984). And, in all the unifying theories, the categories in use, such as utility, need, equality, or contribution, may inevitably be too imprecise or ambiguous to sustain any total claims built upon them. Typically, when we reach the limits of workability of one concept we turn to another, because we have to make decisions, ration resources. Similarly, when cases rank equally on one criterion and we must still ration further, we turn to another criterion.

So each criterion is relevant, but each is insufficient by itself, in terms of persuasiveness, conceptual clarity, available information, and rationing power.

Rae et al. (1981) analyses internal tensions in the ideal of equality, stemming from these many types or dimensions of equality. We have to ask: equality in which respects, at which level of objectives (from inputs through to impacts), and between which groups? For instance, increasing equality between different parts of the middle and upper classes, by levelling up, can sometimes increase overall societal inequality. 'In the urban areas [in Zimbabwe], very high standards of housing, with electricity, water and sanitation, are insisted upon, in part so as not to be seen to be providing facilities inferior to those built in the [white settler rule] era, but the unseen consequence of this is a lack of resources to provide even the basics in the rural areas' (Robinson 1988: 2). While 'people in towns enjoy highly subsidised piped schemes, rural dwellers are now called upon ... to contribute' to capital costs of improved supplies and for maintenance (ibid.: 7).

Rae et al. concludes that 'to boil things as complex as equality down to two or three headings is inevitably too far from the truth to serve even as a sensible approximation' (1981: 144); and that, since there is no single essence of equality, its greatest rival proves to be not order or efficiency or freedom, but instead, paradoxically, itself (ibid.: 150).

SOCIO-POLITICAL CONTEXTS

David Miller (1976) discussed 'Social Justice in Sociological Perspective'. He argued for example that the criterion of needs is more prominent in small-scale relatively egalitarian non-market societies, such as some tribes. The favourable conditions there appear to be that people know each other, often work jointly, and share some notion of the common good. Next, he holds that the criterion of rights in respect of one's position in society (similar to Blanchard's norm of ascriptive status) is fundamental in stable hierarchical non-market societies, for example feudal or caste societies. He holds that the criterion of individual deserts is more fundamental in cases dominated by the market, where people interact as formal equals and typically know neither each other as individuals nor each other's needs. In contrast, under state capitalism and late capitalism, individuals' contributions become much less separable, and one might find a mixture of sanctioned distributive criteria including a quasi-feudal distribution according to position (for example perhaps for ruling party officials) and a specification of one's deserts according in part to how far one has helped to fulfil others' needs. Finally Miller suggests that a purer egalitarianism often emerges in times or contexts of social dislocation, but only temporarily.

In Zimbabwe, according to H. S. M. Ushewokunze when a Minister, socialist groups in the ruling party were united by a recognition 'that society must be re-organised in such a way that it is the people's needs that are paramount' (1985: vii). In contrast other groups 'joined the struggle because business [and job] opportunities had been closed to them by a racist government' (ibid.), and were mainly concerned with rights of equal opportunity and of equal return for equal work. Many of the leaders who spoke of needs criteria seemed to believe that they too should enrich themselves as part of the continued struggle. Ushewokunze was amongst various government and party leaders reported in the Zimbabwean press to have encountered difficulties on the commercial farms they had acquired in the name of their family members (given the ruling party's Leadership Code to limit property acquisition); it was also reported that they did not pay workers and eventually dismissed them *en masse*.

There are a number of shortcomings or gaps in Miller's theory. Claims of rights based on past events are also very important in market societies but are based on arguments from liberty and fair procedures rather than only from deserts (e.g. Nozick 1974a; this was criterion 9 in section 4.3). Clearly, though, there is some value in his approach. We can see that different distributive criteria tend to be found in different settings. But also in any single society there will be a number of criteria with relevant claims. Every state needs to consider production and distribution, growth and social services. Every society inevitably includes a number of over-lapping social contexts, with a number of modes of production and allocation, from the family through informal associations to many types of formal organisation. Even within a single mode, various considerations are found to be relevant: human nature and human concerns are not as one-dimensional as assumed by a unitary theory like utilitarianism. People are interested for example in each of past-, present- and future-oriented criteria. And being open to different kinds of value and meaning may be important for a society's ability to adapt and grow as conditions change.

4.5 CONCLUSION

The main objective of this chapter has been to help readers to recognise different criteria of equity and appropriate distribution. Does it matter who annexes the label of 'equity', so long as we are clear on what different people mean? Yes, for who gains 'ownership' over a key term – like 'equity', 'development' or 'efficiency' – which has wide authority and popular appeal does make a difference. Secondly, we saw reasons to doubt that the various criteria can be justifiably reduced to one or two via a unifying theory. Familiarity with all the criteria is important. Great dangers arise when they are not viewed in relation to each other, when any is proclaimed as a monotheism.

In a book of policy analysis one would go on to consider operational-isation of equity, the making of general concepts measurable or in other ways operationally defined by a set of procedural steps; and to identify and discuss policy options – institutions and actions, national and inter-national – to define, establish, and defend entitlements. One would look at the capacity of possible policy tools, at their possible disincentive and other undesirable side effects, and so on (see e.g. Drèze & Sen 1989; Nagel 1984, 1997).

For some policy analysts, including in parts of economics, equity is not considered at all. We saw that this position goes with implicit adoption of the values of private business, or with abnegation of equity questions, which are left for politicians. If the politicians do not change something, that is read as its endorsement. A more serious stance considers equity as a technical issue, as an objective to be defined, measured, and weighted. A third stance, as adopted here, tries to combine technical and political awareness, and sees an adviser's task as to clarify issues about equity by elucidating a range of relevant concepts. This provides a basis for more intelligent political debate and choice.

DISCUSSION THEMES

1. Is there any difference between equity and equality? If so, what?
2. Suggest criteria for:
   (i) Allocation of parks and allocation of policing, between different areas in a city in a low-income country;
   (ii) Allocation of land to different potential recipients in land reforms in southern Africa;
   (iii) Who should receive priority in a specified affirmative-action programme.
3. Should a country's government or foreign aid agencies offer inducements to expatri-ate professionals from the country to return?
4. Utilitarianism is part of the ethical basis of mainstream economic evaluation (inclu-ding financial and economic cost–benefit analysis). One objection to utilitarianism is that it is willing to sacrifice individuals for a greater good. Some people reply that 'we can't develop without breaking some heads'. Give your reasoned comments, with illustrations.
5. To whom should medical knowledge belong? Does not patenting of indigenous medical knowledge by foreign corporations help to make it internationally available?

READING SUGGESTIONS

Dasgupta (1993) shows how hundreds of millions of people are, through no fault of their own, locked into extreme poverty and in many cases, destitution (see e.g. Chs 9, 10 & 12). Many studies have done this; Dasgupta's deserves mention as an exhaustively documented and tightly reasoned work by an 'Establishment' figure in economics, who has tried to extend the subject's boundaries in terms of value assumptions and empirical scope. Davis (2001) extends the perspectives of economic history, by showing how the pattern of the 1840s Irish famine was repeated on a vastly greater scale in much of Asia, Africa and South America in the last quarter of the nineteenth century. Imperial rule and market forces stripped away the social defences against the effects of natural hazards, and provided no alternative security.

A rich systematic literature exists on the meanings of equity and the normative theory of distribution. Roemer (1996) gives a formal analytical survey. Blanchard (1986) is an elementary introduction with examples from urban policy. Beatley (1984) valuably compares Rawlsian, utilitarian, and egalitarian principles in urban growth management, with reference to a range of objectives levels (from input to impact) and indicators. Sillince (1986), written for British-type urban and regional planners, critiques the utilitarianism that has been taken for granted as common sense. Amartya Sen (1984) gives a more rigorous critique, with an economics orientation; his Ch. 12, which we built on in section 4.3, is widely accessible. Another paper (Sen 1979, reprinted in Sen 1984) launched his attack on unconsidered utilitarianism in mainstream economics. Brittan (1983) offers a partial defence.

Gasper (1986) is a wider, non-technical survey, that goes on to assess and apply some of the distributive criteria seen in literature on Third World development. It criticises the purely procedural ethic of Robert Nozick (1974a), who emerged as a guru of Reaganism. Nozick's forceful attacks on equality were broadcast in development studies by Deepak Lal (1976). The works of Nozick, Lal, and the often sloppy but influential Peter Bauer (e.g. Bauer 1981) were all pointed and readable. Other assessments of the ethics of the New Right are in Riddell (1985, 1986, 1987), with special reference to the case for international aid, and White & Tiongco (1997), concerning attempts to separate the 'deserving' and 'undeserving poor'. Riddell (1987) has a general survey of claims for redistribution, with special reference to international aid. Each of the various criteria are adopted by some Marxist or another; Nielsen & Patten (eds 1981) gives a good cross-section of opinions.

From the perspective of practice, Rae et al. (1981) makes a profound analysis of difficulties in the concept, and hence also the application and organisation, of equality. Elster (1992) is an outstanding study of the varieties and combinations of allocation criteria used in diverse situations, and an attempt to explain them; Elster (1995) gives a shorter introduction.

CHAPTER 5

VIOLENCE AND HUMAN SECURITY

5.1 THE REEMERGENCE OF VIOLENCE AND SECURITY AS CENTRAL CONCERNS

For several decades the world has been ruled to a considerable degree according to figures about Gross Domestic Products. A measure of levels of monetised activity is taken as a measure of welfare. But the level of monetised activity is a seriously unreliable proxy even for the welfare generated by that activity, let alone for the content of whole lives that contain more than economic exchanges. Physical violence is amongst the clearest instances of where one-dimensional measures of social progress through GDP or the like prove unacceptable. The suffering from violence is neither to be ignored nor to be captured by a money measure; nor, most people would say, should it be fed into an aggregation of costs and benefits, for the costs and suffering have been or are borne by specific people (Amerindians, for instance), different from those who benefit. Consider South Africa or Brazil, where multi-faceted violence has been endemic, to support or replace particular socio-economic models, or as their pathological effect.

Post-1945 development policy and studies have inherited eighteenth- and nineteenth-century Western optimism. Like it, they have held that material progress is possible and essential, and can bring with it most other good things, including peace, liberty, tolerance, equity, even wisdom. But whereas violence was an explicit and leading concern in the work of earlier centuries, as something that progress leads us away from, it has been less attended to in modern development studies. Phenomena of violence were central in earlier social philosophy, from Thomas Hobbes's vision of a war of all against all, to Karl Marx and Friedrich Engels's witness to the brutal extension and policing of capitalism and colonialism inside and outside Europe. In contrast, the economics-dominated main-stream of post-1945 development policy and studies has presumed that economic growth – and whatever social and political restructuring it might require ('modernisation') – would sooner or later dissolve societal conflicts. This has been the picture assumed in most textbooks of development economics or manuals of development planning. Violence has been a minor focus, if mentioned at all.

Awareness of conflicts and their costs reappeared in significant degree in the 1990s. Compare two notable book-length policy analyses from the Netherlands Ministry of Foreign Affairs, guided by its then Minister of Development Cooperation, Jan Pronk. In 1990 *A World of Difference* spoke of a world of wide variety, which if carefully understood and engaged with can be greatly improved. Its successor, *A World in Dispute*, spoke in 1993 in a changed voice, of the world of the conflicts in Somalia, the former Yugoslavia, the Caucasus and many other parts of the former Soviet Union, and ongoing mayhem in Afghanistan, Algeria, Colombia, Liberia, Sierra Leone, Sri Lanka, various parts of India, and elsewhere. Later Rwanda, the former Zaire and others joined the list.

Part of the broadening of ideas of 'development' involves matters of personal security and societal peace: 'everyone should enjoy [at least] a minimum level of security' (UNDP 1996: 56). The separate listing of security as a component of human development recognises that it is valued in itself, not only as a condition for empowerment. Violence becomes treated as a central focus for reduction in its own right, even if doing so does not increase or even decreases measured economic growth.

This chapter considers physical violence as an ethically central (section 5.2) and, unfortunately, major (section 5.3) aspect of people's experience. Physical violence is considered in particular, for it frequently involves a special painfulness and traumatic quality. The importance in principle of physical integrity and security is unlikely to be disputed; but the scale of physical insecurity for many of the poor, and many women, is often overlooked. More controversial are the causes and remedies for insecurity. Economic change is widely presumed to be no part of the causes of violence; instead economic growth is considered to be a major part of its solution and central to all improvement. Even if it is recognised as a contributory cause of violence, that violence is taken to be short term and – since there is no alternative path seen for human fulfilment – unavoidable. With such a perspective in much development analysis and policy, violence and the resultant suffering have been marginalised, ignored and downgraded (sections 5.3 and 5.4). Furthermore, if violence and death are treated only as cost categories like others in an economic calculus, they can be too readily outweighed (when counted at all) by calculations of the benefit of others. The chapter does not attempt policy design. Its point instead is that adequate policies must rest on adequate conceptua and explanation. Section 5.5 looks at alternative ways of trying t about the value of physical security and at some of the problems

The chapter thus extends arguments of Chapter 3 on the narrowness of the predominant economics world-view, causes of that, and steps beyond it. It follows Chapter 4 because we will use Amartya Sen's deconstruction of utilitarianism.

5.2 DEVELOPMENT AND VIOLENCE AS VALUE-RELATIVE? ON CONCEPTS

We saw that one part of the core agenda for development ethics stresses attention to costs of development and how they are distributed across people. A second starting point was the demand for attention to what the values contained in the ideas and programmes of development are, and to alternative value stances within and/or against 'development'. A tension can arise between these agenda items if all possible value stances are considered equally valid, including for example a stance that treats indigenous peoples as sub-human and considers costs inflicted on them as insignificant or even praiseworthy.

VIOLENCE

Like 'development' in the sense of societal improvement, 'violence' and 'cost' are value-relative terms. Typically 'violence' has a negative connotation – violence is what damages something of value, according to one definition – though it can potentially be justified by its instrumental role and thus by what it may permit or enforce. This is the standard view of war. In some cultures, however, war has been glorified for itself, just as in some sub-cultures violence is glorified. What is disapproved of, and hence liable to be called violence? Nigel Dower (1999) observes that at root there is a link between 'violence' and 'violation', for example of rights. He stresses, however, the existence of a range of conceptions, as for any major category in ethics and social philosophy. Such categories are 'thick', meaning at least that they have multiple aspects or components. Different weightings of these components produce different interpretations and usages of a concept. Each interpretation of a thick concept such as violence or development gives a way of describing, a way of grouping instances, which reflects a theory that is open to debate. If the concept contains an aspect of normative attractiveness, as for example do development or freedom, then each interpretation reflects also a set of values, also open to debate. That each interpretation reflects a package of theory, perspectives, values and selected experiences, a vision, implies that the concept is typically 'essentially contested'. Its meaning is perennially in dispute (Gallie 1962; Connolly 1993).

The concept of violence is, however, not merely a matter of taste. The degree of value relativity of key concepts here does not take us even close to the point of emptiness. A robust core area can be identified even if there is disagreement beyond it. We see overwhelming rejection of involuntary seizure and trafficking of human body parts, for example. O'Neill (1996) argues that the assumptions we tacitly make in practical dealings and positive analyses, about the agency and vulnerability of others with whom we interact, cannot be dropped when we move to discussions of ethics and justice. A concern for individuals' agency and autonomy leads to a concern with the conditions that promote agency and autonomy (see Doyal & Gough 1991), and with the obligations binding on individuals to accord to others rights similar to those that they claim for themselves.

Cameron (1999: 31–2) focuses on physical violence as more observable, and on the issue of consent:

> Is any form of exercise of power 'violent' *per se*? Is any form of action on a human body without the clear consent of the possessor of that body an act of violence? … [Does] violence then [occur] wherever a person is not being con- sulted about life-changing processes? … This abstract principle is difficult to use in practice as people's views can be muzzled, ignored, obliterated, repressed … By comparison, the bruise or slash, chains or prison bars, or the instruments of execution are clearer evidence of human agency under stress … For the purposes here, the concept of violence will be restricted to situations of activities between human beings where at least one person becomes physically damaged or is physically restricted without giving consent to the activity … Certainly [however] violence has several dimensions which a purely physical perspective may not capture.

So consent under conditions of threat and ignorance is not sufficient. One would require informed and uncoerced consent.

DEVELOPMENT AND PEACE

Dower argues that development and the reduction of violence should be seen as intimately and favourably connected with each other, and also with justice and environmental protection, even though development, narrowly conceived as economic growth and betterment, is in many cases to the detriment of the others. There remains a strong leaning to say that 'real development' involves peace. How could this be?

From Chapter 2 we can see that the term 'real development' marks a switch to a normative concept of improvement, away from a more neutral descriptive concept of economic growth and associated social change. This normative idea of 'development' is not reducible to economic growth, or even structural economic change, for which we have adequate terms already, and which can often conflict with the other elements. 'Develop- ment' typically represents instead a multi-dimensional vision of societal progress, within which various components figure – comfort, peace, environmental balance, and more – all considered as major parts of a good life.

If we simply had a pair of concepts, one descriptive and one normative, why would they not just go under the separate names 'economic growth' and 'societal improvement'? Why they are so often treated in fact as components of a single term, 'development'? The combination has reflected an underlying theory that economic growth in general brings social improvement, and indeed is an indispensable condition for major improvement. This motivating vision then requires a 'protective belt', to cope with what are considered exceptions; hence the categories of 'not real development' and 'mistakes'. Into this protective belt go cases of economic growth and modernisation that do not bring social improvement, whereas 'real development' is the embodiment of the vision, seen as realisable when 'mistakes' are not made.

'Development' typically functions thus as a synonym for, and also a theory of, progress: it incorporates many values, and presumes that these are – in general and in the long run – mutually supportive. Dower finds this plausible, otherwise the term would probably have disintegrated. Some others assert that, as with religions, the more a vision fails the more it may be clung to, as a way of facing adversity and uncertainty. Dower suggests, however, that in general the major components can over the longer run be mutually supportive in sustainable societies, *regardless* of how they are precisely conceptualised:

> Even if there are significant variations in the way human flourishing, peace, justice, and care for the environment are understood, the framework of societal order is still needed. ... That a society here and now must have *some* commitment to peace, justice, environmental care and the pursuit of [economic] development and see a kind of incoherence in failing to see the joint necessity of these conditions, is my contention ... [So] we have the basis for the claim that [economic] development, peace, justice, and environment, whilst not inevitably mutually supportive, will come to be seen as [generally] such ... Development [more broadly] potentially relates to the whole picture – general human flourishing in conditions of peace, justice and care for the environment. (Dower 1999: 57, 60, 61).

5.3 DEVELOPMENT AS VALUE-DAMAGING?

VARIETIES OF VIOLENCE

The twentieth century was very likely the most violent yet (MacRae 1998). Whether casual intra-national violence declined, we do not know for sure; levels of domestic violence appear high. Wars between states were waged at new pitches of intensity and destructiveness, with an ever-greater proportion of civilians amongst the casualties. Wars within countries have proliferated, including some waged by states upon sections of their own populace (such as Armenians in late Ottoman Turkey, Jews in Nazi Europe, Chinese and Russian landowners after the revolutions, educated Cambodians under the Khmer Rouge, Tutsi Rwandese in 1994). In South Africa a minority built a more subtle, routinely brutal system of oppression of the large majority, a system now only painfully and partially dismantled. Yet while George Orwell's *1984* offered as one image of human history a boot grinding a face for ever, the victory of the anti-apartheid struggle impressively showed a different path.

Many types of violence demand attention. Those mentioned below overlap, and other types exist too. The list serves simply to mark a series of overlapping universes of suffering.

- Violence against workers. Slavery and the slave trade were one enormous variant or sister type.
- Violence against indigenous peoples. Encountering these peoples and desiring the resources where they lived, desiring also their labour to exploit the resources, European powers rationalised violent seizure and the use of almost (and sometimes completely) unbridled power in various ways: 'the lands were empty'; 'the people were vicious savages'; 'we brought peace to chaos'; 'the savages reneged on agreements' (often spurious); and so on.
- Violence against other civilisations. Rationalisations such as 'they broke agreements' and 'we brought peace' were still used in European dealings with evidently non-empty, non-primitive lands. (V. G. Kiernan's *The Lords of Human Kind* gives a compilation of cases.) Hardened in centuries of intra-civilisational wars in Europe and wielding superior military technologies that emerged in the competition betwen emergent states, European powers moved on to subdue the world.
- Violence against other races or ethnic groups, including within given political frontiers (as in South Africa and the former Yugoslavia).
- Violence against women – a massive, worldwide phenomenon. Across the world many armed conflicts appear to unleash tidal waves of rape, some planned from above. Do soldiers feel desire for those whom they have never met before and instead proceed to hurt and abuse? The desire seems to be for violence and to humiliate and humble others, and the expression is of hate, resentment, anger, power and self-exaltation.
- Violence against children, another possible pandemic.
- Violence against oneself, including through 'substance abuse' from alcohol and other drugs. These forms of violence underline the inadequacy of the 'economic man' model of personhood. The drugs trades,

centred on filling gaps of meaning left in the homelands of economic-man ideology, fund worldwide systems of physical violence.

Why list these universes of suffering? One reason is in order to consider which pictures of human nature and potential can accommodate the realities of violence, which others can not, and which corresponding models for development (as a direction of improvement) are therefore adequately grounded. And second, to ask what the relation is between particular paths of development (meaning here economic growth and corresponding social modernisation) and these realms of suffering. If the suffering is the same in all cases, or unavoidable, or determined entirely by forces other than socio-economic development – say, by unchangeable features of human nature – then it becomes partly irrelevant for policy, except to stimulate our concern to tend to the damage and to promote countervailing realms of satisfaction through development. But what if this is not so?

VIOLENCE AND THE ECONOMY

Is violence integral or accidental in a particular development path, and on what scale? Is the violence only temporary, part of a transition phase of restructuring, or is it a permanent product, a structural feature of the type of society created? The question of relationships between paths of development and realms of suffering is raised not to be settled here, but to indicate a permanent agenda for attention.

Certainly in some cases a link from the type of socio-economic development to resulting violence is evident, in some other cases proba-ble, in further cases more debatable or absent, and sometimes develop-ment is conducive to peace and security. Pakistan in the 1960s was lauded by many abroad; but the development imbalance between East and West Pakistan, in great favour of the latter, culminated in the more populous East launching its own political movement, murderous repression by the forces of West Pakistan, and a bloody war. The explosion in the 1990s of states such as Yugoslavia and Rwanda was significantly related to massive economic stresses acting on inflammable divided societies which were struggling to fulfil their aspirations, and debt schedules, in the face of severely adverse external conditions.

> The real origin of the Yugoslav conflict is the disintegration of governmental authority and the breakdown of a political and civil order ... A critical element of this failure was economic decline, caused largely by a program intended to resolve a foreign debt crisis. (Woodward 1995)

The international Joint Evaluation of Emergency Assistance to Rwanda concluded the following:

[Explanatory factor 6 behind the 1994 Rwanda genocide of almost a million people in a few months was] the economic slump starting in the late 1980s and the effects of the actions subsequently taken by the government in consultation with the international donor community, i.e. the structural adjustment programmes of 1990 and 1992. The economic deterioration, largely due to a sharp decline of world market prices for coffee – Rwanda's prime export earner – as well as to unfavourable weather and economic policies such as increased protectionism, price controls and other regulations, affected the whole society. In US dollar terms, *GDP per capita fell by some 40 percent over the four years 1989–1993* ... The international community, including the World Bank and the International Monetary Fund, overlooked [the] potentially explosive social and political conse-quences when designing and imposing economic conditions for support to Rwanda's economic recovery. (Eriksson et al. 1996: 15; emphasis added.)

Peter Uvin (1999) elaborates on the factors besides international debt which made Rwanda explosive:

[If] we define structural violence as consisting of the combination of extreme inequality, social exclusion, and humiliation/assault on people's dignity ... [then] notwithstanding positive macro-economic indicators, Rwanda has been charac-terised for decades by a high degree of structural violence: during the years prior to the [1994] genocide, this structural violence greatly intensified. This reality contrasted sharply with the dominant image of Rwanda, shared by donors and government officials alike, of a country in which development was proceeding nicely, under the capable leadership of a free-market oriented government ... [First,] according to 1988 Ministry of the Plan data, the lowest paid 65 percent of public employees earned less than 4 per cent of all salaries, while the share of the top 1 percent was 45.8 per cent [implying a per capita ratio around 1:750] ... approximately half of all Rwandans are ultra-poor, i.e. incapable of feeding them-selves decently or investing productively ... and perhaps 1 per cent are positively rich ... [Second,] social exclusion was deeply embedded ... [and] foremost of a social and regional nature ... from 1982 to 1984, nine-tenths of all public invest-ments [was in four out of the ten provinces] ... while Gitarama, the most popu-lous province after Kigali, received 0.16 per cent ... more than a third of the 85 most important government positions, as well as the quasi-totality of direction functions in the army and the security apparatus, were held by people from Gisenyi, the president's native province ... [O]fficials' scornful attitude to farmers brings us to the third element of structural violence, i.e. humiliation. Prejudice existed in Rwanda not in one but two forms. One was the official racist 'Hutu' ideology ... [which] constituted the moral basis for the genocide. The other is the prejudice of what are locally called the *évolués* – the urban, educated, modern, 'developed' people – versus their backward, rural, illiterate 'underdeveloped' brothers ... an often extremely condescending, rude and manipulative attitude toward the masses ... [This] interaction between structural violence and racism created the conditions necessary for genocidal manipulation by the elites to be successful ... Structural violence is what provoked a need for scapegoating among ordinary people: the existence of a longstanding racism is what allowed parts of the elite to build a genocidal movement on the basis of this need. (Ibid.: 50–2, 54)

The development aid system, adds Uvin, has remained dominated by a narrow economic-technical perspective which cannot conceive of how issues such as he describes might connect to economic development. It thus 'allows the processes of exclusion and humiliation to continue unabated, if not to become strengthened [and thus] helps to lay the groundwork for further ... structural and, eventually, acute violence' (ibid.: 55).

If some might claim that Yugoslavia and Rwanda are special cases with peculiarly inflammable political heritages, let us take the case of Sri Lanka. In 1977 Sri Lanka, noted for its smooth transition to independence, its stable parliamentary democracy, and its European-type longevity and education standards despite low-income economic status, embarked on major economic liberalisation. It moved towards freer international trade, and reduced subsidies and taxes, especially food subsidies; and through the 1990s privatised much of the very extensive state sector. Sri Lanka has now the most liberalised, market-oriented economy in South Asia. But its economic performance has been patchy and not come close to the expectation of liberalisation's proponents that this well-educated country would join the East Asian tiger economies. The explanation by the economic reformers has been that a promising economic experiment was undermined by exogenous factors: a determined, well-organised and ruthlessly violent secessionist movement, the Tamil Tigers, amongst a substantial ethnic minority; and an almost equally disruptive armed uprising during 1987–9 amongst young unemployed from the ethnic majority, organised by a revolutionary group left from Sri Lanka's socialist past but converted to an ethnic agenda.

David Dunham argues that in fact the content and implementation of the 'promising economic experiment' contributed to a downward spiral of conflict and corruption. 'A mutually reinforcing process of economic "reforms" and socio-political decay was ... set in motion' (2001: 2). An economic reform package is inevitably also a political package which particularly benefits some groups and typically harms or is resented by some others. It is usually part of the programme of a political movement, since it requires and rewards a political support base. Economic liberalisation in Sri Lanka was central to the programme by which the United National Party (UNP), leaders of the country into independence but largely out of power from the mid-1950s, recovered power in 1977 and held it until 1994. It created enormous opportunities for gain by favoured groups. Reductions of tariffs and subsidies were concentrated on sectors which hit only the government's opponents, including Tamil farmers. The attractiveness to Western governments of a former socialist bastion adopting the language of market economics led to major foreign funding for the UNP's public infrastructure investments. These, in particular the huge Mahaweli irrigation and settlement programme, provided lavish government patronage to selected Sinhalese supporters. The new Sinhalese settlers were perceived as a threat by Tamils who considered the area as part of their homeland. When violent conflict erupted in 1983, the government used this to extend its powers and term of office. The cycle deepened: economic reform → patronage → conflict → authoritarian measures to entrench rulers in power → more conflict → new authoritarian trends, new opportunities for patronage and corruption (e.g. in military procurement), and new economic reforms in order to maintain or generate bases of internal and external support. With the first phase of economic liberalisation exhausted by the mid-1980s and the country slumped into civil war on two fronts, the government turned to a second phase of reform with privatisation prominent. This allowed patronage and personal gain on a new scale, both in the process of sale of public enterprises and during subsequent regulation, thus further raising the ruthlessness of the fight for political office. The system continued after the transfer of power to another party in 1994. Ironically, an economic programme supposed by market theorists to reduce state patronage and rent-taking instituted it on a far greater scale (Dunham 2001).

Analytically, violence and security are not 'luxury items' for consideration – if and when one has the time, perhaps after economic 'take-off' – separately from economic policy and impacts. In some cases economic change and growth contribute to peace and personal security, but one needs to understand how, and how a negative cycle was avoided. Perhaps governments were more skilful and far seeing, not only lucky. Possibly they were also better counterbalanced and constrained by civil societies and legal systems. Prescriptively, a complex agenda on governance and the defence of human rights arises: difficult and far from clear, but essential.

5.4 DOWNGRADING THE COST OF VIOLENCE

One major type of response to violence and to the suffering it produces is to downgrade and ignore them. Part of this denial derives from world-views in which improvement equals economic growth, and the conception of people has been reduced to that of assiduous pursuers of commodities. Such world-views also generate powerful incentives to minimise estimates of the costs of economic change and to exaggerate the benefits.

MARKET THEORY: ONLY INTERESTS, NO PASSIONS

In conventional modern economics, human beings appear as the species *Homo economicus*, 'economic man': commodity- and comfort-seekers, usually implicitly conceived as law-abiding and peaceful. (Only in more extreme models does *Homo economicus* seize any opportunity to break the law and misuse other people if it will work to his own gain.) Their identity is as producers and consumers, no more; their activity is utility maximisation, and they operate within mutually agreed and respected contracts. They are endlessly motivated by the lure of more commodities. The model fits much of life poorly. In reality, although money is frequently a good motivator, it achieves that by offering generalised command over commodities which are desired in important part in the hope of identity, status, novelty, security and other forms of meaning – as business marketers know but many economists do not, although Adam Smith himself stressed it (Hirschman 1977).

Early market theorists were typically aware that *Homo economicus* was a stereotype (Rothschild 1994). But they held that a focus on commodities and private material gain through market exchange did make people more rational, prudent, and peaceful. The market helped to control and replace 'the passions' by 'the interests', they believed. 'Interests' were seen as the reasoned variants of some calmer passions, but were accorded a new name to give them a greater acceptability and authority (Hirschman 1977: 28–43).

In reality, the market might only be an attractive alternative to the violent pursuit of gain if it offers adequate possibilities for profit, and this depends on forces of production and powers of exploitation. Further, the market must be instituted and regulated; people must be restrained from using violence as a business strategy. In many colonies there was little restraint, rather in fact active state support for violent colonisers, but this was to institute particular exploitative forms of market relations; and the surpluses thus generated played a role in sustaining pacification 'back home'. Elsewhere Hirschman concludes (1986) that market activity is conducive *both* to peace and order (the *doux-commerce* thesis), *and* to undermining its own moral foundations (the self-destruction thesis); and that where the balance lies in particular cases requires historically specific investigation. Economics, the predominant social science of market activity, has until very recently screened out such issues.

Smith considered that drives for meanings underlay the drive for economic gain, giving the latter its unceasing energy and centrality in marketised societies. Does such centrality imply that if all passions are channelled through the market, then social scientific attention can centre on market mechanics? (Hirschman 1977: 108–13). That conclusion, and the programme for a separate science of economic behaviour focusing only on more material interests (comfort, money and commodities), lived on even after the reasoning was forgotten and superseded by nineteenth-century loss of belief in the calming effect of commerce (ibid.: 128). Most modern market theorists forgot the passions altogether. The rational bargainers in their models either had no proclivities for violence, or were restrained by states with sufficient capacity which floated in an explanatory vacuum and themselves had no proclivities for violence other than as required to restrain the violence of others. This thinking continued on even through the most violent century in history.

Overall, the mainstream vision of development from the 1950s through to the 1980s – human fulfilment through the peaceful pursuit of investment and industrialisation – was insufficient as a description, as a prediction, and as a prescription. Theories of 'basic material needs' in the 1970s hinted at something more when they emphasised security too, including security against violence and deception. Theories of 'basic human needs' went further, and brought back the passions: impulses for esteem, status, identity, novelty. The darker passions and potentials still tended to be passed over: wishes for domination, superiority and exclusion of others and of the unfamiliar. The neo-liberalism of the 1980s reemphasised *Homo economicus* as theoretical foundation – while those passions mounted and then spilled out in the 1990s. Viewed globally, the market does not appear to have displaced the passions with the interests, whether in the past century as a whole or the present era in particular. Movement may even have occurred in the contrary direction.

THE DOWNGRADING AND DEFINING AWAY OF COSTS AND ALTERNATIVES

Ignoring likely or actual costs because of a deficient conception of persons is different from ignoring the costs of others because of self-interest. Granted, underestimating costs certainly also often applies to the costs of not changing; and the violence of the status quo can be worse than the violence of change. In both cases, downgrading of costs can have a motor propelling it: the large gains that relatively small groups can or already do reap from the situation or from the change. They have a high motive to defend the situation or to 'sell' the change. Concentration of benefits, which is the motor that drives the downgrading and denial of costs, is often particularly intense for changes. To highlight the costs of change – such as 'external' costs inflicted on innocent bystanders – would reduce the public attractiveness of the investments and thus their chances of sustained support, approval and funding.

The neglect of non-commoditised suffering (and happiness) applies more broadly still in economics-dominated evaluation. Consider a notional case. An enraged and jobless young man robs and murders a sickly retired person. No one withdraws from paid employment as a result; instead resources are expended for the funeral and the police investigation, so GDP could rise. Further, a transfer of resources out of health care and into 'productive' investment might result, leading to later GDP rise. ('Productive' here in practice means conducing through monetised activity to the increase of GDP.) The enriched young man proceeds to entertain and then rape a series of women. GDP is unharmed, for the women continue to carry out all their commitments; in fact it rises due to monetised medical treatment. Interrupted during one rape, the young man kills a policeman and sells his body parts in the international market – an activity likely to boost GDP, and increasingly practised. Recruitment from the ranks of the unemployed soon restores the wage bill of the police force. The net result is: unemployment down, GDP up, two people dead, several raped, others afraid. The example is not remote from some current realities (see e.g. Truong 2001 on international trafficking).

Sister to the exclusion by definition of costs is denial of the existence of alternatives, past or present. Such denial perhaps most often involves simply turning a blind eye, not looking. It can also use arguments. First, that alternatives exist but are not serious, due to alleged internal contradictions. There is only one viable path, all others self-destruct, and so whatever one's values one must agree on that one path, say the free-market order or 'the' Islamic way. Second, the argument that alternatives are inconsistent with fixed and overriding moral tenets. One example concerns the claim by some relief agencies that 'the humanitarian imperative' leaves them in all cases no ethical alternative except to try to provide succour to and save the lives of those who are in distress, regardless of possible overall negative consequences when we take into account the actual capture and use of the resources by warring parties (Gasper 1999a).

5.5 REAL ALTERNATIVES AND PAINFUL CHOICES

How can we combine due weight to the special undesirability of physical violence with an ability to think constructively about what can bring improvement when we face 'tragic choices', where all options involve major costs?

NOTIONS OF TRAGEDY, EVIL, DILEMMA

The notion of tragedy refers at least to great costs and misfortunes. The economics sense of tragedy goes a bit further. First, it sees costs as unavoidable to obtain benefits; second, the two can be compared; and third, they are not proportionately distributed between people, but situations can still be compared (when this is not prevented by the strongest party). In pure utilitarian versions, everything is open to comparison. Costs are just to be summed and then compared to benefits; there are no types of cost that are categorically unacceptable – such as killing and letting die. A business analysis of costs and benefits can be applied equally to trade in body parts or in dead children (as in Jonathan Swift's satire about famine in eighteenth-century Ireland). The thought processes of a profit-seeker in a commoditised economy become applied to all choices.

Suffering is a theme central to utilitarian ethics. It is partly represented in economics, although its operationalisation by reference to commoditised transactions introduces great distortions – non-commoditised parts of life can be ignored, the commoditised parts weighted in proportion to ability to pay, and creative accounting plays a part since markets generate incentives to manipulate their own categories. However, violence in itself is not a category in utilitarianism, which contains no inherent restrictions on what is acceptable, only the principle to increase utility and reduce disutility. If violence brings greater utility then it is considered desirable; if a sadist damages a masochist we might have a 'win-win solution'.

Other perspectives add ethical constraints from outside utilitarianism and economics. Their conceptions of tragedy thus go further, to argue that sometimes costs cannot be compared on a common scale with benefits, and that some types of cost are intolerable and cannot be outweighed by however much benefit. The removal of body parts from an unwilling innocent to save however many others is never considered justifiable (let alone as operationalised in the world human-organs market via ability to pay). Choices have still to be made, but rather than running on the smooth calculation of maximum advantage they may sear the psyche and the community. Evils might not be comparable, if of qualitatively different kinds, or not comparable in the same way that we make other cost comparisons, if the choices include choices of loyalty and identity. Choosing 'the lesser evil' is not like other choices. The concept of a dilemma can arise here: where each option available involves damage to values that are deemed fundamental – such as life and, for Kantians, non-deception and non-coercion. If these human values are fundamental then they must be separately studied, not concealed or lost under the calculation of market values (Cameron 1999).

So violence is a category of significance in itself in some ethics. It has a special degree of undesirability for Kantianism, as an infringement on the autonomy and dignity, and frequently the capability, of a human being, a creature endowed with reason and the potential to set and pursue her own ends (Baron et al. 1998; Cameron 1999; O'Neill 1991). Kantianism is deontological (an ethics of duty) and in general rejects violence even if its effects are good. Similarly, good effects obtained by evil means – say the pleasure derived by the executors of illicit violence – are not accepted. But some quasi-Kantian positions accept violent action which really leads to the reduction of violence overall.

Sarah White and Romy Tiongco (1997) warn that violent resistance to violently backed injustice often carries dangers that are overlooked. It assumes that while one type of violence calls forth a violent response, the violent response itself will eventually end violence rather than call forth more. It assumes that violence removes a delimited evil and leaves everything else unchanged, whereas in reality societies are moulded and scarred through conflict. It can lead down a path of mutual demonisation, escalation and brutalisation. Victory, if ever achieved, leaves many deaths and embittered enemies. The resort to violence assumes that power rests at a centre which must be captured, as prelude to redistribution. In practice the violent battle against power creates a counter-power hierarchy which itself becomes centralised and authoritarian. If it triumphs it inherits a reinforced government hierarchy and has little inclination towards any other form of organisation. These are reasons then for the alternative of non-violent struggle expounded by Mahatma Gandhi and others, which seeks to build on the potential power held by myriads of people if they resist and attempt to persuade in coordinated fashion. It has its own limitations, remark White and Tiongco: it is hard to initiate, hard to sustain, hard to make effective. The crushing of the peaceful anti-apartheid movement of the 1950s in South Africa illustrates this. However, insights from the philosophy of non-violence helped in that country's remarkable transition in the 1990s.

TOWARDS A CALCULUS OF PAIN, WITH A RESPECT FOR PERSONS

Wilhelm Verwoerd (1999) considers the debates in South Africa about what to do about past violence. He widens the horizons of assessment beyond the traditional ethical–legal level of justice for directly harmed individuals, and places responses to past violence in a context of long-term development implications, with attention to what are feasible paths of social betterment and greater overall social justice. This, he argues, helps to defend the South African Truth and Reconciliation Commission (TRC) against the claim that it was part of an abandonment of justice for the sake of peace and a spurious reconciliation.

Verwoerd deepens too the content of assessment, by analysis of what drives societies in their long-term development paths. The importance for individuals and all South Africa of an uncovering of past gross human-rights violations is, he argues, to further delegitimise the past, to establish trust between state and citizens and, by respecting families' right to know, to help unblock social energies. The TRC's opponents argue that the feelings of meaning and dignity require a fuller settling of the past than just truth without sanctions. Here Verwoerd refers us back to the horizons: to the nature of the political compromise that permitted the transfer of power, the more inclusive development that the transfer in turn permits, and the vital potential contribution of this to social justice and dignity.

The South African TRC path represents a set of hypotheses, a major 'experiment with truth', to use Gandhi's phrase. The content of this set reflects a Kantian concern for individual dignity, but goes beyond rigid deontology ('thou shalt never do X', 'thou shalt never balance evil 1 against evil 2'). It seems to reflect – like Peter Berger's calculi of pain and meaning – a post-utilitarian consequentialism. Policies must promote the good, not only respect the right; the content of the good is broader than utility, and much of what promotes the good is found to be precisely that which respects the right, including respecting people's dignity (Gasper ed. 1999).

Utilitarianism uses a particularly narrow picture of personhood. The Kantian picture is richer: the rational actor is not only a calculator of satisfactions, but is self-conscious, able to reflect on and choose ends as well as means, able to sympathise with others and to consider the consistency between his actions towards them and the principles he demands in respect of himself. But while richer, this picture is still somewhat thin. Religious or Aristotelian positions, and theories of basic human needs, for example, have fuller pictures of personhood and thus generate further ethical and policy propositions.

Consider one example. Interviews with a variety of women in India suggest that basic education and access to support networks are more effective than paid employment in helping women respond to and remove domestic violence (see e.g. P. Sen 1999). This fits a picture of people as limited, thinking, feeling agents, who live in groups. Capacitisation requires the acquisition of skills, confidence, emotional support and access to alternative viable identities, even more than of a wage.

The richer the picture of persons, the greater the dangers of specifying as essential some features which are too culturally contingent. A vision of personhood that can sustain a widely persuasive ethic might require an intermediate degree of specification (Gasper 1996b, 1997a). We will look at this in Chapters 6 to 8. A Kantian-style emphasis on real ability to choose is reflected in the influential work of Amartya Sen on 'capabilities' and in the UNDP *Human Development Reports* which have recognised security as an essential part of human development.

5.6 CONCLUSION

While this chapter, like the rest of the book, does not focus on designing policy proposals, a likely policy upshot of our discussion of violence is a human-rights agenda. A common conclusion in development ethics is the importance of the category of basic economic and social rights: that the sorts of norms of basic human needs that we look at in the next chapter may require institutionalisation through the language and machinery of rights – including statements of policy principle, constitutional commitments, justiciable claims. The chapter's main conclusion complements that. Protection from violence is already an officially acknowledged civil and political right, but for it to be taken more seriously and more adequately fulfilled, it must be a major focus of attention in social and economic analysis too.

DISCUSSION THEMES

1. What do you mean by violence and security?
2. Do you agree with the theory that peace and economic development are mutually supportive in general and/or in the long run?
3. Do you see other important types of violence besides those listed in section 5.3?
4. How convincing do you find the arguments that economic stresses are often major factors contributing to violence? Identify and comment on possible counter-arguments.
5. Hirschman proposed that market activity can have both favourable and negative impacts on peace and order, and that the balance varies between cases and historical eras. Try to find some cases with different outcomes, and examples of the factors which determine such different balances.
6. If one accepts the special importance of physical integrity and security for all, can that concern be given a workable policy formulation?
7. Assess Verwoerd's defence of the Truth and Reconciliation Commission's attempt to come to terms with past violence in South Africa despite major political constraints.

READING SUGGESTIONS

Papers in Gasper (ed. 1999) go further into the issues raised in this chapter, including on alternative responses at individual, agency, and societal levels, to past, present and prospective violence. John Cameron presents the centrality of violence in development ethics from a Kantian perspective; Nigel Dower probes the relationship between concepts of peace and development; Purna Sen looks at individual Calcutta women's responses to ongoing domestic violence; Willem Verwoerd examines the societal level response in majority-rule South Africa to its past of apartheid violence; and I discuss different responses by humanitarian relief agencies to dilemmas they face in emergency situations involving violent conflict, such as after the Rwanda genocide of 1994. Each paper provides an entrance point to work in those areas. Slim (1997) and Moore (1998) examine ethical dilemmas in humanitarian assistance. Asmal et al. (1997), Krog (1998) and James and van de Vijver (eds 2000) treat the tasks, strategy, achievements and limitations of the South African Truth and Reconciliation Commission. Galtung (1994), the *Human Development Report 2000*, and Gasper and St Clair (eds 2000) provide overviews of the agenda of universal human rights.

CHAPTER 6

NEEDS AND BASIC NEEDS

6.1 FIRST THINGS FIRST

Probably the central, though certainly not the only, set of issues in development ethics concerns massive, remediable, undeserved suffering, and how to facilitate rather than evade response to it. During the 1990s more than 10 million children per year died from readily preventable causes: 3.5 million from pneumonia, three million from diarrhoea, one million from measles, and so on. Such figures are widely reported by UNICEF in its *State of the World's Children* reports, and by other agencies. Peter Unger in his book *Living High and Letting Die* (1996) asked why less than 1 per cent of the Americans who received informative appeals from UNICEF responded, despite convenient preaddressed envelopes for reply. Issues arise concerning whether the rich far away have any duty to respond, and then whether such responsibilities lie directly with individuals or with collectivities.

In the year in which Unger wrote, 1995, the UN summit on social development in Copenhagen consolidated a set of targets for tackling poverty in the world in the next twenty years. The targets included:

- Halving the proportion of people in extreme poverty
- Universal primary education
- Cutting mortality of under-fives to one-third of the 1990 level
- Cutting maternal mortality to one-quarter of the 1990 level.

In 1996 the Development Assistance Committee (DAC) of the OECD, the secretariat of the economically rich countries which provide concessional loans or grants to poor countries, adopted the targets. The rich countries, as collectivities, committed themselves to supporting the poor countries to achieve the targets for 2015. These became known as the International Development Targets (IDTs) and later as the Millennium Development Goals. They represent an international commitment to meeting basic needs – or at least meeting many basic needs to a large extent.

In this chapter we consider the ethical claims in the basic needs approach, its value and limits, the objections that contributed to its sidelining during the so-called 'neo-liberal' ascendancy of the 1980s and early 1990s, and the replies and rethinking in the new wave since then. The new wave has various names and members – 'human development', the IDTs, the 'rights-based approach', and so on – but basic needs thinking is a major shared intellectual source and component. Basic rights, for instance, may have to rest on well-theorised claims of basic needs. One may disagree about matters beyond those basics but, the basic needs approach (BNA) argues, basic needs are the prerequisites for all other normative criteria and development perspectives to become relevant. First things first, declared the title of one important exposition (Streeten et al. 1981).

The claim of special priority is consistent with ordinary language usage of 'need': the term 'need' is normatively stronger than 'want'. Indeed, 'development' as a normative concept is sometimes defined as whatever economic growth and social change fulfil human needs, or basic needs in particular. 'Needs' appears also as one of the major types of equity claim, notably to argue why the outcomes of legal market transactions, and even equality of receipts, are often inequitable.

Partha Dasgupta's magisterial *An Inquiry into Well-Being and Destitution* appeared in 1993. Modern economics at last took centrally into account that the agents in economic life have bodily needs. Work capacity and health depend on food intake; very poor people cannot mainly adapt by using food even more efficiently. Dasgupta confirmed how market equilibrium wages for rural labour often do not cover the worker's subsistence. Subsistence refers to more than mere survival: people may survive through losses in body weight and lowered activity levels, and with malnutrition, which is reflected in higher rates of sickness and shorter life expectancy. In the case of children, malnutrition affects their long-term physical and mental capacities. In situations of pressure of population on land, there are some families who, to survive, will accept a market wage below subsistence level since they can compensate by access to common property resources or other assets. Other families without equivalent access or assets, or with greater needs, cannot compensate. If they accept the market wage, they will work but be malnourished, with the consequences described above. The worst cases eventually lose the physical strength to do the work required of them and are forced to scavenge or beg. Scavengers, the malnourished and their children do not fit the equal-opportunity assumptions behind norms of distribution in proportion to contribution. Such findings are not new (see e.g. work summarised in Kurien 1996), and not dependent on high mathematical technique; a willingness to observe was more important. But Dasgupta's mobilisation of the abstracted formalised language of 'modern resource allocation theory' (his phrase) for this theme commanded much attention.

Needs theories have remained a perennial contender in social policy, although marginalised by the branch of 'modern resource allocation theory' which focuses on preferences backed by money. The needs approach reached a peak of prominence in development policies in the late 1970s (e.g., ILO 1976, Lederer 1980). It was marginalised in the 1980s by neo-liberalism, which accuses needs analyses of being rigid, asocial and authoritarian (e.g. Fitzgerald ed. 1977, Springborg 1981). Debates derived from welfare states in rich Northern countries invaded and dominated the discussion of absolute poverty and destitution in the South. In section 6.4 we will see a range of doubts about ideas of 'needs', doubts not held only amongst market liberals. Some for example hold that ethics of needs danger-ously diverge from the expressed wishes of subjects. Further, human behaviour and motives cannot be well captured by simple models and it has been easy to criticise the descriptive–explanatory psychologies sometimes used in BNA, for example the Maslow model (Maslow 1954, 1970). Such models are best seen as introducing a counter-agenda to the still simpler models of human personality which have been used in economic theory.

In response to these various attacks, the needs approach was rethought and deepened. Work by David Braybrooke, Len Doyal and Ian Gough, Amartya Sen and Frances Stewart, amongst others, systematised and better justified BNA's concepts and focus. They distanced themselves from psychological theories in terms of needs, and concentrated on clarify-ing the structure of needs ethics. In the 1990s these stronger and successor forms of normative needs analysis appeared, partly under a new flag, 'Human Development', which we will consider in Chapter 7.

The new versions deal with a set of underlying problems in debates about needs. One problem has been obscurity about the meaning of 'need'. We should distinguish three versions or modes: 'need' as a descriptive and explanatory category, 'need' as a prerequisite for doing something else, and 'need' as a prerequisite which has special normative priority. The three have linkages – the second mode connects to both the others – but to think clearly we must initially differentiate. A sister problem has been obscurity about the meaning(s) of 'basic'. We have to ask: 'basic for what?' and 'why is the what (the thing for which we need this) of basic importance?' That helps us to tackle the last problem, 'the lack of a unify-ing conceptual framework' (Doyal & Gough 1991: 154). Sen's capability approach now helps to provide such a framework. Concepts of need become more precise through the use of some other concepts, including 'capabilities', 'functionings', and 'characteristics'.

This framework for normative discourse on needs is presented in section 6.2. The contemporary Human Development stream of work, coordinated by the United Nations Development Programme (UNDP), draws also from the other modes, which give a richer picture of human personality and sharper data and models of the requirements of health and welfare; section 6.3 (which is optional reading) refers to such richer work. Section 6.4 considers criticisms of needs theory in both the explanatory and normative modes. Section 6.5 clarifies needs theories' specific roles, as an alternative to economism. The chapter's final section sums up attractions and limitations of the basic human needs stance for research and policy.

6.2   THE LANGUAGE OF NEED

MEANINGS AND SYNTAX OF 'NEED'

Analytic philosophy looked from the 1950s at the concept of 'need'. Taylor (1959) lists four types of meaning of the noun. For us three are important:

- needs as factual entities, related in some way to wants or desires (mode A); here 'need' is a descriptive and explanatory category;
- needs as requisites for meeting a given end (mode B); here 'needs' are instrumental;
- needs as normatively justified requisites or priority requisites (mode C); here 'need' is a normative category.

The fourth meaning is: need as something required by a rule or law. It can be treated as a special case in mode B.

Table 6.1 groups around forty observable meanings of the nouns 'need' and 'needs', under these three generic senses. (An asterisk in a name indicates that a meaning is a variant or partner of the other meaning specified in a cell.) Meanings on the same row have similar foci. The sets of meanings in a column each reflect a distinct, established and legitimate stream of work. In mode A we try to explain wants and behaviour by reference to underlying human traits. While in certain ways problematic this advances one beyond 'economic man' models and cruder pictures of asserted universal wants. In mode B, as for instance in Dasgupta (1993), we try to identify requisites and determinants of physical and mental health and well-being. Mode B leads into the policy-oriented concerns of mode C, where we attempt to specify justified priority requisites. It is our main interest here. Much work on needs has jumped without specification or explanation between these modes. Admittedly the distinction between positive and normative is imperfect; but it is a relevant contrast. To try to operate without it here gives far less insight.

Table 6.1 Different meanings given to 'need(s)' as a noun

A. IN DESCRIPTIVE AND EXPLANATORY ANALYSES OF WANTS/DESIRES/BEHAVIOUR	B. IN INSTRUMENTAL ANALYSES: REQUISITES FOR MEETING A GIVEN END	C. IN NORMATIVE ANALYSES: JUSTIFIED/PRIORITY REQUISITES
A1. Wants, desires	B1. Requisites for meeting wants	C1. Requisites for approved wants
A2. Those wants which are felt earlier than others	B2. Requisites for survival B2*. Requisites for 'maintenance of human capital' (Pyatt 1995)	C2. Requisites for survival, when justified (e.g. high cost prolongation of the life of a critically ill 100–year old might not be)
A3. Wants whose non-fulfilment results in (significant) suffering A3*. Strong wants (Friedmann 1992: 61)	B3. Requisites for avoiding suffering B3*. Requisites for lowering of tension	C3. Requisites for avoiding excessive/unjustified suffering
		C4. Requisites for avoiding harm (a different and broader category than suffering) C4*. Requisites for minimal decency
A5. A behaviour tendency whose fulfilment results in satisfaction	B5. Requisites for satisfaction, fulfilment	C5. Justified requisites of desirable satisfactions
A5*. A behaviour tendency whose continued denial results in pathological responses (Bay 1968; however, some criteria for pathology are culturally relative)	B5*. Requisites for avoidance of pathology (subject to a similar comment as for A5*)	C5*. Requisites for 'flourishing' (whose meaning depends on norms which will be in part culturally relative or otherwise open to dispute; this is close to C7)
	B6. Requisites for participating in a given way of life	C6. Justified requisites of a way of life C6*. Requisites of a justifiable way of life
A7. Human potentials (not all are desirable)	B7. Requisites for fulfilling (a conception of) the human essence (Springborg 1981:109) B8 (& B8*). Requisites for pursuing very many (or even any) other ends, or many (or even any) ways of life	C7. Justified requisites for fulfilment of desirable human potentials C8 (& C8*). Justified requisites for pursuing very many (or even any) other ends, or many (or even any) ways of life (cf. Ramsay 1992: 6)
A9. A political claim for priority use of publicly managed resources (Friedmann 1992)	B9. Requisites for meeting a law (Taylor 1959: no. 1)	C9. Requisites that should be ensured by state action C9*. Normatively agreed entitlements (Friedmann 1992)
A10. Factors ('drives'/ instincts) that (are claimed to) underlie and generate wants		C10. Basic rights

Source: Based on Gasper 1996b

We use 'want' here in the everyday modern sense of 'wish' or 'desire'; not the archaic sense of 'want' as 'lack' or 'need'. The earlier identity between the terms 'want' and 'need' matched eras when subsistence was not assured and ordinary people had little or no space for non-necessities. In the nineteenth-century language of economics the terms were used interchangeably (see cell A1 in Table 6.1), or together as the portmanteau 'wants and needs'. This contributed to lack of clarity later, when most usage of the two terms diverged as wealth grew, at least amongst some groups, and as active desires and their promotion grew for most groups.

Each mode contains a distinction between 'needs' and 'wants', as shown in Table 6.2. In all three modes, the sense of 'wants' remains this: wishes, desires, impulses. The sense of 'needs' varies between mode. In mode C, needs are priorities for a person, according to some judge (herself or another person or body). The person may want those needs, but not all needs are felt needs, wanted. A child may not want education, an adult may not want medical treatment for a serious disease. A gap between perceived needs and wants can apply even when the judge is the person concerned. One may need and even want to stop smoking, yet actively want to smoke.

In prescriptive mode, claims about need fit a 'relational formula' (Braybrooke 1987): 'I need S – in order to do D, which is of special importance'. S is a satisfier, to be used; D is the doing, or the thing done. When someone says 'I want S', it requires no debate as a descriptive statement. But when they assert 'I need S', their position is as yet incomplete. Need is a priority term and so the question arises 'why is S a priority?'. The implicit or explicit response is 'because it allows me to do D'. This too is not yet enough. We could accept the response but still ask 'but do you really *need* it?' (Wiggins 1985). So there are two asserted links, around both of which disagreement might arise. One claim is empirical: 'I need S in order to do D'. Will S really permit D? And are

Table 6.2 Needs versus wants

THREE TYPES OF NEEDS–WANTS CONTRAST	*NEEDS*	*WANTS*
Mode A – explanatory	Needs are what explain wants	The wants themselves
Mode B – instrumental	Needs are things required in order to do other things	Those other things that are wanted for themselves
Mode C – prescriptive	Needs are those things considered (very) important for people to have/be	Wants may not all be needed: and may not not include all needs

there other routes to D? The second claim is normative: 'D is of special importance'. Is it really? Sometimes we formulate the second claim as 'D brings E, an end or goal which is an evident priority'. So the overall claim contains at least three levels: S-D-E. In the attempted justification of priorities we often have more than three. A multi-level structure brings scope for confusion, as the entities at every level may then be called needs. This indicates the importance of refined terms. Partha Dasgupta remarks that the complexity of a concept is no reason to dispense with it; few good ones would survive. The advantage of the normative concept of needs is precisely its complex relational structure, which interconnects 'commodity consumption as an input, political and civil liberties as the background environment, and welfare and individual functionings as an output vector ... Needs provide a most valuable marker for guiding public policy' (Dasgupta 1993: 37, 40).

The empirical component behind mode C needs-claims lies in mode B: what is really needed to do what? How much food, of what types, do people need in order to live on average a specified lifespan in a specified lifestyle, with only specified 'normal' levels of illness? Mode B's instrumental investigations can link with the explanatory work of mode A, but have to be distinguished. The mode B work on nutrition, health, education, childcare and so on which underlies contemporary mode C policy prioritisations – such as reported in Doyal & Gough (1991), Dasgupta (1993), Drèze and Sen (1989), and the *Human Development Reports* – is explicitly not mode A theory, not an attempted explanation of all human motivation along the lines of a Freud or Maslow. This new wave of mode C work proposes that we do not require a universal mode A theory of human needs in order to establish some mode C policy claims of massive significance; mode B data suffices. Psychological and cultural–theoretical critiques of mode A needs theories do not affect mode C ethical theories of need.

A UNIFYING FRAMEWORK FOR NEEDS ETHICS AND POLICY

A Theory of Need by Len Doyal and Ian Gough (1991) propounds a normative (mode C) sense of needs as the requisites for fulfilling fundamental human interests. From an argued specification of these interests they derive a reasoned, not *ad hoc*, list of proposed human needs. This is 'a theory of need', which examines the implications of a normative criterion, rather than a theory of 'needs' as supposed universal behavioural tendencies. Although it talks of needs as nouns, such needs are derived through the relational formula: the verb language of needing has primacy. David Braybrooke's *Meeting Needs* (1987) has a similar approach. He sums up normative needs discourse as a schema which involves: a criterion of need, a set of types of need derived from that criterion, and a family of levels, indicators, and provision targets; all as specified in a particular political community for a certain target population. Table 6.3 integrates these insights from Braybrooke with ideas from Doyal and Gough (1991) and later work by Gough and Thomas (1994).

Doyal and Gough operationalise their theory by distinguishing five levels, derived from Amartya Sen's rethinking of the economics of welfare and consumption, and use the social indicators literature to measure achievements at those levels. Sen amongst others had criticised 1970s basic needs work as too focused on commodities rather than on the lives which they enable people to live. He stressed that besides commodities, and the levels of satisfaction or preference fulfilment from their consumption, we must look at the *characteristics* which the commodities provide; at the *capabilities* – the range of alternative attainable life paths – which people thus acquire; and at the *functionings*, the ways in which people actually live as a result. (We examine the concepts further in Chapter 7.)

Table 6.3 distinguishes these five levels in discourse on 'needs', and illustrates how different normative criteria imply different needs, each with their own indicators. It does not try to specify targets, which typically will depend on context; although one could insert some globally accepted targets, such as concerning access to safe water by a particular date.

The levels of need can be further described as follows:

1. A topmost level of *proposed universal human interests, priority functionings.* 'Universal' means: for all members of the political or moral community which is referred to or assumed in the particular exercise; it could extend as far as all human beings. Doyal and Gough specify these interests as 'avoidance of serious harm' and 'minimally impaired functioning', but sometimes more extensively as 'human liberation'. The third column refers in italics to a yet more ambitious goal conception, 'human flourishing', as adopted in some of Martha Nussbaum's work. Each specification of interests leads to different derived needs. Needs of sheer survival are less than the needs which must be fulfilled to allow basic levels of participation in a given society; the latter are less than the needs implied by critical participation, which in turn may well be less than those implied by a conception of human flourishing.

2. A level of *'basic needs', which are the 'capabilities' required for the universal goal(s).* Here Doyal and Gough propose health (physical and mental) and autonomy. Autonomy of agency, being able to act and function effectively in one's society, in awareness of its values, is required for avoidance of serious harm; and critical autonomy, being able to reflect on and intelligently choose values, is required for 'human liberation'.

3. *'Intermediate needs'* are sets of 'characteristics' (e.g. shelter) which are necessary for fulfilment of those basic needs/capabilities. This level matches most of the traditional specifications of basic needs in development policy, though those also mixed different levels. For autonomy of agency Doyal and Gough specify

Table 6.3: A framework for normative needs discourse and policy
(for a particular political/moral community deciding for a particular reference group)

LEVELS OF NEED	CONTENT OF NEEDS, AT THE VARIOUS LEVELS, ACCORDING TO DIFFERENT NORMATIVE CRITERIA		INDICATOR CONCEPT *(Gough & Thomas 1994)*	OPERATIONAL INDICATORS *(Gough & Thomas 1994)*	TARGET LEVELS
1. PRIORITY FUNCTION-INGS	Criterion 1: 'Avoidance of serious harm'	Criterion 2: 'Human liberation' *[Criterion 3: 'Human flourishing/ fulfilment']*			
2. Implied REQUIRED CAPABILITIES ('Basic needs' in Doyal & Gough's usage)	Health, autonomy of agency (Doyal & Gough 1991)	Health and both agency autonomy & critical autonomy *[& belonging, understanding…]*	E.g.: • birth weight • life expectancy • adult literacy	E.g.: • % of births at low weight • literacy rate for 15+	
3. Implied REQUIRED SATISFIER CHARACTER-ISTICS ('Intermed-iate needs')	Food & water; housing; secure environment & work; health care, education; childhood security, etc.	Plus: additional education *[& additional medical care etc.]*	E.g.: • access to safe water • adults' mean years schooling • primary school completion	• % of population with safe water	
4. Implied REQUIRED SATISFIER COMMODI-TIES	[These vary, per criterion, according to the geographical, socio-economic and cultural context]				
5. Implied REQUIRED SOCIETAL CONDITIONS	Conditions concerning: • production • reproduction • cultural transmission • political authority		E.g.: • GDP per head • taxation • women's position • rights	E.g.: • logarithm of of purchasing power parity • tax/GDP • gender equality index • human rights index	

Source: Based on Gasper (1996b)

the required characteristics as: nutritious food and clean water; protective housing; a non-hazardous work environment and physical environment; appropriate health care and education; security in childhood; significant primary relationships; physical and economic security; safe birth control and child-bearing. (1991: 157–8)

4. *Goods* that provide these intermediate needs. The specific goods ('commodities' in Sen's economic parlance) required – for example to provide adequate nutrition and appropriate education – vary according to culture, context, and the person concerned.

5. *Societal preconditions* (or, less rigidly stated, conducive factors) for the provision and use of such goods.

The framework helps in analysing patterns of variation and similarity. Within a given interpretation of 'need', space for inter-community variation exists at the lower levels (3, 4 and 5). In Nussbaum's terms there is 'local specification', to take into account distinctive local conditions (for example, heating is a priority in countries with hard winters), and 'plural specification' of how to meet universal requirements, to take into account local traditions and tastes. Space exists also for inter- and intra-cultural variation at levels 1 and 2, in so far as cultures or persons set different criteria concerning priority functionings and capacities. Even if there were complete variation between cultures, the framework of prioritisation would remain important in each. In fact all leading world bodies accept that we can identify some vital universal requirements. Gough & Thomas (1994: 744) concluded from cross-national empirical work that 'the concept of [intermediate needs, i.e.] universal satisfier characteristics that in all cultures and social settings contribute to final levels of welfare is supported insofar as we can model these relations with the data at our disposal'.

Each of the following positions is then a needs ethic, although their emphases differ. Authors such as Doyal and Gough argue that there are universally relevant normatively required functionings, from which we can derive implications about the required capabilities, characteristics and commodities (all of which will be situationally and culturally relative). Some others argue instead that only the type of format is universally relevant and acceptable, and stress that different normative stances on required functionings will generate different views of needs. And some, like Braybrooke, do not make explicit claims for the format outside the Euro-American culture area. Moore (1978), Küng (1997) and others conclude, however, that diversity in this respect is exaggerated: all societies use pictures of legitimate needs, and all share certain types of moral feelings.

The leading variants of *basic* needs ethics hold that they are concerned not with very culturally specific priorities, but rather with the requirements for survival and for basic participation in one's society (autonomy of agency); and that any differences at levels 1 and 2 will not bring differences in many of the requirements at lower levels. We will in all cases need food and water, basic health care, nurturance during childhood, and so on.

MEANINGS OF 'BASIC'

In all modes of usage, needs are already seen as in some sense more basic than wants: as causally or ethically prior. Why would one add further emphasis and prioritisation *amongst* needs by speaking of 'basic needs'? The answer is that some needs might be identified as causally or ethically fundamental, or as the most general formulation, which will be concretised differently in different circumstances.

In descriptive mode, contenders for being called 'basic' include prepotent felt needs: those which are felt first. Thus if we are extremely hungry or cold we automatically focus on remedying those lacks, before thinking of any other goals. In explanatory mode, some theories posit that there are source needs – for instance, for power or for self-expression – which underlie particular felt needs. This was Abraham Maslow's type of usage.

In instrumental mode, one may call 'basic' those things – notably survival – which are prerequisites for very much else. In normative mode, one will call 'basic' the prerequisites for fundamentally important outcomes, including the top priority needs which a government or society must try to ensure. The framework we derived from Braybrooke (1987) and Doyal & Gough (1991) already focuses our discussion of normative needs on 'basic needs' in those senses. Len Doyal and Ian Gough reserve the term for their level 2, the most generally specified requisites for whatever are specified as the normatively fundamental outcomes. We have seen alternative specifications of such outcomes and thus of the criteria for why something would be considered 'basic'. In increasing order of ambition and implied demands, these criteria are:

1. To be able to survive.
2. To avoid 'serious harm' where serious harm may mean death or abnormal/deranged functioning or failure to achieve (mental and physical) health and autonomy of agency (Doyal & Gough 1991).
3. To be able to participate adequately in one's society's way of life. This does not suffice as a normative criterion if no exclusions are set concerning what is unacceptable as a way of life, e.g. slavery or genocide. Or, to be able to fulfil basic social roles (e.g. 'parent, householder, worker, citizen', according to Braybrooke 1987). We saw in Chapter 3 that capable agency is one of the unstated prerequisites for markets to function acceptably.
4. To be able to fulfil or at least competently pursue one's life project. Again, this is too permissive a criterion if it gives no attention to what is unacceptable as a life project.
5. A 'fulfilling life', 'human flourishing', or 'full development of positive potentials'. David Braybrooke warns that consensus on the meaning of such criteria will often be too little. He advises that needs ethics should not try to cover all of life, but should limit themselves to providing a basis and complement to other ethics. (Adapted from Gasper 1996b)

Nussbaum [handwritten margin note]

So there are reasons to focus on criterion (2), health and autonomy, as not too extended or permissive. But its spirit is close to that of criterion (3), competent participation in one's society. Ramashray Roy argues that 'efficacy [has] constituted an important component of the modern identity of man' (1994: 141). Both when acting in the public sphere as community-oriented citizen, and in the private sphere as self-interested entrepreneur, he requires an ability to form and fulfil goals, otherwise he 'would be incapable of sustaining a modern identity or else would be deeply humiliated in [his] identity' (ibid.: 141).

To answer then the question 'specifically what are basic needs?', one has to clarify which mode and which level one focuses on. For the explanatory mode A we will look briefly at some evidence in the following section. For the normative mode C one must further clarify which criterion of fundamental importance is used. Partha Dasgupta's list – 'a class of commodities to which people have positive rights, such as nutrition, shelter, clothing, primary and secondary education, basic health care, and legal services' (1993: 149) – is consistent with the criteria of competent membership and autonomy of agency within one's society. He derives it from a Rawls-type thought experiment concerning a fair social contract: 'Under the terms of the social contract, an individual's access to them at an acceptable level should not depend upon an ability to pay' (ibid.: 149). Dasgupta still talks of 'commodities'. Doyal & Gough's framework helps us to identify also non-marketed goods and services which have vital roles, including in meeting emotional needs; for instance, care during the upbringing of children, and respect from others.

6.3 A RICHER PICTURE OF PERSONS

Looking further at what the requisites are for avoidance of serious harm, for competent participation in one's society, or for whatever else are specified as fundamental interests, leads us to seek evidence in the instrumental mode B, and indirectly from mode A on explanation of behaviour. But it is easy to over-generalise, especially in mode A. Here we will take a comparative stance, contrasting a basic human needs (BHN) approach with two common alternative positions in mode A: a pure situationalist view that there is no inbuilt human nature, that people are 'plasticine men' who totally adapt to their physical and societal environments; and an essentialist view common in economics, that people are unchangeable 'economic men' with a pre-social universal human nature of calculating self-interest. In both the alternatives social and ethical analysis become oversimplified by ignoring the interaction of psychology, society and economy. (We will see comparable debates in mode C, ethics, between needs ethicists, pure inter-societal relativists, and those who use the world-view of mainstream economics.) BHN theories can give a better picture of human motives and interests than the two extremes of infinitely malleable 'plasticine man' and pre-social 'economic man'. (This section is optional reading.)

DO WE REQUIRE A PICTURE OF PERSONS?

Explicit theorising on motivation is superior to inexplicit smuggling in of assumptions on human nature and needs. As we cannot avoid a 'theory of man', we had better make it considered and open to examination and refinement (Wade 1976; Forbes & Smith eds 1983). We require a richer, more realistic, more social, picture of persons than is typical in economics or even in much of moral theory. Absence of serious discussion of human nature can lead to 'the ethics of fantasy' (Mackie 1977); for example, Karl Marx's inspirational vision of man having the means to cultivate his talents in all directions in community with others could be turned into a dogma of perfectibility.

Many modern humanists yet hold that: 'conceptions of a good do not require a belief in human nature ... [for example] societies can be judged on internal consistency ... [and conformity] to the "human nature" they have created' (Stafford 1983: 68). Attention to the created needs would remain important. In this 'plasticine man' model, human nature is over-whelmingly the product of its physical, technical, economic and social environments. The model implausibly neglects non-nurture factors. If human nature is totally malleable then perhaps any social set-up could satisfy the requirement of conformity with the inclinations of its members. The view leaves little motive force for social transition, since pure plasticine can be moulded to accept anything (Lane 1978). Nor does it allow singling out some state as 'truly human' and 'natural' – although many utopians, including some Marxists, still tried to do so; C. S. Lewis (1947) noted the contradiction. Judgements that while members of a certain society are habituated to it they are not truly satisfied require some further picture of human nature, between crude essentialism and pure situationalism: noting common needs and potentials while acknow-ledging malleability and variation.

A BETTER EMPIRICAL BASE FOR PREDICTION AND EVALUATION

The *Homo economicus* model has an explicit picture of persons, but a crude one: (1) individuals each have a set of personally specific and exogenously given preferences, but (2) everyone is predominantly (or exclusively) interested in income, wealth and security; and typically (3) individuals unerringly know and choose their own good (see e.g. Weigel 1986, 1989). Let us look at the second feature, strong material preoccupations. We saw in our discussion of violence that people have other concerns besides material well-being: 'passions' and not only 'interests', in Albert Hirschman's terms. That recognition distinguishes a basic human needs (BHN) approach from a basic material needs (BMN) one as well as from *Homo economicus*. BMN was prominent in the 1970s basic needs approach as interpreted by large donor agencies, but it did not exhaust the content of the basic needs approach or of needs analysis in general (Wisner 1988). The BHN approach includes for example participation as an end and not only a means; indeed as an important end, and therefore as an important means because it can be a major motivator.

For a fuller working out of Hirschman's point, we can refer to Abraham Maslow's (1908–70) theory of needs, since it continues to be widely used. Later we mention its pitfalls. While written as mainly a mode A theory about human urges and motivation, it can also or instead be seen as a mode B checklist about requisites for personal fulfilment. The very term 'need' suggests a lack or deficiency and hence mode B, so why use the term in mode A, about behaviour? Because of a hypothesis that thanks to evolutionary selection, combined with intelligent upbringing that reflects societal and parental learning, our main inner motors, conscious and unconscious, seek to promote our well-being by remedying deficiencies. Maslow derived this optimistic stance from following a principle that psychology should learn from healthy people, not predominantly study the disturbed. 'Any theory of motivation that is worthy of attention must deal with the highest capacities of the healthy and strong man as well as with the defensive maneuvers of crippled spirits' (Maslow 1970: 33). Some who study human evolution worry, however, that much of our mental hardware and software reflects the aeons of hunter–gatherer life and not present-day requirements.

Maslow proposed five types of basic need. He also speculated on others, including meta-needs, which lead towards self-transcendence. Here is part of the summary of his original statement of the theory (1943):

(1) There are at least five sets of goals, which we may call basic needs. These are briefly physiological, safety, love, esteem, and self-actualization. In addition, we are motivated by the desire to achieve or maintain the various conditions upon which these basic satisfactions rest and by certain more intellectual desires.

(2) These basic goals are related to each other, being arranged in a hierarchy of prepotency. This means that the most prepotent goal will monopolize consciousness and will tend of itself to organize the recruitment of the various capacities of the organism. The less prepotent needs are minimized, even forgotten or denied. But when a need is fairly well satisfied, the next prepotent

('higher') need emerges, in turn to dominate the conscious life and to serve as the center of organization of behavior, since gratified needs are not active motivators. Thus man is a perpetually wanting animal... The average member of our society is most often partially satisfied and partially unsatisfied in all of his wants. The hierarchy principle is usually empirically observed in terms of increasing percentages of non-satisfaction as we go up the hierarchy ... an individual may permanently lose the higher wants in the hierarchy under special conditions. There are not only ordinarily multiple motivations for usual behavior, but in addition many determinants other than motives.

(3) Any thwarting or possibility of thwarting of these basic human goals, or danger to the defenses which protect them, or to the conditions upon which they rest, is considered to be a psychological threat. With a few exceptions, all psychopathology may be partially traced to such threats ...

Table 6.4 Maslow's list of types of basic human need

SETS OF BASIC (SOURCE) NEEDS	*TWO GROUPINGS OF THE SETS*	
[Meta needs]	*Growth needs*	*Enhancement needs*
Self-actualisation needs (for activity, expression, inquiry, use of one's potential, etc.)		
Esteem needs (autonomy, respect from others, self-respect)	*Deficiency needs*	
Affective needs (love, friendship, belonging, etc.)		
Security/Safety needs		*Physical subsistence needs*
Physiological needs		

Let us look at some of these posited types, starting from the bottom. Survival needs consist of not only the needs of physical subsistence – the physiological and security needs – but some 'enhancement needs' from the other sets. People can die or go mad from extreme isolation, ignominy, monotony or restriction, and some risk death to avoid them. Survival is still sensibly called a (mode A) need – understood as a near-general motive – as well as (in nearly all cases) a mode C justified requirement.

'Affective needs' is a broader and more adequate label than 'love'. Here we move decisively beyond the 'economic man' picture of motivation. Economists offer some reasons for sticking to a picture of self-interest. One is 'the considerable merit of being parsimonious', wary of adding any extra assumptions (Dasgupta 1993: 212). Such a simple picture of motivation aids mathematical formulation of the behaviour implied. But the resultant model of 'economic man' unacceptably overgeneralises the occurrence of another dictionary meaning of 'parsimony': meanness, stinginess. Economists' second argument is that social norms of more altruistic behaviour exist but probably derive from, or at least have to be consistent with, long-run self-interest. Partha Dasgupta proposes that we have no need to assume more than self-interest to explain internalised norms. He discusses for example scenarios in which norms of looking after one's elders, subject to certain conditions, could have emerged purely from self-interest. But the underlying concepts of 'self' and 'interest' remain bizarrely unexamined in economics (Douglas and Ney 1998); nor are emotions considered (Elster 1999). Dasgupta notes in passing the presence of emotional bonds in families (1993: 224–5), but these go far beyond mere respect for norms. Parents do not relate to children solely in terms of internalised norms, but also out of strong affection. Its attention to these elementary facts of life makes a theory like Maslow's a more reliable guide than the economic-man model.

Self-actualisation needs refer 'to the desire for self-fulfillment, to become everything that one is capable of becoming' (Maslow 1943: 383). This can be through serving others or a cause, not only through self-orientation. Maslow's article went further:

> Curiosity, exploration, desire for the facts, desire to know may certainly be observed easily enough. The fact that they often are pursued even at great cost to the individual's safety is an earnest [token] of the partial character of our previous discussion ... Rather tentatively ... we shall postulate a basic desire to know, to be aware of reality, to get the facts, to satisfy curiosity, or as Wertheimer phrases it, to see rather than to be blind.

Denis Goulet's *The Cruel Choice* elaborated the picture of needs for meaning. People seek 'significative values' that reinforce the performative values (a better term than Goulet's 'normative values') which are implied in their activity choices, and vice versa. Goulet suggested that a gap had opened, notably but not only in developing countries, between people's significative values and the new performative values required in economic development. This could undermine both sets of values, whereas: 'every society must feel that its values are worthy of respect if it is to embark on an uncertain future with confidence in its own ability to control that future' (Goulet 1971: 49).

The neglect of significative values brings deep failings in understanding and in policy. Despite the preeminence of religions historically and still in the lives of vast numbers of people, development discourse has largely ignored them (Gunatilleke 1983; Baha'i International Community 1999). Both Marxism and market liberalism were long puzzled by the power and persistence of nationalism, religion and other such sources of concrete identity and meaning. For they both were heirs to an Enlightenment notion of 'man' as sufficient identity in itself. Marx overemphasised the self-actualisation needs of creative activity, in comparison to, or in isolation from, the significative need seen in the 'self's irreducible interest in a definition of itself' (Cohen 1983: 233). Similarly, BHN analysis can help us understand part of the attractions of liberal societies, in terms of their satisfaction of certain *non*-material needs.

It is not needs for conflict and aggression but thwarted basic needs that generate violence, argued Maslow. And thwarted or unrecognised needs cannot be assuaged by further gratification of needs which are already satiated.

> Some conflict theorists – referred to as 'human needs theorists' – argue that the most difficult and intense conflicts, such as racial and ethnic conflicts, are caused by the denial of one or both groups' fundamental human needs: the need for identity, security, and/or recognition. In order to resolve such conflicts, ways must be found to provide these needs for all individuals and groups without compromise – as human needs 'are not for trading'. (Conflict Research Consortium 1998)

Sixty years on, Maslow's model of motives continues in widespread use, refined in some details but easily recognisable. Easy too to criticise (see e.g. Douglas et al. 1998), it nevertheless remains superior to reasoning in terms of economic or plasticine men, although its claimed hierarchy of prepotency is problematic. It has proved a durable tool for thinking beyond psychological models which are based on studying rats or the emotionally disturbed, or which take the deliberations of a businessman in an anonymous market to be the paradigm for all behaviour.

We must accept that 'a single theory could not hope to explain all motivated behaviour. ... Some behaviours are programmed into the organism, while others are learned or depend upon social interactions or environmental conditions' (Petri 1981, cited in Baxter 1988). A range of personal, social, and species 'programmes' are at work. BHN theories in modes A and B (i.e., explanation and means–ends analysis) do not seek generalisations at the level of behaviour or desires, but at deeper levels of capacities and urges, or requirements. They are compatible with cultural analyses, and with enormously diverse behaviours. Diversity arises in response to different environments and as expression of the open, creative aspect of higher needs, and persists through the tenacity of cultural traditions.

Mode A needs theory analyses variety across cultures by distinguishing (1) source/fundamental needs, such as hypothesised in Maslow's list; (2) concretised forms of those needs, as shaped in a given socio-cultural context; and (3) the specific satisfiers to fulfil a concretised need in the given context. Baxter (1988) offers an elaboration: Person, with inborn features, plus Environmental influences → Needs, plus further Environmental influences → Wants/Desires → Choice and use of Satisfiers → Effects on the person. Most research on basic needs accepts that needs are bio-social rather than only biological; they are partly created in processes of social interaction (Handy 1969), but the interaction moulds and focuses rather than creates from nothing. The resulting concretised needs will be socially and historically specific.

Nurtured differences may eventually not be reversible by new experiences. 'Give me the boy until he is seven and I will give you the man', and the society, and the plan for a good society of such men. Even if produced values are in principle reversible by new experiences, some new experiences do not get a chance. Many sets of values generate a style of life and thought which excludes other styles (Hampshire 1983).

So, more adequate but more complex explanatory alternatives exist than basic needs lists of motives (see e.g. Etzioni 1988; Douglas et al. 1998). Those interested in improving on the model might turn for example to the school of humanistic psychology led by Edward Deci and Richard Ryan (1985, 2000). But BHN lists can be readily grasped by a range of audiences who are beyond the reach of most cultural and psychological theory. Whether for explaining behaviour or satisfactions, BHN lists of human motives and interests are a simplification but more adequate than some very influential views. They are largely consistent with the picture of values from over 60,000 interviewees in the World Bank's *Voices of the Poor* study (Narayan et al. 2000). While the source–needs notion is a crude summary of complex plural causes, the lists lead to a set of vital reminders: don't forget security, don't forget identity, don't forget religion, don't forget esteem.

REINTERPRETATIONS OF POVERTY, LUXURY AND LIMITLESS DEMAND

Ideas of poverty link directly to ideas of need, for typically by 'poverty' we mean shortage of something necessary or required, in other words the non-fulfilment of needs. An idea of absolute poverty, not merely low income compared to other people, implies a concern with certain priority needs. Consequently ideas about poverty can be clarified by the same framework as for (mode C) needs. BHN theory helps us to see poverty as both absolute and relative, and as multi-dimensional.

We have at least three types of relativity: relativity to the society's circumstances (e.g. one needs more energy in a cold climate), relativity to the society's culture, and relativity to the position of others within the society. The following views are all common.

1. Poverty is purely subjective, a matter of individual feelings; within any society there is no consensus on it.

2. Within any society, poverty is purely inter-personally relative, i.e. a matter only of one's relative position in the society, and thus dependent on what others possess (see e.g. Griffin 1990). Sen (1981, 1984) has definitively refuted such attempts to *equate* poverty and inequality – starvation for example is a matter of absolutes – while also clarifying how poverty in some respects is indeed inter-personally relative.

3. Poverty is an absolute matter within a society, but culturally and situationally relative (e.g. one might say that Americans without a car are poor, but Dutch are not, because of differences in norms, distances and public transport conditions); also, ideas and conditions change within a society over time.

4. Poverty is an absolute concept even across societies (e.g. concerning vitamin requirements). An absolute concept of worldwide poverty rests on a picture of universal human needs.

Once we introduce levels into our conception of need, we can have a universal conceptualisation of needs and poverty but accept culturally relative detailed specification of what the needs involve – and hence what poverty is – in a particular society. Poverty could then be both intra-societally absolute and inter-societally relative (O'Boyle 1990; position 3 above). The scale of the needs (e.g. how much transport or heating or clothing) is society-specific; and the acceptable satisfiers are culturally relative and inextricably involve non-material considerations, as seen in Adam Smith's example of the need to be able to present oneself without shame in public and in modern children's demands for the latest fashions. So 'basic needs is a country-specific and dynamic concept' (ILO 1976), but for a specific time, place and social group, basic needs are more definite (Sen 1984).

Given different types of need, we are led towards Manfred Max-Neef's view that 'we should speak not of poverty, but of poverties. In fact, any fundamental human need that is not adequately satisfied, reveals a human poverty' (1989: 21). Each poverty generates a pathology. Some poverties are more absolute (like lack of vitamins) whereas some are more inter-societally relative. With non-material needs we face more relativity: the expression of needs for dignity, friendship, membership, or creativity is highly culturally specific, and their fulfilment is often affected by the relative position of others (e.g. social hierarchy may affect dignity and fraternity).

In sum, an inter-societally relative concept of poverty is compatible with a belief in shared human needs; and an intra-societally relative concept requires such a belief, for the relative incomes of persons are not the crux but serve as imperfect proxy measures for fulfilment of non-material needs of dignity, esteem and membership.

Let us look next at luxury and affluence. We earlier saw Easterlin's paradox, that what is recorded as growing affluence brings no sustained increase in levels of satisfaction, and how this is consistent with Abraham Maslow's needs hierarchy hypothesis (section 3.4). However, serious objections arise to the idea of prepotent hierarchy, especially the simplified Maslow model's version. One danger is that needs for meaning could become seen as marginal, with 'cultural needs' treated as a separate set that require attention only at a later stage than material needs or at higher income levels. But culture is all-pervasive rather than supplementary; each broad need requires and receives more concrete specification in light of local culture and circumstances. Further, searches for meaning are important at all material levels of living: arguably they are even more intense amongst the poor. Maslow himself always allowed for co-occurrence of needs. Psychological research has found much co-occurrence of felt needs and little support for five or more different levels or stages, but does suggest two or three, not just one level (e.g. 1. physiological and safety needs, 2a. affective needs, 2b. other needs; Lea et al. 1987; Baxter 1988, 1993).

A needs-based perspective without the prepotent hierarchy might yet explain a drive for unending economic expansion which continues regardless of satisfaction. For Immanuel Wallerstein it is

> not hard to understand why people feel so passionately about development ... Development as the achievement of 'more' is the Promethean myth. It is the realization of all our libidinal desires. It is pleasure and power combined, or rather fused. The desire lies within all of us. What the capitalist world-economy as a historical system has done is to make these desires for the first time socially legitimate. (1991: 107)

Tibor Scitovsky proposed a more complex resolution of Easterlin's paradox. Scitovsky (1910–2002), a leading American welfare and development economist (see Scitovsky 1952, 1992; Little et al. 1970), came in the second half of his career to query conventional economics' understanding of well-being. His study *The Joyless Economy* builds on neurological research which has physically located two types of pleasure system. Satisfaction in the primary system depends on relation to an optimal level of arousal, and can be called 'comfort'. Satisfaction in the secondary system relates to change and variety, and can be called 'stimulation'. Success in a need satisfaction search restores comfort; plus the search itself gives pleasurable stimulation, both during the mobilisation phase and, after success, during the phase of declining arousal, disappearing pain, and relaxation. A habit of immediately removing pain and discomfort and reaping primary pleasure will be at the expense of losing greater satisfactions from stimulation and of probably creating deep frustrations. The psychological theories which Scitovsky drew on have limitations (Lea et al. 1987), and his argument is perhaps better read in mode B, concerning sources of satisfaction and dissatisfaction, than in mode A as a model of mechanisms. But he provides an advance on mainstream economics since that presumes a single type of satisfaction (or that all types are commensurable).

The economics definition of 'luxuries' is products whose share in consumption rises as income rises. What is on the list varies according to time and place. The luxuries vary with income level and social habits: tobacco may be absent and unlamented in some societies, a 'luxury' good in yet others, and a 'necessity' with near-satiated demand in yet others. In contrast, Scitovsky defined 'luxury needs' as the urges to comfort beyond the needs of survival. This sort of psychological definition probes behind variation in habits to look for possible commonality of urges: tobacco might be one satisfier of universal urges for arousal and displacement activity. Urges to achieve comfort through luxury are real urges produced by real discomforts. Other things being equal, meeting many of them is legitimate. But there is a frequent tendency to overindulgence, including from habituation to immediate removal of discomfort. This is at the cost of activities (like exercise and education) that bring temporary discomfort but stimulation and delayed pay–offs, and of attention to needs of other types. In so far as people are using material luxuries to try to satisfy these other needs, there are typically better ways of satisfying them.

Economics usually assumes that wants are limitless, and typically interprets this as meaning wants for comfort-giving commodities. Economics-dominated policies have thus relatively neglected enhancement needs – affective, esteem, self-actualisation and inquiry needs – which are at risk too because of habituation to immediate comfort restoration. We see, in Max-Neef's terms, provision of pseudo- and inhibiting satisfiers: goods which fail to satisfy but which block access to effective satisfiers. So, the behaviour referred to as showing limitless material wants can be reinterpreted as part of the unending alternation of temporary consumerist novelty and recurrent inevitable dissatisfaction, since non-comfort needs are neglected. André Gorz argued that reduction of working hours in Europe could not only reduce unemployment but increase satisfaction better than does endless acquisition of commodities (see e.g. Gorz 1989). For it provides time for satisfaction of other needs, and for less alienated forms of care and solidarity than an overwhelming reliance on a welfare bureaucracy. It is the needs of activity, inquiry and signification, not of comfort, which are less limited, and can take forms with less environmental impact. They are more ongoing and open: interesting experience adds to the interest of later experience. The pre-eminent economist Alfred Marshall (1842–1924) stressed these open needs, in the non-formalised parts of his theoretical system, using a mild version of prepotency theory

(Douglas et al. 1998). According to him, after the level of biological needs comes the level of utility-seeking wants. But the 'real aims of life lie in the [higher level] of activities pursued as ends in themselves … [the] healthful exercise and development of faculties which yields happiness without pall' (cited in Parsons 1968: 141). The required precondition is the partly painful acquisition of skills to use capacities and make new things meaningful. Advice and training may be important, including to raise vague urges to the level of directed consciousness and sometimes to unlearn dysfunctional habits.

6.4   DANGERS IN NEEDS THEORIES AND ETHICS

We have already assessed criticisms that supposed needs are totally variable across different individuals, societies and times; we noted significant underlying unities, through distinguishing different levels. Other major criticisms are diverse and mutually contradictory. One set holds that needs discourse treats people as if they are crops or animals: relatively simple beings, not able to know their own good, and better understood by external experts. Needs discourse can then become a tool of domination, used by elites and technocrats to legitimate their hold on power and to give themselves work, telling other people what they should want and have. A famous critique of the former Soviet bloc, by Agnes Heller and others, was entitled *Dictatorship over Needs* (1983). Another set of criticisms argues, in contrast, that needs discourse is a tool of self-interested and far from passive bargainers, and inevitably becomes misused. Children soon learn to say 'I *need* it' when 'I want it' hasn't worked. So-called needs, say the critics, are the wants that people try not to pay for; needs claims are merely a tool of negotiation for getting more, a cover for people to demand that they must get what they want, as a top priority and free of charge. A 'so what if you need it?' position rejects such bids and sees needs as claims without corresponding responsibilities, and binding on nobody else. Let us look at these two sets of criticisms in turn.

IS BASIC NEEDS ANALYSIS PASSIVE AND PACIFYING?

Is the needs approach a model of passive individual receipt-need, which neglects the primacy of human activity? Is the 'satisfaction of existing needs a specification … [that distracts attention from] the removal of obstacles to the negotiation of social demands' (Schaffer & Lamb 1981: 122)? Some voices declared that planning for basic needs, as taken up by the World Bank in the 1970s, was an inexpensive sop to the poor to keep them quiet and divert them from more fundamental demands (e.g. Roy 1979/80). These criticisms could apply to the basic material needs (BMN) variant, but not to the basic human needs (BHN) stream, which stresses expression, participation and self-determination (Hettne 1995; Galtung 1978/9; Green 1978). Further, analyses of needs feed into negotiations. Some feminist authors argue that dominant definitions of need are an element in patriarchal control of women (see Fraser 1989), but the real issue is who defines needs, rather than the need category itself. For there is no good alternative to seeking public priorities. Not everything that people want constitutes a valid claim in a public arena, and while markets serve in many ways, leaving them to do all prioritisation fatally marginalizes some people and grotesquely magnifies the interests of some others.

BHN approaches provide for participation in defining one's own needs, take as open questions what are acceptable and effective means to fulfil more general needs, and often simply aim to provide opportunities without enforcing their use. Manfred Max-Neef's work takes BHN analysis further, analysing each posited fundamental need in terms of 'being', 'doing', and 'interacting', as well as 'having', in other words also in more active modes. A priority to economical provision of basic material needs is largely compatible with an emphasis on self-determination in programmes with poor people. For people can discuss their preferences between different needs, and between the means for meeting each more general need; and the resulting mobilisation of their energies is likely to be economical too. This illustrates Max-Neef's idea of synergic satisfiers, activities which fulfil more than one need. Harrell-Bond (1986) gives an example from refugee camps in Sudan. Refugees outside the camps did better than those inside, in material welfare, mental health, self-reliance, and local integration; for their knowledge, skills, initiative, and preferences were respected and used. Internationally the trend – where politically tolerated – has been towards having refugees themselves partly manage external aid, as amongst the vast numbers of Afghan refugees in Pakistan.

The famous Austrian–Mexican critic of advanced technological societies, Ivan Illich (1926–2002), claimed that the policy language of 'needs' is control-speak. In his view, expounded in *The Development Dictionary* (1992), it refers to desires that have been fostered and turned into addictions by modern industrialism but which now have to be controlled and managed. '"Basic needs" may be the most insidious legacy left behind by development.' (Ibid.: 88). Industrialism's attempt to substitute through technology a world of liberty for the traditional world of necessity has ironically brought 'the reconstruction of desires into needs' (ibid.: 90). So:

> Most people who are now adults are addicted to electric power, synthetic clothing, junk food and travel … they accept unquestioningly their human condition as one of dependence on goods and services, a dependence which they call need. In just one generation, needy man – *homo miserabilis* – has become the norm …

man, the needy addict ... needs are a social habit acquired in the 20th century and a habit that needs to be kicked in the next. (Ibid.: 89, 90)

Illich tried to link the use of needs theories to the requirements of national and world-system managers. Since by the 1980s 'an economy based on wants ... now inevitably leads [in the South] to socially intoler-able levels of polarisation ... an economy based on needs – including their identification by experts and well-managed satisfaction – can provide unprecedented legitimacy for the use of this science in the service of the social control of "needy" man' (ibid.: 97). He added: 'The subtle and asym-metrical power relationship implicit in the concept of needs was clearly perceived by S. de Beauvoir in *The Second Sex'*, in her discussion of the relation of master and slave. But the asymmetrical power relationship lay in the master–slave relation rather than in the concept of needs. Slaves themselves have employed concepts of needs to support demands for liberty and equality.

One can sympathise with Illich's concern at consumerist addiction, yet his treatment of 'needs' as its Trojan horse misused language and was out of touch with current debates. Even for the technocratic BMN approach, preoccupied with reducing malnutrition and disease, the language of 'addiction' to basic needs was absurd. Illich himself presented people as dummies: 'that many people today already recognize their systemic requirements ['needs' as defined by global managers for compatibility with operation of the global system] principally argues the power of pro-fessional prestige and pedagogy, and the final loss of personal autonomy' (ibid.: 98). He thus agreed with what he had attacked needs discourse for: 'the needs discourse implies that you can become either more or less human', as in increase or loss of personal autonomy (ibid.: 98). He speci-fied needs discourse as 'professionally defined requirements (needs) for survival' and contrasted it with 'personal claims to freedom which would foster autonomous survival' (ibid.: 99) – as if Marx, Maslow, Fromm, Max-Neef and the entire body of BHN work, through to Sen's theory and the *Human Development Reports*, had not espoused the latter. In contrast to Illich, elsewhere in *The Development Dictionary* Gustavo Esteva used the concept of 'needs' approvingly. For him the issues were instead: that people must indeed escape from the cultural straitjacket of 'economic man', prisoner to an unendingly reinvented scarcity and to externalised or externally specified 'needs'; but they must recover 'their own definition of needs' (Esteva 1992: 21), including through activities of gaining and using skills, and interacting with others and with nature. In Chapter 7 we see how the human development ethics of Amartya Sen and especially Martha Nussbaum respond to these challenges.

OVEREXTENDED?

Some allege that the needs concept provides an open door to justify keeping whatever one has ('the needs of my way of life'), and to demand more (e.g. 'my need to be kept alive' however old and sick I am). We have seen that modern basic needs discourse in fact gives a framework to debate bids for priority treatment, with attention to the values, data and logical connections claimed. It helps to strengthen the priority of education for future mothers, and of the easily arranged and extraordinarily low-cost measures to reduce child mortality which Peter Unger pointed to. David Braybrooke warns that needs reasoning is, however, in danger on some other frontiers: for example as the numbers of very old people escalate, each of whose lives could be substantially prolonged at very high cost by new medical technologies. Feasible provision targets could be derived from a criterion of need that prioritised preservation of life until for instance eighty years of age, or of lives up to, say, ninety years if healthy; however, such line-drawing could be unsustainable politically and in other ways.

So how important are needs in ethical terms? Basic-needs ethics argue that *basic* needs have a special, though also delimited, importance. Since they are the requisites for functioning as a competent member of a society, their fulfilment should be supported by people of many viewpoints even when they disagree about life beyond basic needs. We will look at this key idea in section 6.5.

Needs theory brings an expectation that there will be such disagreements beyond the stage of (mode C) basic needs. While complete malleability is not the case, humans clearly are malleable, unlike economic man. This is fortunate for policy: human nature is sufficiently mutable to be satisfiable in various ways, depending on the specific opportunities that are current (Hollis 1977). But the idea of a unique social optimum is then undermined, at any rate for ethics which focus on people's desires or specific needs. When desires and people's concrete natures are moulded by the social choices – for example of types of production (Dobb 1969) – which one wishes them to determine, there is an irreducible degree of relativity. Scope exists for partial ordering of alternative social states by reference to fulfilment of basic needs, but the remaining ordering should then be by other types of normative principle.

There is a great temptation to broaden specifications of needs: for more ambitious explanation, or on grounds of equity, or in elaboration of a vision of 'human flourishing'. The purposes should be clearly separated. In positive analysis the incentive to explain may generate longer lists of substantive needs. However, while a useful list must not leave out major types of dimension, it cannot become very complex. Psychologists suggest that lists longer than seven become difficult to use for most people. Lea et al. (1987) argues that Maslow's theory stimulated research and refinement since it is neither so detailed that testing is bound to refute it, nor so vague that testing can never do so.

In normative analysis, definitions and lists of needs and levels are parts of a schema of social assessment that has to be operationally and politically feasible. Needs as well as targets can get specified on an overblown scale. Needs ethics which go beyond basic needs of decency or autonomy of agency may bring in non-universal norms, and may not be accepted widely in the foreseeable future. For example, in the state of Kerala in southern India, the requirements for women's autonomy of agency appear well met, yet women participate little in many aspects of public life (Mathew 1995, Gasper 1996a). Some observers, both outsiders and insiders, ask: Do they happily choose such an outcome? Do they lack *critical* autonomy, capacity to assess their society and choose values? But others ask: Shouldn't local culture rule when we are beyond the level of basic needs seen as *agency* autonomy, sufficient capacity to act as an adult in one's own society? We look at these questions in Chapter 8.

An equity purpose should confine itself to specifying modest basic needs, advises Braybrooke. Too extended an interpretation of basic decency will undermine the political consensus required to legitimise and implement the claimed normative needs, and can politically endanger the very idea of 'basic needs'. In contrast, too narrow a view of human personality and potential (and too little attention to positive theory) may rob a picture of human flourishing of its plausibility and motivating force. These two major roles of needs analysis will be weakened by not clearly distinguishing them.

6.5 THE DISCURSIVE AND PRACTICAL STRATEGY OF BASIC HUMAN NEEDS

A REQUIRED BASIS FOR OTHER ETHICS

David Braybrooke and Peter Penz argue that a priority to basic needs fulfilment can attract or demand support from a wide range of philosophical positions. Unlike many other ethical positions, basic needs ethics do not try to provide a full ordering of possible actions or states of the world. They simply seek to establish a minimum level of capability (attainable functionings, or, in some variants, actual functionings) to which all community members are entitled; beyond that they hand over to other types of ethic. Ethics of such a type are deliberately restricted in scope, in order to fulfil the role of obtaining sufficient consensus around them in plural societies. Quite the opposite of ignoring that plurality, they are designed to respond to it.

Further, non-needs ethics themselves require a basic needs ethic in order to become plausible: for instance a deserts ethic which says that people should be rewarded in proportion to what they contribute, or a libertarian ethic which says that people are entitled to whatever they obtain through legal voluntary transactions, require as a starting point that people are in a position to make contributions or to transact in an informed and capable way – which implies that they have at least a basic education and the conditions for a minimum decent level of physical and mental health. Basic needs have priority because their 'fulfilment provides the necessary background environment for persons to be capable of deliberating and acting upon considerations such as utility' (Dasgupta 1993: 44). Basic needs guarantees are also essential parts of any plausible social contract. That guarantees are not absolute, having overriding force in every situation, does not make them empty (ibid.: 46). Much writing on ethics from rich countries has simply ignored this priority of basic needs, taking it for granted that they are already fulfilled for all (ibid.: 68), which is untrue even for the rich countries, let alone for the South.

Penz extended the argument from national to international settings. He urged that 'the identification of the priority of basic needs as a rough consensus, and taking them into – no, pressing them upon – the "real world" of development practice must not be postponed' (Penz 1991: 66). There would be disagreements about the details of lists of priorities, target levels, and who should be involved in such choices, but there could be very significant agreement 'about the priority of basic needs in general' (ibid.: 56). What emerged in the 1990s, propelled by the second basic human needs wave in development thinking, was formal international consensus on a broad set of targets, the International Development Targets (IDTs) or Millennium Development Goals.

OPERATIONALISING BASIC NEEDS: TARGETS, RIGHTS, RESPONSIBILITIES

Policy and planning raise many questions beyond ethics and values: measuring needs, comparing them, devising strategies and tactics and procedures, setting targets. We have looked at (1) concepts of needs, and (2) ethics of need, with some reference to (3) needs-based theories of behaviour. All of these are relevant to policy, but that must draw also on (4) evidence on prerequisites, (5) ideas on the availability and efficacy of alternative policy means and measures, (6) reference also to other relevant policy criteria, and so on. Tibor Scitovsky treats area 3, and Abraham Maslow areas 3 and 4, from behavioural science; Amartya Sen treats areas 1 and 2 from philosophy, and together with Jean Drèze also areas 4 to 6, reaching into policy analysis. Len Doyal & Ian Gough and

Partha Dasgupta treat all the areas except for the theories of behaviour. Thus Dasgupta (1993, chs 6 & 17) provides criteria for which basic needs goods should be provided in kind (those where resale is not possible), and which should be supported by cash transfers (only those where the persons concerned know their requirements well). Such issues from areas 4 to 6 go beyond the scope of this book. We should, however, make a few connections.

First, policy naturally involves a combination of needs criteria with other criteria, as we saw in Chapter 4 on equity criteria, and in section 6.4 on the danger of overextending needs claims. Blanchard (1986) and Elster (1992, 1995) provide illustrations.

Second, these other criteria link to the question of where responsibility lies for promoting need fulfilment. People who have neglected good opportunities would have a weaker claim upon their community. But children and the disabled or infirm are not in a position to care for themselves, and malnourished and uneducated parents are often not in a position to care adequately for their children. Dasgupta refutes the market theory claim that people can borrow to cover all their needs. Credit markets in poor countries are too thin and flawed, poor borrowers lack collateral, and health and education are not goods that can be repossessed by a creditor.

Third, 'the supposedly rival concepts of basic needs, capabilities, and human rights... are not really rival concepts at all, but are essentially complementary' (Penz 1991: 36), as we will see further in Chapters 7 and 8. There may be good reasons for institutionalisation of basic needs as rights. In his companion volume in this series, Peter Brown proposes a set of three basic rights (subsistence, bodily integrity, and moral, political and religious choice), compatible with Doyal and Gough's conception which we used in section 6.2.

Fourth, while targets are sometimes a crude policy means (Rhoads 1985), they provide a focus for attention and pressure in truly basic priority areas. Some economists hold that to set policy target levels is overly rigid, as seen in Soviet planning; we need more flexible ways that take into account the changing trade-offs between different needs. But practical decision-making can try to reflect such issues in the targets it sets for a given situation, while probably often sticking to targets as a practicable as well as secure form for specifying basic needs objectives. Without targets, and with instead the pull of market forces, national and international authorities have left many millions of children to die prematurely each year and tens of millions more to grow up physically and mentally stunted. While international action to support fulfilment of the IDTs has so far been poor (Mehrotra 2001), the targets have fixed attention and helped to mobilise extra resources at the UN's Monterey conference in

2002. The World Bank has become a belated advocate of free primary schooling. In some African countries, numbers of children in school have quickly doubled as the school fees imposed by the World Bank and IMF in the 1980s and 1990s have been withdrawn.

Fifth, needs policy analysis now uses a vast body of work on social indicators (see e.g. Miles 1985, Doyal & Gough 1991, and the *Human Development Reports*). Sometimes comparison between needs is unnecessary: often a modest minimum standard of provision in each need area suffices for a decision, or can lead us to devise a satisfactory solution (Braybrooke 1991). The literature on both aggregating and non-aggregating multi-criterion assessment helps here, if we remember that the exercise is to establish orders of magnitude and to increase transparency and reflection, not to produce assertions of exactitude such as in much economic cost–benefit analysis. David Braybrooke speaks of 'utilitarianism without utility', meaning that we can retain a systematic consequentialism in identifying relevant effects, and when necessary also aggregate across cases and people; but should not adopt pure 'sum-ranking' (for that implies absence of minimum-needs guarantees), nor a 'utility-base', the supposed currency of comparison which is so difficult to measure, other than by unacceptable willingness-to-pay proxies, and so tenuously connected to people's life conditions.

Sixth, as Braybrooke underlines, these activities – negotiation of indicators and indexes and targets, inter-relating different criteria, and so on – are not impossibly difficult: they are done every day in every administration (see e.g. Witkin & Altschuld 1995).

Most needed in policy is creative thinking on possible means. Max-Neef (1989) illustrates how needs analysis can itself become a means, when applied as an exercise of self-diagnosis by local (or higher-level) groups. The groups work to construct a matrix of needs and satisfiers for their situation, especially to identify the destructive satisfiers, those that undermine the possibilities of satisfaction of the need they are supposed to serve and of other needs, and then the opposite category, the synergic satisfiers. Such group analysis can itself be synergistic.

A PROGRAMMATIC ALTERNATIVE TO ECONOMISM

Some critics of the economistic mainstream forget that a superior alternative is the best criticism. Debunking current practices and theories is not enough; they will not be amended if better alternatives are not clearly available. Longstanding powerful attacks on many uses of the GNP concept had very limited impact, for example, until the gradual emergence of alternative measures able to perform similar roles. Even the 1980s 'UNICEF [adjustment with a human face] approach provides neither a real critique of structural adjustment as a principle nor a solution to previous problems with conceptualising inequality and poverty. ... To broaden and deepen qualified criticism into a full critique demands a counter philosophy' (Cameron 1992: 9, 11). It provides a framework and so can stimulate and integrate concepts, measures and alternative plans; and it builds credibility and encourages participation in the required work. In that way, nothing is more practical than a good theory.

An attractive alternative theory requires the following: (1) a strong and clear conceptual basis; (2) methodological and theoretical elaboration, in ways that match the various allures of dominant approaches, their air of being both 'science' and common sense; (3) operational wings that are well linked to the theoretical base, yet still practical, with simple versions available for simple cases and audiences, and sophisticated versions for the more demanding; and (4) the ability to absorb or annex some strong areas in competing approaches. Economistic ideas (like GNP and growth-manship, long-term time discounting and cost–benefit analysis) have exercised dominance because they have strength in all four respects. They represent an elaborated yet graspable, battle-hardened yet flexible package with great staying power.

BHN analysis has met to an important extent the requirements for an effective counter-attractive theory to compete with economism and utilitarianism. It combines enough empirical reference and conceptual basis. Thus it has had the ability to generate an ongoing research programme or programmes, especially in Amartya Sen's capabilities work, the related UNDP *Human Development Reports* and work on social indicators, and Martha Nussbaum's existentially richer sister theory. Sen's research programme in particular, to deepen and humanise welfare economics, has had a central role, linking the worlds of economic theory, philosophy and policy. We turn to that in Chapter 7.

6.6 CONCLUSION: BEGGARS CAN'T BE CHOOSERS

Work in development ethics often stresses needs, because dominant economics can understate the range within people's motives and personality, and overweight the importance of marginal costs and benefits as expressed in terms of money (section 6.1). An important distinction exists between narrower conceptions, of more material needs, and wider specifications that include 'open' needs for activity and 'passions' in addition to interests. This underlies the gap between basic material needs and basic human needs approaches.

An essential step in discussing 'needs' is clarity on differences concerning (1) mode (positive/normative) and (2) level (section 6.2). Regarding modes, we must distinguish positive understanding of human behaviour from moral philosophy on required goals. In normative analysis, needs is a prioritising notion. Levels help us to understand elements of variety around elements of unity. Amartya Sen, Len Doyal and Ian Gough give a workable universal framework for normative needs analysis, with a set of levels from functionings down to commodities and societal precon-ditions, that provides great scope for cultural and contextual variation. The schema can be specified in many different versions: from proposing requirements of a fuller human flourishing, to negotiating a politically feasible set of welfare minima. None of the elements of normative needs analysis has a uniquely correct version: the lists of levels and types, the criterion of priority, or the targets for provision.

Employing such distinctions and related theory, needs analyses offer important pay-offs (section 6.3). These include: a better basis for explan-ation and for normative analysis than either 'economic man' or 'plasticine man'; useful first approximations in positive analysis for understanding the substance of choices; a grasp of poverty as simultaneously absolute and (inter- and intra-societally) relative; and reinterpretations of luxury (as comfort-oriented) and its dangers (the neglect of enhancement needs) and of 'limitless demand' (as the fruitless attempt to satisfy other needs through comfort-giving commodities).

Needs approaches have limits, and needs criteria must be combined with other ethical criteria (section 6.4). There are limits to the under-pinning from behavioural science, and to trans-cultural sharing; and dangers of misuse of needs formats and of neglect of cultural analysis. Who is involved in the discussion of needs makes a crucial difference.

Basic needs ethics have wider acceptability if they try not to cover all of life, but to draw out the common requirements behind a wide range of possible ethics. A narrower picture of needs is appropriate for establish-ing a consensual priority to requirements for basic decency, as opposed to when trying to explain human behaviour or advise on 'the good life'. While attractive in other ways, extended needs ethics – with criteria of required functionings beyond those of survival and minimal decency, to cover 'liberation', 'human flourishing' or 'human fulfilment' – serve less well as an area of consensus between otherwise conflicting positions.

Assessment of needs theory should be comparative, against leading alternatives in explanatory and normative arenas. To only emphasise limits brings the danger of leaving us with weaker but already entrenched theories. A refined form of human needs theory might provide a com-petitive alternative to conventional economism, spanning principle and practice, political appeal and research appeal. It can offer a plausible ethical rallying point in a plural world – provided that needs claims are not overextended – by giving a basis for alliance between different philosophies and world-views, each of which contains or requires for its own coherence a basic needs component (section 6.5). Beggars can't be choosers.

1. Do you find the idea of 'basic needs' helpful or not? 'Basic needs' in what sense? (Can we define clearly their meaning or meanings?)
2. Specifically what things do you think are basic needs, in an ethical sense? (Can we specify certain things, and which ones?) Why?
3. Are basic needs universal or do they totally vary according to the individual/the society/the historical period …?
4. In which ways is Maslow's theory of needs helpful and in which ways is it perhaps crude or misleading?
5. Are there any persuasive ways of setting limits to the claims made in terms of 'needs' (for example, claims about 'the needs of my way of life')?
6. How far can arguments about the ethical priority of basic needs in a national or local political community carry over to the international arena?

For lucid introductory perspectives, see Crocker (1996), Goulet (1995, especially Ch. 4), Finnis (1987), Rahman (1992) and Stewart (1989); and as more advanced reading, Braybrooke (1987), Doyal & Gough (1991) and Gray (1993). On concepts: Plant (1991) shows how well established are the everyday language distinctions (in English) between 'wants' and 'needs'; Braybrooke (1998) sustains the distinction, despite overlapping labels, for French and German too; and Gasper (1996b) gives a fuller treatment of the ideas here in section 6.2. On the needs approach to understanding and mitigating conflict, Burton (ed. 1990) is a helpful collection. On trying to deepen or go beyond needs theory: besides Deci & Ryan (2000), see Douglas et al. (1998), which assesses how far existing needs theories, explanatory or normative, might help in understanding and responding to global climate change. While the section on concepts of need (pp. 203–18) is subsidiary to Gasper (1996a, 1996b) and superseded by the treatment in this chapter, later sections sketch a socially embedded type of needs theory. On how far needs worldwide establish moral claims on the rich, see e.g. O'Neill (1985, 1996, 2000), Gasper (1986), Unger (1996). Hicks (2000) makes good points on the rationale of building alliances between different philosophies and world-views.

CHAPTER 7

'HUMAN DEVELOPMENT': CAPABILITIES AND POSITIVE FREEDOM

7.1 FROM BASIC NEEDS TO A FULLER PHILOSOPHY OF DEVELOPMENT

We introduced contents and justification of the field of development ethics by presenting a series of issues in Chapter 1. Many of the issues concerned basic material needs, including those around health, shelter and physical security. We began with shelter and saw Ammajan Amina's loss of her home, stemming from her lack as a widow of property rights, and leading to her beggary and the death of her daughter. We highlighted the many millions of deaths a year in poor countries that are preventable by treatments which are inexpensive by world economic standards, though not by the standards of the poorest countries, and noted the further legions of deaths which could be prevented if research was directed to the diseases of the poor rather than overwhelmingly to the lesser ailments of the already long-lived rich. The issues have been elaborated in subsequent chapters.

Chapter 2 noted the gradual evolution of concepts of 'development', towards a 'human development' conception which includes the aspects of a decent human life, and away from a central focus on the growth of monetised activity. Chapter 3 examined that conventional central focus and its underlying values and assumptions, including its disinterest in inter-personal distribution. Chapter 4 illustrated the associated appalling neglect of the poor and vulnerable, seen at its most extreme in cases like the Great Irish Famine and the Great Bengal Famine, and at work on a global scale in the extraction from the South of vastly escalated debt service payments since 1980. Chapter 5 looked at physical security and insecurity, and their links to both material and non-material deprivations, including indignity and humiliation.

Chapter 6 has presented basic needs ethics which explicitly prioritise and defend fulfilment of people's basic needs, material and non-material. It clarified the different components, strands and levels in needs discourse, and argued that rigorously structured and carefully delimited basic needs ethics – such as in the work of David Braybrooke, Len Doyal and Ian Gough – can provide an important core for development ethics. However, we noted also various pitfalls and limits for needs discourse, including dangers of its being operationalised in monological elitist form, and the limit (for many basic needs theories) of not commenting beyond relatively low levels of minimum decent provision.

The work of the Indian economist and philosopher Amartya Sen (1933–) has been pivotal in several ways in development ethics, and has enriched our discussion in nearly all of the previous chapters. He also offers one way of building on the strengths in needs discourse while avoiding its dangers and extending its scope. Sen has reestablished the close links necessary between ethics and economics, to the benefit of both (Sen 1987). As we saw in Chapters 3 and 4, he has memorably analysed several major famines as the 'side effects' of 'efficient' market functioning (Sen 1981), and precisely identified the utilitarian and/or market-liberal ethical assumptions typically made tacitly in the economics of welfare and policy, which have dominated much of development planning and practice (Sen 1982, 1984). By theorising the structure of utilitarianism and alternatives to it, he has emphasised the many relevant types of information besides those considered in previous welfare economics, and has reconceptualised equity and equality as having many aspects, so making us always ask 'equality of what?' and understand each version of equity as involving equality of something (Sen 1992). All of this showed the importance of more explicit and argued choices of ethical assumptions and a richer range of sources.

Highlighting two particular categories of additional information, his capability approach leads us to look at the set of life options that a person has, and the actual things the person does and achieves – not only at income or the declared or imputed state of satisfaction, each of which can be misleading as a welfare measure. Sen's categories have helped to put normative needs theory on an adequate footing, as we saw in Chapter 6. The reconceptualisation of poverty and development in such terms was adopted in 1990 for the UNDP's annual *Human Development Reports*, as outlined in Chapter 2. Under the inspirational and astute leadership of the Pakistani economist Mahbub ul Haq (1934–98), the reports made a decisive breakthrough in the campaign to fundamentally see development as more than, indeed distinct from, economic growth. The conclusion was not new, but the strength and breadth of the coalition behind it was. By the late 1990s some of this thinking was officially proclaimed by parts of the World Bank too.

Sen now integrates many of his insights under the attention-catching and widely appealing label 'Development as Freedom', the title of his

1999 book. He stresses not only negative freedom, meaning the formal absence of interference or restriction, but especially positive freedom, capacity to achieve things which one has reason to value. He consistently champions reasoned freedom rather than the freedom of caprice or the assertion of identity as something beyond reason (Sen 1998).

The related work of writers such as Denis Goulet, Doyal and Gough, Manfred Max-Neef, Martha Nussbaum and others also has impressive scope and potential. However, for the key shift of momentum, authority and influence we are indebted to the alliance of ul Haq and Sen. Sen in particular spans and links work on concepts, explanatory theory, normative theory and policy design, offering in each case both simple and sophisticated versions, in languages that can speak to and persuade important audiences. He has combined the rigour of formal economics with the conceptual sensitivity of philosophy and the practical focus and urgency of development policy, in a way not bound to preexisting doctrine in any of these areas but able to draw creatively from many earlier sources. He addresses various longstanding themes in social philosophy – from Aristotle, Immanuel Kant, Adam Smith, John Stuart Mill and others – in a way oriented to development concerns. This often proves to bring fresh insights.

Section 7.2 will look at the *Human Development Reports*' rethinking of the concept of development to focus on the contents of people's lives, and at this work's linkage to human rights discourse. Section 7.3 considers Sen's capability approach, which underlies the reports. We have already seen how Doyal and Gough integrate reason and freedom in their schema of needs, building on Sen's categories. Sen has built his own, even more flexible and capacious integrative structure, seeing development (as a state of affairs) as freedom to attain whatever one has reason to value. His thinking, like that of Doyal & Gough and Nussbaum, extends beyond the zones of more basic needs and subsistence. The structure is so flexible that it also leaves significant doubts. Section 7.4 discusses these objections and looks at how Nussbaum builds from Aristotle, Sen and others, to propound a more specific conception of human development, with more attention to personhood, emotion, and the textures of lived experience, not only to the formal notions of reason and freedom. Despite – or because of – her Aristotelian roots, she has sometimes been attacked as culturally parochial and imperialist. Chapter 8 will take such issues further.

7.2 THE UNDP HUMAN DEVELOPMENT SCHOOL

THE *HUMAN DEVELOPMENT REPORTS*

The adjective 'human' in 'Human Development' suggests that development previously had not been human-centred but instead interpreted predominantly as economic growth. The *Human Development Reports* (HDRs) reconceive development-as-product to mean human well-being, and development-as-process to mean its increase. Economic growth is at best a means towards human development. The HDRs have still for poor countries emphasised economic growth but stress too the importance of what are its specific contents and distribution and of much else besides growth. They have taken East Asia as their main model. They show that economic growth is neither sufficient nor necessary for improvements in quality of life (various countries have achieved dramatic human development gains without fast or even any economic growth), but argue that continued rapid gains require (and contribute to) growth. For rich countries ul Haq (1998) stressed the evidence that further economic growth was not raising the quality of life, but, perhaps unfortunately, this theme has not become central in the HDRs.

Human Development is not seen as merely a means towards economic growth, as in the language of 'human resource development'. But the school does emphasise the role of 'human capital' in long-term economic growth, as in the East Asian success stories, and in fact greatly broadens this idea. Just as free and educated agents can make economic choices that take into account their specific circumstances and aspirations, so, more widely, can informed and capable persons contribute more effectively to human development, as better parents, citizens and members of associations, not only as better employees or entrepreneurs. Education levels, for example, affect the ability to discipline power-holders; and women's education affects their self-confidence, their status, the use of their knowledge, and very much else, including child health and fertility patterns.

We saw in Chapter 2 that the HDRs adopted the conception that 'Human development can be expressed as a process of enlarging people's choices' (UNDP 1996: 49). Some options are undesired and some are insignificant. So, more precisely, the HDRs stress valued options and 'people's capabilities to lead the lives they value' (ibid.: 49). This is a liberal position, which trusts people's own priorities. We saw also how the HDRs moved to add a series of other concerns beyond choice: equity, security, community membership, and sustainability. They then synthesise a mass of information on these concerns.

Their best-known measure is the Human Development Index (HDI), but it is only one of a family of summary indexes (see Table 7.1), and has

Table 7.1 Some indicators from the *Human Development Reports*

CONCEPT	INDICATOR (see e.g. UNDP 2000: 269ff.)
Economic activity	GDP
Choices/Capabilities	HDI (a mean of indexes of: mean longevity; mean schooling enrolment & literacy; GDP/capita adjusted for purchasing power)
Choices and equity	HPI (Human Poverty Index: a mean of the percentages deprived in terms of longevity, literacy, and three other basic needs) GDI (Gender-related Development Index = HDI adjusted for degree of gender equity) GEM (Gender Empowerment Measure)

a specific, limited role: to dethrone GNP/GDP, rather than to replace it as the supposed summation of nearly all that is important. It has succeeded in that role, by highlighting in a vivid accessible way the frequent significant discrepancy between human development gains and economic growth. Some economists have devoted effort to showing that the HDI is an imperfect indicator and that they had long accepted that GDP is not a sufficient measure of development. But GDP had remained predominant in most practice and the HDI has made a stronger point – that GDP in many important cases seriously misleads as a welfare measure – to a wider audience, of politicians, policymakers, financiers and the general public. As to the imperfection of the HDI, it claims only to be an *indicator* of *part* (the part that stresses possession of valued options) of the UNDP concept of Human Development. It incorporates life-span and education as centrally important both in themselves and as the basis for most other valued options; and also, perhaps unfortunately (but on grounds of familiarity and universal availability), includes GDP per capita as an indicator of the other bases and options. The Human Poverty Index (HPI), introduced in 1997, makes a thorough break from GDP and shows how much more widespread poverty appears when we measure fulfilment of basic needs rather than just levels of income. The 1996 HDR already reported that in South Asia 29 per cent of people were officially income poor but 62 per cent had one or more very basic need unfulfilled. Many basic goods cannot be bought with money.

There are several other non-commodity dimensions of the HDRs' Human Development concept, outside the scope of the HDI. One early HDR attempted to include civil and political rights, negative freedom, but the measures were too controversial to sustain. The topic receives attention in the HDRs now in other ways than through the HDI.

None of the summary indexes is meant to replace attention to the mass of specific indicators on diverse aspects of living; and none of the indicators is to be fetishised as a perfect representation of those aspects. Indicators will frequently be culturally specific, and contentious within societies too. But they give a focus for reflection and debate, which contributes towards more conscious and informed value choices and response.

Every attempt at taking an aggregated index as a synthesising indicator faces similar problems to those of GDP: the danger of thinking that all values can be measured and compared in ways that do not undermine the values themselves; and the fact that aggregates hide the distribution of benefits. Aggregation is so problematic that some consider it a mistaken method. However, while always imperfect, aggregation too can be part of a strategy of encouraging debate, if – unlike in most economic accounting – one highlights the choices of weights and thus of values. Aggregation allows league tables which grab public attention and can promote useful discussion, as the HDI and sister indexes have done. Some of the sister indexes take account of distribution of benefits: the Gender-related Development Index adjusts the HDI in light of distribution between men and women. The HDRs also espouse disaggregated social reporting: to show distributions as well as averages, and to distinguish the positions of important social groups.

For Paul Ekins and Manfred Max-Neef (eds 1992) an adequate overall set of societal indicators will cover:

- Security: physical security, including life expectancy, deaths due to accidents and murder; and economic security matters, including employment, poverty, wealth distribution, homelessness;
- Welfare: ownership of durables, health, nutrition, housing conditions;
- Identity: suicide rate, hard drug use, mental health, job satisfaction, loneliness, etc.;
- Freedom: mobility, equality of opportunity, gender discrimination, leisure, access to culture, access to birth control, political and civil rights, etc.

This will give a picture of quality of life in terms of more objectively measurable welfare features rather than only more subjective personal feelings. It should be complemented by a modified picture of production, in which GDP figures are drastically modified to become better indicators of economic welfare (e.g. Daly & Cobb 1990), and by a picture of ecological, human, organisational and physical capital stocks. Such an overall set of indicators is now feasible for many countries and gives a proper basis for discussions of priorities, in contrast to an automatic devotion to the growth of economic activity levels.

HUMAN DEVELOPMENT AND HUMAN RIGHTS

Indicators and indexes must be seen only as tools within an overall Human Development approach. The *Human Development Report 2000* reached the conclusion that the most essential tool for human development (HD) may be the reassertion, institutionalisation and implementation of what are already formally accepted as human rights. The HDR work must link to the longer-standing discourse of human rights, championed by some other wings of the United Nations and many other institutions.

Emphasis on an HD–human rights linkage has come from the growing attention to economic and social rights in addition to civil liberties and political rights, and through theorisation of a strong link from civil and political rights and democracy to sustained economic and social development, not only vice versa. This makes Hans Eggil Offerdal (2000) mistrust the dominant motivation within the system of international organisations, which he sees as instrumental: to harness human rights to economic advance. He distinguishes that motivation from the idealistic intentions of many individuals within the system. Similarly sceptical, Camilo Perez Bustillo (2000) attacks the HDR 2000's historical perspective on human rights. International human rights doctrine and international law have emerged over centuries and even millennia through the interaction and conflicts between imperial states and conquered peoples, as well as from a dawning recognition of some shared principles and a single humanity. For Perez Bustillo the paradigmatic figure is the sixteenth-century Spanish friar Bartolomé de Las Casas, who became a defender of the rights of indigenes of the Americas; and the key struggles include the subsequent anti-slavery and anti-colonial movements, hardly mentioned in the HDR 2000's Eurocentric history of human rights.

Bas de Gaay Fortman (2000) acknowledges that the language used at many points in the HDR 2000 dilutes the content of the 1948 Universal Declaration of Human Rights. But, he stresses, the HDRs have the great merit of reintegrating concerns about economic and social development, human security and human rights, which in the 1940s were unfortunately divided within and between the various United Nations organs and Bretton Woods institutions. This integrated perspective leads the HDRs to raise fundamental critical issues. The HDR 2000 sees that of present international declarations only WTO rules are 'truly binding on national policy – because they have enforcement measures' (UNDP 2000: 9), as seen in the recent battles over the supply of patented drugs in health crises in poor countries. It concludes that human rights obligations must enter trade rules and their application. The same applies in debt repayment.

Fortman addresses more generally the HDRs' shortage of policy instruments to fulfil the rights of the poor, and the weak or missing links from indicators to instruments to action. These concerns – who has the obligations which correspond to declared rights, and what are the instruments for action? – mark relatively weak points in human rights discourse too. The HDR 2000 thus leads to an agenda to investigate and establish instruments and systems for the respect and implementation of human rights, including, Fortman adds, specified responsibilities in the case of global injustices too.

Karin Arts (2000) warns that twenty-five years of formalised cooperation between the European Union (EU) and countries in Africa, the Caribbean and the Pacific (ACP) has involved sustained dialogue about human rights and development, but has yielded very modest results. She notes problems in setting standards, collecting authoritative information and establishing agreed judgements through international consultation; continuing conceptual disagreements; the distorting force in these relationships of the EU's dominance over ACP countries; and the inconsistency of EU practice, including sometimes supporting regimes which are clear major human rights violators, thanks to priority to business interests, WTO principles, and other foreign-policy concerns.

While the HDR 2000 set a welcome direction, these commentaries reflect long and painful experience of what is needed to go beyond a humanist manifesto. The programme of human development is, as seen in the battle for formally acknowledged human rights, in substantial part a process of political and legal struggle. Fortman observes that within these struggles, statements of human rights help, as established standards of legitimacy and hence as vital legal resources in bringing pressure on the advantaged to acknowledge the dignity of the poor and their dues towards them. The HDR 2000 emphasises promotion of an HRs culture and a language of human rights, as a framework for strengthened global campaigns.

Support will run both ways. While human rights help to implement human development, HD theory can strengthen the legitimacy of human rights. Human rights discourse has been something to which a majority of people could apparently accede without necessarily agreeing on an underlying theoretical basis. But, as noted in the previous chapter, there may be nothing so practical as a good theory. Stronger theory will help to integrate and systematise ideas, and to buttress the human rights language against those who dislike its practical implications.

The version of human development theory which is linked closely to the HDRs comes from Amartya Sen. Equally prominent and somewhat different is the version by Martha Nussbaum. We examine these in the next two sections.

7.3 SEN'S CAPABILITY APPROACH AND 'DEVELOPMENT AS FREEDOM'

FREEDOM AND REASON

Much of earlier ethics has tried to order the welter of declared needs and other claims by reference to criteria of reason and/or freedom. Some proposed a fundamental priority to freedom; Denis Goulet for example declared that 'the most basic human need of poor people is the freedom to define their own needs, to organise to meet them, and to transcend them as they see fit' (1983: 620). The principle of priority to freedom helps to organise many other claims: it combines substantive implications of many 'freedoms from' (e.g. from hunger) with a large degree of openness and flexibility ('freedoms to'), as we saw in basic human needs theory. The Marxian priority to free activity is similar. The precondition 'freedoms from' are not exclusively material but include freedom from ignorance and from arbitrary power, as necessary conditions for autonomy or 'freedom to' (Lesser 1980). Freedom in the sense of autonomy gets priority because it is seen as the basis for pursuit of all other goals; it clearly does not displace them. However, if freedom is not to be a tautology then one must be able to distinguish it from bondage, by reference partly to how preferences are formed. Were needs or desires generated by means that respected the autonomy and dignity of the people who have them (Dandekar 1991)? Criteria of rationality in the use of freedom are similarly required (Elster 1984). Needs analysis tries to do some of this. Further, we require criteria for the trade-offs we face between the many different freedoms, and between different people's freedoms.

So, reason is another eternal candidate to guide and order the variety of needs and desires. This again may be on the grounds that it is supposedly humans' highest and distinctive feature. We find it at work in prerequisites analysis. Reason works with evidence, and behavioural science provides some grounds for ordering (as we saw when discussing the concept of luxury), but, currently at least, only limited grounds. In general, alternative reasoned orderings of conflicting impulses and interests are possible. Aristotle's conception of the 'good life for man' recognised this. His ethics involved reasoned ordering of a plurality of different goods, to ensure decent and complete individual life cycles within an overall societal balance (Nussbaum 1990). Since humans are social animals, the full definition of the good life for them was specific to and within a particular society's way of life. People's personalities, mind-sets and wants are partly determined by their way of life, as well as determining it. We noted in Chapter 6 this inability to uniquely define an optimal order, given the relevance yet endogeny of what people actually want. It has some compatibility with the emergent, expressive aspects of human nature. For Aristotle, like Marx, the good life was primarily activity oriented, not end-state oriented. It involved the exercise of appropriately trained – rationalised, socialised – human capacities, notably those of practical reason and judgement. Much of human fulfilment comes through these non-specific forms – freely and rationally chosen activity and inquiry – which people necessarily concretise in diverse and individual ways.

Amartya Sen, Martha Nussbaum and others have clarified and extended several of these themes. Sen developed his capability approach to evaluation from the late 1970s. In work with Jean Drèze, a Belgian economist based in India, he has strikingly applied it to India's socio-economic development and policy options. His 1999 book *Development as Freedom* extends the approach into a social philosophy for development policy. Let us start with the broad philosophy. It allows us to see the evaluation approach in perspective.

DEVELOPMENT AS FREEDOM

'Expansion of freedom is viewed, in this approach, both as the primary end and as the principal means of development' (A. Sen 1999: xii). Drèze and Sen have subsequently reduced freedom's status somewhat, to 'among the principal means as well as the primary ends' (2002: 4), but the earlier quotation better represents most of Sen's statements. People want freedom; and their intelligence as well as their wilfulness imply that providing and using such freedom is essential for formulating well-informed and widely accepted statements of purposes and priorities, and should be a principal instrument for acting on the purposes. Sen proposes three major roles of freedom and democracy. Sometimes he stresses these roles as 'of public participation in particular' (ibid.: 33).

First, freedom and democracy have *direct importance*, as valuable in themselves. Part of the desirability of markets is in so far as they give space for exercise of free choice, regardless of the results. Sen asserts that all available evidence shows that very poor people too place significant value on political and other freedoms. He frequently cites the shift of some percentage points in Indian voters' choices in 1977, away from Indira Gandhi's Congress Party at the end of her period of authoritarian emergency rule. (Three years later she was triumphantly reelected.)

Second, freedom has *instrumental importance*, as often conducing to the attainment of other desired ends. The approach 'puts human agency … at the centre of the stage' (ibid.: 6). Free discussion and choice in southern India have led to larger and better-sustained declines in female fertility than compulsion in China has achieved. For women's education and out-of-home employment are better 'contraceptives' than is economic growth, and far more significant in reducing infant and child mortality and anti-girl bias than are general economic and social development (namely, growth of production, urbanisation and access to health facilities). Free discussion and circulation of information, followed by democratic decision-making, are presented as potent also in overcoming Pareto's paradox, that a measure that benefits one powerful person by 500 francs, at the expense of a one-franc loss to each of a thousand poorer persons, is likely to be established and maintained, because the gainer has high motivation to mobilise forces to that end. Drèze & Sen's *India: Development and Participation* takes as its 'main theme ... [that] through democratic practice ... there is some hope of addressing the prevailing biases of public policy and development patterns' (ibid.: viii).

The centrality accorded to democracy is a bold generalisation to all public policy from Sen's earlier theses that there has never been a famine in a democracy whereas China's Great Leap Forward of 1958–61 brought the greatest famine in history (Drèze & Sen 1989). Democracy provides for free circulation and testing of vital information, and for incentives to decision-makers to anticipate or respond to the informed pressures from their electorate. Banik (1998) and Currie (2000), however, with reference to ethnically marginal groups in the state of Orissa, argue that in some cases democratic independent India has not ended famines but instead simply not reported them, or else reported but ignored them.

Third, freedom has – or can have – a *constructive role*, in building views about desired ends and drawing validated moral conclusions. Free exchange of views influences and modifies opinions and social values, and this is a vital arena in policy. Not least, 'public discussion and participatory interaction can make citizens take an interest in each other' (Drèze & Sen 2002: 378). Circulation of information about famines would not enforce government response if the unaffected majority remained indifferent to those who starve, as is often the case on a world scale.

ASPECTS OF THE CAPABILITY APPROACH

Sen's capability approach in evaluation has several features or aspects, which we can present as follows (based on Gasper 2002), with illustrations drawn from Sabina Alkire's synthesis and application (2002).

Aspect 1 is the principle that there are more types of information relevant for evaluation of well-being and quality of life than those considered in mainstream economics (people's assets, incomes, purchases, and stated or imputed levels of satisfaction), let alone those included in pure financial calculation. We should especially also look at how people actually live, and at what range and quality of valued options they have to choose between. We saw for example in Chapter 3 the neglect of the non-financial costs of the 'involuntary displacement', or in other words forced resettlement, that has been associated with large infrastructural projects in many countries – including not only landlessness, joblessness and homelessness, but destruction of communities. For assessing options Sen further stresses, as we saw in Chapter 4, that besides impacts we must also consider their inter-personal distribution, persons' rights and other features of the decision situation.

So to assess a series of small Oxfam-supported community projects in Pakistan, Alkire collected information on many aspects other than the conventional economic ones: impacts on the quality of human relationships, the status of women, the growth of knowledge and of self-confidence, satisfaction with work, and more. A female-literacy programme, for example, failed to move women into paid jobs, given the absence of market demand; but it empowered its graduates in several other ways. In the words of one woman:

> Now I have learned to trust my own talk, and ability to judge that this is good and this is bad … My heart has become strong. I can speak about my rights, can even slowly, politely, tell my parents that they have done something wrong. We have begun now to talk with them about the difference between sons and daughters, that we are equal. 'Literate people can solve their own problems.' (Cited in Alkire 2002: 267)

The example highlights expression by people of their previously neglected concerns. We saw that Drèze and Sen hope that strengthened participation will then also bring more awareness of and sympathy for other people's concerns too.

Aspect 2: Sen provides a set of concepts for describing some of these types of information. *Functionings* are components of how a person lives – for example, one's health status, or speaking about one's rights. Together a set (or vector) of such functionings makes up a person's life. A person's *capability* ('capability set') is the set of alternative vectors of functionings she could attain, in other words the alternative lives open to her; this is the extent of her positive freedom. *Capabilities* in the plural refers for Sen to the particular functionings that may be attainable for a person; for example, the ability to appear in public without shame, or the ability to speak up about one's rights.

More precisely, Sen argues that an agent's situation can be relevantly evaluated in a number of ways: by how much personal well-being she achieves (her 'well-being achievement'), and here one should look especially at her actual functionings, not only her felt or imputed satisfaction; secondly, by what she was free to achieve, both in terms of her own well-being (this is her 'well-being freedom') and with respect to her actual values, which include her values for other people and entities (this is her 'agency freedom'); and finally, by what she achieves with respect to her values (her 'agency achievement'). Of the two freedom categories, Sen's main attention has been on well-being freedom, which concerns the attainable (valued) functionings for the agent herself; but agency freedom is also important. Hence Sen talks of development as freedom rather than development as well-being.

Sen presents a general language rather than a theory about substantive capabilities. Alkire therefore adds John Finnis's method, which we saw in section 2.4, to establish a list of fundamental types of capability and functioning. Finnis asks what the types of functioning are that constitute basic motives needing no further explanation. He proposes that they are: preserving life and health; obtaining knowledge and understanding; using one's skills; exercising friendship; sexual union; achieving balance between one's emotions, judgements and actions; and seeking harmony with the universe (Alkire 2002: 48).

Aspect 3 is an informal ranking of the normative priority of some of the various facets of a person's situation, in descending order: (1) capability (as personal well-being freedom), in other words the set of life paths a person *could* follow; (2) (valued) functionings – how people *actually* live, which is ranked below capability due to a stress on freedom and self-responsibility; (3a) utility, whether interpreted as declared feelings of satisfaction, or the fulfilment of preferences, or the fact of choice: all these are placed relatively low, because choices and declared and even felt preferences may have been formed under situations of deprivation of exposure, information or options; and (3b) goods/commodities used – this is ranked low because these things are means, not ends, and because people have different needs and wants. Thus utilitarianism's central category, utility, is somewhat downgraded. Expressions of personal satisfaction can be biased by fear, politeness, stupefaction, or adaptation to misery. Even more dangerous is to presume a person's satisfaction ('she must have chosen what she has, so it must make her happy'), as if agents make only conscious and error-free choices. Despite these dangers, satisfaction can still be treated as a special and significant type of functioning (Clark 2002). But human rights for specified priority functionings and capabilities will provide a better defence of basic human interests than a focus on utility.

Sen and his school are ambivalent about their recurrent prioritisation of capability as 'our paramount interest' (Sen 2000: 3). It is an optional feature, but it typifies his work ('central as it [capability] is for a theory of justice', Sen 1992: 87) and that of his expositors, and it motivates the very title 'the capability approach'. Alkire refers to capability space as 'primary', the focus to which we 'largely' look when evaluating well-being and advantage, since expansion of valued capabilities provides 'the objective' (2002: 13, 34, 88, 172, 205). Her checklist for evaluation is organised in terms of these categories and priorities: it focuses on valued capabilities and functionings rather than on material or financial achievements in themselves. In practice, those achievements are sometimes used as proxy measures for capabilities and functionings, and Alkire still executes conventional economic cost–benefit analyses, to check on financial viability and to meet the expectations of funders.

The normative priority to capability can be read as a policy rule to promote people's capability and then 'let them make their own mistakes', rather than as an evaluative rule that 'capability is more important than functionings'. Capability is then proposed as an appropriate measure of advantage rather than of achieved well-being or quality of life, though it might contribute to them. Yet, for example, children cannot always be left to make their own mistakes. Thus even as a policy rule, Sen does not propose that we look *only* at the capability level. Such a stance is, however, quite widespread, as in the slogan 'development is the expansion of capabilities', and in some of Sen's own formulations ('The issue ultimately, is what freedom does have a person have …', Sen 2000: 29).

Aspect 4: Priority amongst capabilities is determined by the criterion of what 'people have reason to value'. So Sen's book could strictly be called 'Development as Reasoned Freedom'. Matching its interest in multiple types of information, the approach expects that people find reason to value a wide range of features of life, not only material ones. This is corroborated in many studies, such as *Voices of the Poor* (Narayan et al. 2000). To collect data on this range of valued features requires use of a range also of methods.

Aspect 5: In multi-agent situations the criterion 'what people have reason to value' is to be operationalised by public procedures for prioritising and threshold-setting. Sen here moves far from the tradition of seeking a mathematical formula for calculation of aggregate goal achievement. Specifications of needs should arise from democratic debate, as statements of community priorities; and in general, value-laden community choices between competing goods and the associated unequally distributed evils should be through open discussion, rather than concealed by pseudo-neutral techniques. (One disturbing example of such concealment, which we saw in Chapter 3, concerned use of economic cost–benefit analysis to justify pro-car transport investments in Calcutta.) Certainly, however, techniques can support discussion and open choice. Capability analysis should move beyond the incomplete coverage, the inequitable but veiled weightings, and the all-too-ready comparisons seen in markets' financial calculations, to more informed and open political choices about some values. Given, however, the range of capabilities and the massive difficulties in structuring political choice processes in ways which are simultaneously feasible, participatory and equitable, one expects workable operationalisations of capability analysis to be rather simplified. One central role then, as in other multi-criteria evaluation, is simply to demystify the financial analyses and reveal the particular, limited values behind them (Nijkamp et al. 1990).

Alkire (2002) connects Sen's work also to that of the participatory appraisal and evaluation movements, for these provide relevant methods for discussion and prioritisation in local projects. She uses Finnis's list of types of consideration to check the scope of the participatory discussions by adding questions of the form 'what do or did you experience and value, if anything, also of features of types R and S?'.

Aspect 6 is a category, or even a list, of priority capabilities. This aspect can be competitive with aspect 5 and Sen makes no such list, unlike Nussbaum. Alternatively put, he leaves these lists to emerge from democratic discussion and decision-making. While he draws quietly on background ideas about human motives, potentials and requirements – to support his emphases on freedom and agency, and on how they can fail – he refrains from precise substantive formulation of them: he fears over-simplification and cultural parochialism. However, he periodically refers to a category of basic capabilities (basic for survival and dignity) for which there are minimum required attainment levels for each person. Explicit specification of these capabilities and levels would guard against cases where the 'reasons to value' held by a majority of agents could – especially if agents are weighted by their wealth, as in market calculations – lead to serious damage to other agents (or sometimes even to themselves).

POLICY ORIENTATION

Is the philosophy practically applicable? Operationalisation refers to the conversion of concepts into identifiable, preferably measurable and influenceable, variables; to institutionalisation; and to consolidation as coherent, feasible strategy. The work of the UNDP, Drèze and Sen (e.g. 1989, 2002), Alkire (2002) and others (e.g. Clements 1995; Comim et al., eds 2004) indicate that these are possible. Alkire and Paul Clements focus on project-level appraisal and evaluation, while Drèze and Sen and the HDRs take up the more important areas of broad policy analysis and design, for example for nutrition, education and health. The capability approach helps them to focus their investigations. Martha Nussbaum applies her version to a complementary, equally fundamental area: basic legal principles and constitutional guarantees. The capability (or capabilities) approach offers justifications for specific human rights, and also must work through such legal instruments.

In his book in this series, Peter Brown fears that capability theories give no guidance on how to balance the many different relevant capabilities, or that the approach leads into a sea of indicators and becomes too complicated. He argues that the approach creates too many duties – even a duty to maximise capabilities of people around the globe – and fails to specify who bears the obligations. In reality, it highlights basic needs (aspect 6 above), not the ocean of duty that Brown fears, and priorities derived from democratic public process (aspect 5); and Sen is explicit that it must be complemented and balanced by other criteria of inter-personal equity. Certainly, like human rights thought it requires a complementary theory of obligations (see e.g. O'Neill 1996, Drydyk 2000). Brown considers that the gap concerning obligations reflects a lack of attention to institutional and social context, just as in the welfare economic theories which capability theory reacts against. But while Sen does not specify one particular context in his theorising, he is aware of the need for specification in each concrete case. Brown does not refer to Sen's detailed applications to particular contexts in India (Drèze & Sen 1995, 1996, 2002); and he wrote before the appearance of Sen's consolidated statement of his social philosophy in *Development as Freedom*.

The capability approach can be seen as having a pragmatic policy focus in another respect: its emphasis on opportunity as the foremost aspect in assessing people's situations (aspect 3 above). In a public policy context, mature autonomous agents are deemed responsible for the use they make of opportunities. However, formulations in which achievement falls away altogether and only opportunity is declared important for evaluation are dangerous (Gasper 2002). Various of Sen's statements lend themselves to that unfortunate reading. A recent example from Drèze and Sen illustrates the problem: economic advances 'can be very important "instruments" *for the enhancement of human freedom*. But they have to be appraised precisely in that light – in terms of their actual effectiveness in *enriching the lives and liberties of people*' (2002: 3, italics added). The second italicised clause covers more than the first: lives and liberties are more than just liberties; and we should be centrally interested in both.

Sen deals effectively with bogey-men arguments about policy that became common in the 1980s and 1990s: that effective public action is ruled out by incorrigible inability to predict and control unintended consequences – whereas in reality we are able to learn; or by utter selfishness – whereas in fact 'space does not have to be artificially created in the human mind for the idea of justice or fairness ... That space already exists' (A. Sen 1999: 262). Public expenditure on human development does not bring an inevitable slide into destructive inflation, stagnation, and the 'serfdom' of a state that must define and enforce fairness down to the distribution of the last dollar. He notes the numerous major examples of large-scale beneficial purposive change and the high cost-effectiveness of many public programmes (such as anti-famine measures and for public health) and underlines that support to the weak is a precondition for them to take up individual responsibility. Like Mahbub ul Haq he directs those concerned with fiscal restraint to look more at military expenditures (Gasper 2000d).

Overall, Sen provides us with an advance beyond mainstream economics and utilitarian philosophy: a focus on more than income and felt utility, by examination of the contents of the life options available to people. He does so in ways that maintain a conversation with mainstream economists and hence have been able to influence them. In profiling his ideas as 'Development as Freedom', he has sought to recapture the term 'freedom' for positive and not only negative freedom; and he has made major progress in doing that.

7.4 DOUBTS AND ALTERNATIVES

SEN'S PICTURE OF PERSONS, CAPABILITIES AND FREEDOM

One set of doubts concerns the picture of persons which underlies Sen's treatment of freedom, capability and well-being. The picture is richer and more adequate than that behind mainstream economics, but is it sufficient for a theory of human development? Sen, like many economists and philosophers, provides a theory of *well*-being on the basis of relatively little explicit discussion of simply being, or of good lives – in his case more, it is true, than in mainstream economics but still very incomplete compared to studies of what brings people satisfaction. (High quality of family life and fulfilling work have central importance here, reported Argyle (1987) for modern Britain, for example.) Let us examine these doubts with reference to the concepts of capability, freedom, 'human' and well-being.

A person's capability, in Sen's language, refers to his or her set of attainable life-paths. It provides an extension of the economist's concept of real income, by reference to the substantive functionings a person could attain: life of how long, of what health quality, with what mobility, and so on. It diverges from the main everyday concept of capability: a skill, aptitude, strength or ability. I have called this S-capability (S for skill; Gasper 1997a); Nussbaum (2000) uses the term 'internal capability'. The interaction of these capacities with the possibilities provided in a person's environment generates a person's capability in Sen's sense, which we can call O-capability (O for options or opportunities) or, with Nussbaum, 'combined capability'. Sen, ul Haq, the HDRs and many others periodically use 'capability' with the first meaning, not only the second, but without distinguishing the two.

The ambiguity affects the depth of thinking about human action and welfare. In the economics tradition itself little is said (even in so-called consumer theory) about human actors, except that they have desires, great powers of calculation and (nowadays) sometimes limited information. If we consider also skills in learning, reasoning, valuing, deciding, operating and cooperating, Sen periodically raises such issues, but without sustained attention (Andersson 1996). Yet motivation, morale, imagination and self-image play vital roles in personal and human development (see e.g. Carmen 2000, Giri 2000, Nussbaum 2000, P. Sen 1999).

These issues about capability take us to the conceptualisation of freedom. Does an ever-greater range of choice constitute an expansion of freedom, and therefore an increase in development? In Sen's approach the key is what 'people have reason to value'. But unless we both interpret this as 'good reason to value' and add a richer picture of human personality, with categories concerning skills and empathy, confidence and shame, habit and addiction, we will be liable to conclude that an American or European consumer stranded in front of her television set for five to six hours every day represents a fulfilment of reasoned freedom. (The mean viewing figure per American is four hours a day, with the set turned on for longer, reports *The Economist*, 13 April 2002; millions watch much more.) In Chapter 3 we saw, with the example of casinos and gambling palaces in southern Africa, that capable and responsible agency is required in order to buttress the claims of the principle of consumer sovereignty. Further, even if each additional alternative – each extra television channel, every extra consumer option – appears attractive in isolation, its addition in a given context is not necessarily desirable. Sometimes extra alternatives divert and distract.

Even as a prescriptive stance, a criterion of assessing only people's opportunities is not appropriate for children, especially younger children; and it is inappropriate for adults too in any situations where they lack the capacity to understand or cope. Alternatively stated, the capability set should be seen realistically, in light of agents' actual (lack of) knowledge and skills. The same issues about limited knowledge arise here which Sen used to query an exclusive or primary focus on choice or felt satisfaction.

If Sen's approach uses only a compass of people's reasons to value as set within existing polities, then in a market-dominated, money-dominated world it is at risk of being used to legitimate what comes out of market- and money-dominated processes. Kurien (2000) warns that an insistent language of individual freedom can go hand in hand with a neglect of evaluation and choice about societal systems and a presumption that there is no alternative to present-day global capitalism, including its down-grading of workers and harsher neglect of those without work and money. Devised as a way to think more adequately about the needs of the poor and the lives of all, the approach could be distorted into a too-easy rationale for endless economic growth and consumption – 'the more (market) choices the better' – unless it is combined with richer languages of analysis and evaluation.

The 1998 *Human Development Report* on consumption recognised that we 'must aim at extending and improving consumer choices too, but in ways that promote human life' (UNDP 1998: 1), but it did not offer criteria of good human life. For Sen these must come from or be con-firmed by broad local discussion. The 1998 HDR relied on micro-economics' consumer theory, which has focused not on real consumers but on utility-maximising choice under special assumptions. So despite noting that 'Many opinion surveys show that people place a higher value on community and family life than on acquiring material possessions' (ibid.: 12–13), the report failed to express concern at the projection that industrial countries' consumption might increase four- to five-fold over the next fifty years (ibid.: 8). A plausible hypothesis is, however, that absorption in consumption and possessions is likely to be at the expense of those higher-valued areas. Without substantive ideas about the contents and trade-offs within good human lives one cannot recognise the possibility of consumerism, the unending addictive quest for satisfaction through purchases.

Let us look further at the capability approach's picture of persons and the meaning it gives to 'human'. The actors in Sen's theory remain pre-social, for the theory emerges from and in an ongoing conversation with mainstream economics and retains some of the same limitations. If it tried to abandon them all at once then the conversation would cease. Yet economics is an inadequate basis for thinking about some major features of social life, for example the relations between parents and children. These are not overwhelmingly understandable in terms of self-interest alone; societies would be more unstable and dysfunctional if they were. In Sen's approach, actors can feel for each other ('sympathy', in his terms) and have 'commitments' to causes beyond their own personal advantage; but he does not specify those features as central, as essential for balanced persons or a decent or sustainable world. Recognising that humans have emerged from hundreds of thousands of years of evolution in groups, some writers hold that potentials for sympathy and commitment are basic parts of our genetic inheritance. Others hold that we are members of material, emotional and semantic networks throughout our personal formation (even from the moment of conception), so that 'the more traditional ethical idea of freedom as autonomy has to be articulated with the concern for others, that is, through the idea of solidarity' (Emilia Steuerman, cited in Booth et al. 2001: 27).

Douglas et al. (1998: 235) warns that many economists, psychologists and philosophers 'have been crippled by an ego-focused model of the psyche and all lack a theory about the relations between Ego and Ego's universe of others'. Need becomes conceived as purely individual need, yet many needs (whether in Chapter 6's mode A, B or C) concern relationships between people: for example, esteem. 'A theory of personal development that is not based on a coherent theory of what constitutes a person falls back on ... local, culturally innocent [i.e. ignorant] and far from universal ... judgements of what a person needs' (ibid.: 228).

The Sen–UNDP school of human development responds in effect as follows. First, it uses a core ideal of autonomous choosers, and holds that a picture of personhood that is incomplete as description might yet, for reasons we outlined in Chapter 6, provide a basis for an ethic that is incomplete but can be generally shared. Implications of the core ideal of autonomous choice can be derived using social theory (as we saw in Doyal and Gough's model). Second, it hesitates to specify a richer picture of personhood, for fear of including features which are culturally contingent and controversial. But third, the core theme of choice has been supplemented in several ways. The HDRs for example add community membership and belonging, as essential parts of human development. In Chapter 8 we will see the attempt by the UN's Commission on Culture and Development to take this further than mere acknowledgement. And fourthly, the HD work can be operationalised in culturally sensitive and (yet) in some respects participatory ways, such as illustrated in Sabina Alkire's work.

In some of these areas – the pictures of capabilities, freedom, wellbeing, and of central features of personhood – Nussbaum's variant of human development theory claims to offer us more than Sen's.

NUSSBAUM'S CAPABILITIES ETHIC

The American philosopher and classicist Martha Nussbaum (1947–) gives a conception of human well-being that arises from investigation into 'human be-ing': into the meaning of 'human' and the contents of 'be-ing'. She proposes a set of features to be definitive of a (properly) human existence (e.g., Nussbaum 1999a, Ch. 1). Following a procedure in classical Greek and Roman philosophy, and drawing on insights from literature of that era and from modern Europe, America and India, she asks which are the features without which we would consider a being, or a life, not to be human: for example empathy for others and mortality. The term 'human' here has of course a normative, not only genetic, definition; 'human development' is the opposite of inhuman development.

The procedure leads to a 'thick conception of the good': one that includes multiple distinct major aspects, not only a single one such as utility or freedom. Thus Nussbaum consciously describes hers as 'the capabilities approach' in contradistinction to Sen's 'capability approach'. She argues for a set of central capabilities, none of which can be adequately replaced by more of something else. One could not adequately defend a modern society by saying: 'Our citizens cannot read, but look how healthy they are.'

The result is a richer, more real, picture of what a human life is. Nussbaum highlights for example the importance of play and leisure, and the satisfactions from meaningful work. Mainstream economics in contrast presumes that work is a cost, rather than often a central source of well-being and a priority capability. In recent work she discusses religious and spiritual aspirations in detail and with sympathy, acknowledging the goods they can bring. However, she excludes religion from the conception of basic humanity, since many people manage well without it and some are damaged by it. It is better seen as one possible expression of some more general capabilities; and as subject to principled limits to its exercise, limits set by consistency and humanity.

Nussbaum's criteria for the 'well' in well-being are thus her criteria for what is human, what are essential functionings or, rather, essential capabilities to function. Table 7.2 summarises her proposed list of these essential functional capabilities (2000, 2002a). (All except 7B start with the phrase 'Being able ...'.) It is intended to help in the design of national constitutions and bills of rights and in the judgement of legal cases.

Two capabilities, those for affiliation and practical reason, are accorded central roles and priority; indeed priority is accorded to their exercise, the actual functionings. For as part of the conception of 'human' comes the idea, found in Aristotle and Marx, that there is a human, not merely animal, way of performing the other functionings: as a reflective, self-determining actor who takes other persons into account. So capabilities 6 and 7 are the core of the core. A person who does not think, or does not consider others, falls short of Nussbaum's normative conception of 'human'.

Some writers ridicule explanatory lists of human needs which tack on 'social needs' of individuals as a separate item on the list, as if persons were not comprehensively social beings (Douglas et al. 1998). But Nussbaum's central capability of 'affiliation' is part of a normative set of priorities to be promoted and defended, not part of an explanatory theory on human impulses; and it has the central role just mentioned, that it should influence the exercise of all the other capabilities.

Table 7.2 Nussbaum's list: ten normatively central human capabilities

1. Life	Being able to live for the span normal for the species
2. Bodily health	Being able to have good health (and, in order to obtain this, adequate nourishment and shelter)
3. Bodily integrity	Being able to be physically secure, and with rights over one's own body (e.g. not forced to lose capacity for sexual satisfaction or forced to conceive and bear children)
4. Senses, imagination and thought	Being able to use the senses, imagine, think and reason, and to do this in a truly human way: adequately educated, informed, and free from repression
5. Emotions	Being able to have attachments and feelings for other people and things
6. Practical reason	Being able 'to form a conception of the good and to engage in critical reflection about the planning of one's life' (2000: 79)
7. Affiliation	A. Being able to interact well with other people, and imagine and empathise with their situation B. Having the social bases for self-respect and non-humiliation; not being subject to discrimination on grounds of race, sex, etc.
8. Other species	Being able to live with concern for the natural world
9. Play	Being able to play and laugh
10. Control over one's environment	A. Being able to effectively participate in political processes B. Being able to have possessions, and to seek employment

Nussbaum does engage with explanatory theory very significantly in her work on emotions, including on some of the 'passions' we noted in Chapter 5 (Nussbaum 2001). Emotions are essential parts of normative reasoning, motivation and action: notably the emotions of sympathy and compassion for others. Nussbaum's insights about emotion add to the intellectual power and practical relevance of her ethics.

She argues that her normative model incorporates insights from communitarianism, in its 'thick' conception of the good and its central role for affiliation, while avoiding relativism. She specifies, and illustrates in detail, five ways in which the model is neither paternalistic nor stiflingly standardised (Nussbaum 2000, 2002a). First, its general statements leave significant space for local interpretations during their detailed application, in light of both different material conditions and local traditions. Second, the goal is to seek to ensure capability, not to enforce the corresponding functionings. Third, the list emphasises building people's liberties, their ability to define and construct their own lives. Fourth, the list provides a recommended set of norms, to influence the political processes in each nation, but not a set of commandments to be imposed by force, except in very special and extreme cases.

Lastly, Nussbaum now conceives and constructs the list as an element in a 'political liberalism', as an area for shared acceptance between ideologies which can otherwise differ – the same role that we saw for (other) basic needs theories. 'Comprehensive liberalism' considers that a government should actively promote personal autonomy in all spheres of life. In contrast, political liberalism acknowledges and respects the presence of multiple visions of the good life, and respects persons' decisions to live non-autonomously, provided that the decisions come from 'a background of liberty and opportunity' (Nussbaum 1999b: 110). It makes no attempt to enforce a common metaphysical vision or conception of human nature, but does insist on some minimum of practices and political values. It seeks agreement on a core of principles even if there is disagreement on the premises behind them.

Thus overall, in Nussbaum's view her approach protects each of wellbeing, liberty and diversity. Influenced by her research on and in India, in particular, she has scaled down her earlier externally specified and Aristotelian vision of 'the good life for man', and argues (similarly to Hans Küng amongst others) rather that there is shared commitment in all cultures, actually or potentially, to this core of values. She acknowledges that cultures are internally plural and inconsistent, but emphasises the scope for 'internal criticism' that can use ordering criteria from within the culture to strengthen this commitment (see section 8.3 below). Cultural traditions are far more than a set of petrified practices: they contain sub-traditions of reflection and a potential to evolve.

While Nussbaum practices 'political liberalism', the strength of her position comes from pursuing this search for core areas of potential consensus through intimate attention to the diverse, rich languages of value used in different cultures. If one tried to establish areas of consensus by ignoring and 'quarantining' those languages of value (often religious), and seeking something that is exclusive of them, one may fail to connect to their sources of meaning and motivation, and end by being ignored oneself (Hicks 2000, Ch. 5).

FOR AND AGAINST A UNIVERSAL LIST OF PRIORITY CAPABILITIES

Nussbaum's capabilities ethic has considerably matured, influenced by exposure to debates and cases in law and politics and from India, besides her traditional sources in European philosophy and literature, ancient and modern. Is it wrong even so? Is the aspiration for a universal list of priority (opportunity) capabilities sensible? Why do we need a list at all? And does Nussbaum specify hers persuasively?

Why have a list? First, Nussbaum shows the inadequacy of trying to define justice only in terms of fair procedure. Behind the concept of fair procedure inevitably lie ideas about basic human requirements, which should become explicit and well considered. Second, the role of the list is comparable to that of the Universal Declaration of Human Rights but now with an explicit theoretical basis – the capabilities ethic is to provide 'a [philosophical] basis for central constitutional principles' (Nussbaum 2000: 12). Nussbaum specifies the principles that each person is an end, and that each person should have capability. More generally, such a list sets a relevant starting point for discussion and public action. It focuses us on proposed priorities, as a reminder and basis for discussion. Without a list, policy argumentation can drift into dehumanised abstractions, as in much economics. So when Sabina Alkire seeks to apply Sen's capability theory in project planning and evaluation, she constructs a list of types of basic capabilities fairly similar to Nussbaum's, though rather more general and flexible. Third, Nussbaum stresses that, like (and through) a legal constitution, a list can be interpreted according to context, through due process. The list must itself be 'both open-ended and humble; it can always be contested and remade' (Nussbaum 1999a: 40). The relative importance and even necessity of its different elements can be decided in this way, as Alkire shows. Alkire derives and specifies her own indicative list with care to avoid parochialism and paternalism, and then uses it only as a supportive framework for the required democratic discussions.

Why a *universal* list of priority capabilities? Is not *that* paternalistic? Nussbaum finds the accusation of paternalism itself an assertion of universal values of liberty and choice, and hence supportive of a form of universalism which promotes those values (2002a: 12). She similarly responds to the counter-argument in favour of diversity, by stressing that her universalism precisely promotes the preconditions, capacities and opportunities for diversity. She disposes of the analogy to the virtues of language diversity – 'languages, as such, don't harm people, [but] cultural practices frequently do' (ibid.: 11) – but misses the harder analogy of biodiversity. Evolutionary theorists may claim that diversity of practices, including practices which harm some persons, provides a vital resource of learning and adaptability. One can answer that the analogy requires that learning should continue and that some practices will become invalidated, and certainly not that every current local cultural practice will be endorsed.

So, if we accept that the idea of a universal list is not in itself misconceived – all countries subscribe to the Universal Declaration – provided it is understood as an input to a fuller decision process within each given context, is Nussbaum's particular list misspecified? We must refer here to the sharpened and streamlined current version (2000, 2002a,

2002b), not to earlier versions (e.g. 1992, 1995) which included a partly excessive individualism in their picture of universal requirements for a good life. The list would still benefit, we saw, from a theory of obligations, for while Aristotle could presume 'an intact, functioning community with clear duties' (Brown 2000: 19), we cannot; but that is a separate issue. In presentational terms, while Nussbaum has preferred the Mosaic number of ten, one could make the list shorter (perhaps by merging elements 5 and 9) or longer (by separating the disparate parts of elements 7 and 10). And just as some elements may be more central, some others can be understood as marginal, so that the list fades out fuzzily rather than stopping abruptly.

More importantly, in terms of precision and scope, any such list requires refinements and faces exceptions, or at least encounters cases where its generalities demand intelligent application in light of the complexities of life: for the situations of the disabled or the congenitally ill, for example (which are extensively examined in Nussbaum 2002b). Many societies contain religious hermits, some of whom do not seek societal affiliation, human betterment or sexual fulfilment, and seek affiliation only to a notion of the divine. Nussbaum sometimes asserts that really they have humanistic concerns (2000: 92), but also rather more convincingly replies that the hermit's renunciation would not acquire and retain its intended meaning in the absence of the opportunity to have what he abjures. She claims majority endorsement in nearly all societies of her list's priorities. She accepts that minorities far larger than hermits may dissent, but asserts that 'regimes that fail to deliver health, or basic security, or liberty, are unstable' (ibid.: 155). Historically this has not, however, always been so, and it remains untrue for hundreds of millions of poor people in South Asia. Nussbaum's base of evidence and experience remains rather limited. The list can be seen then not as a headcount of present-day opinions, but as a hypothesis about what would over time become an acceptable starting point for discussions in each society, as a rational interpretation, implication and evolution of their values.

Some commentators deem the list confused, but it derives from a systematic procedure using criteria for well-being and humanity, as we saw. It can be upgraded, clarifying its status as a checklist in evaluations (cf. Alkire 2002) and as one startpoint in constitutional discussions. It can also be subsumed into a more structured basic needs theory, along the lines that we saw in Chapter 6. One persistent issue here concerns the consistency of use of the criteria behind the list. We analysed this issue in needs ethics in section 6.4. Consider four different criteria, each of which can be used to generate a list of priority capabilities: (1) sheer survival; this is not sufficient for saying something is a human life, since one can survive at merely an animal level; (2) living in a way judged as human in quality; (3) a decent life; (4) a flourishing life. Nussbaum seems to merge criteria 2 and 3, yet we may find a life to be recognisably human without it meeting target minimum levels of welfare. In earlier work Nussbaum (e.g. 1995) clearly distinguished criteria 3 and 4, giving two distinct levels of prescribed capabilities/functionings. Her more recent work focuses only on level 3, and emphasises that people may agree on this level without agreeing on the content of the next; but she seems to set the standards for decency (or humanity) rather high, in effect bringing in aspects of flourishing. Thus item 6 in her list seems to extend practical reason to encompass critical reason, by including the ability 'to form a conception of the good', not only to function competently in terms of a societally given conception. For some commentators, the insistence on critical powers is excessively individualistic. We continue with that issue in Chapter 8.

Certain key roles are underemphasised in a purely philosophical discussion around lists. Nussbaum's list is a part of a style of looking and understanding: looking at the content and potentials in diverse important areas of people's lives, with attention to holistic cases and to a broad range of evidence, including from fiction, poetry and biography, as well as from conventional social science sources; and using rich pictures of mind, personhood, emotions and language to explore the human content of evidence, including its emotional content. These features form an interconnected package and are important for building both relevant ethical theory and concern and compassion for other persons, and for motivating and sustaining action. Nussbaum's approach to the ethics of human development thus involves far more than a list of specific priorities.

7.5 CONCLUSION

Amartya Sen's capability approach has had an unusual degree of attention and influence, with numerous attempts to apply it (see e.g. DeMartino 2000 on rules for world trade); it has the ability to appeal both to many mainstream economists and to many of their critics. It offers a widely popular improvement in addressing well-being, for it contains more of a theory of being than does mainstream economics but not one so rich as to lose the ability to have measures. Behind a clear and plausible central focus – human development seen as the expansion of reasoned positive freedom – it has a profound underlying method. It stresses the richness of life and hence the use of a plurality of types of information, and the importance of local democratic process in prioritising and synthesising such information. It distances itself from the basic material needs approach by its emphasis on human agency and its relevance not only to low levels of living.

In Sen's view, Martha Nussbaum's version is just one possible concretisation of his approach, and will not appeal to all audiences. He prefers to leave his version general and flexible. In Nussbaum's view, Sen's version is underspecified in its picture of personhood, motives, emotions and skills, with resultant weaknesses when used in description, evaluation and persuasion, including in defending basic rights, in motivating concern for others, and in understanding and critiquing consumerism. She exemplifies a more elaborated theory of the good, or rather, of goods. Her list of priority capabilities should be refined and partly reconceived; but it must be understood as part of an overall approach, which emphasises use of a broad range of evidence, including from outside conventional social science, and also the analysis and harnessing of emotions.

Sen's version well suits a conversation with the powerful tribe of economists; Nussbaum's better suits an engagement with the humanities and human sciences. Both versions provide elements towards a coherent and usable ethics of human development, but they leave important issues unsettled and requiring further attention. These include the balance or choice between unified and pluralistic conceptions of welfare or development (for example, as freedom or as a diverse set of priority goods); how far should some key capabilities be centrally specified and guaranteed; and the relative importance of capabilities and of basic functionings.

Both writers appreciate that the battle for human development is one of social, political and legal struggle and not only of philosophical and scientific debate. Linkage of their Human Development school to the human rights tradition can provide a more inspirational and also more realistic, more struggle-focused, framework for the project of human development. The hope is that human development theory and the human rights movement can together do what neither could achieve alone.

DISCUSSION THEMES

1. 'The Human Development approach was led by a Pakistani and an Indian, but both were products of Western education (in their own countries and later in England). As a result, the approach is in various ways an expression of Western values, Western economics mind-sets, and Western individualism.' Do you agree?
2. Is moralising about universal human rights counter-productive – part of an imposition of Western values on poor countries, and sometimes an attempt to reduce their economic competitiveness?
3. Do poor people place a high value on (political) freedom?
4. What is the relative importance of (real) opportunity compared to actual achievement (in other words, of O-capability compared to functioning)?

5. Industrial countries' consumption might increase four- to five-fold over the next fifty years (UNDP 1998: 8). If this projection is correct, what do you expect will be the implications for human development?

6. Systematically compare Sen's 'capability approach' and Nussbaum's 'capabilities approach'.

7. '"Development" is a concept that depends on ideas about what is good. But these ideas vary so much between different people and cultures, that we cannot agree about what is properly human and what is proper development.' Evaluate this view.

READING SUGGESTIONS

Haq (1998) is a lucid history and survey of the Human Development school by its leader; Apthorpe (1997) subjects the school to searching critique; Drèze & Sen (2002) is a fine recent example of its work. Also readable and enlightening is Amartya Sen's influential *Development as Freedom* (1999). For a mixture of views, some more sceptical than Sen's, on what democracy achieves, see Shapiro & Hacher-Cordón (eds 1999). Sen's *On Ethics and Economics* (1987), *Inequality Reexamined* (1992) and *Rationality and Freedom* (2002) present his normative theories more technically, in increasing order of complexity. Alkire (2002) provides an important exposition, extension and application; it extends Sen's work by integrating elements from John Finnis, Martha Nussbaum and participatory research. Assessments and critiques of the approach include: Crocker (1992, 1995), Gasper (ed., 1997) and Cameron & Gasper (eds 2000), especially the paper by Ananta Giri; also Clark (2002), Gasper (2002), Gasper & van Staveren (2003) and Shanmugaratnam (2001). Hicks (2000, Chs 8 & 11) provides a more socially and materially situated picture of the self than does Sen, and links certain types of social setting to the formation of persons who show sympathy and commitment for others. Martha Nussbaum's *Sex and Social Justice* (1999a), *Women and Human Development* (2000), and *Beyond the Social Contract* (2002b) merit close attention and have substantially modified her position on human development. They should be referred to before any of her earlier work. See St Clair & Gasper (eds 2001) for several assessments of the 2000 book, and Gasper (2003b) on Nussbaum's work more broadly.

CHAPTER 8

CULTURES AND THE
ETHICS OF DEVELOPMENT

8.1 CAN ONE CRITICISE CULTURES AND YET
AVOID ETHNOCENTRISM ?

AGENDA

How far do the ethical debates which we looked at in earlier chapters involve or even assume some culturally specific values? We looked at perceptions of the costs and benefits of social and economic change, and the content of 'development' considered as improvement (Chapters 1 to 3); the meaning of equity and the significance of violence (Chapters 4 and 5); and the specification of priority needs and 'human development', related to concepts of the person, autonomy, freedom, and well-being (Chapters 6 and 7). In discussing equity we noted how different criteria to some extent fit different sorts of society and context (Miller 1976, Walzer 1983). In discussing needs and human development we considered variation across societies, needs of meaning and identity, and more. The issues of culture demand fuller coverage, as fundamental and complex. For those close to the UNDP's *Human Development Reports* from 1990 onwards, it was clear that 'Building cultural insights into the broader development strategies ... had to be the next step in rethinking development' (WCCD 1995: 8).

'Culture' is an umbrella term which is used to highlight a variety of views, including of the shallowness of asocial explanatory models, the importance of human diversity, and the centrality of aspects besides individual consumption which make life meaningful, cultured. Our concern here is not with every debate about culture and development, let alone every question on culture in low-income countries or in the relations of rich and poor. We will concentrate on matters related to the normative meaning of development and on the challenge posed in development ethics by cultural differences, especially by claims that ethics is entirely culturally relative, i.e. solely depends on what the accepted ways are in each society. The chapter tries to throw light on these questions:

- Are there systems called cultures which view development fundamentally differently?
- If so, are they open to ethical dialogue and comparison? Can one have critique of cultures which is not ethnocentric?
- Which variations in social practices are ethically acceptable? Every variation? Or are there limits to acceptable variation, set by, not least, considerations of basic needs and rights?
- How much ethical weight does culture have relative to other factors?

We will focus on possible inter-cultural differences over the position and rights of women. This is not a divergence from a development ethics agenda. We concluded in Chapters 5, 6 and 7 that economic advance is only a potential – and sometimes counter-productive – means towards human development, and that many other possible means or aspects demand attention. These include the rights and opportunities of all people and the quality of family life and inter-personal relations.

The chapter's coverage can again be seen in terms of the three stages of ethics introduced in Chapter 1. In first-stage work one reacts to experience, to cases and questions, including basic questions such as 'How would I have felt if they did that to me?' and 'How does she feel when we do that to her?'. The questions are basic since morality starts from a willingness to consider other people's situations, costs and benefits, not only refer to self-interest or authority (Nagel 1987). If an adequate range of experience receives attention, such reflection should promote a grounded ethics, germane and realistic. In second stage work one tries to systematise ideas, make them clearer, more consistent, more argued and more principled; and to go beyond reference to untested feelings, by reference rather to feelings that arise in, in some sense, fair and well-informed conditions. Third-stage work applies ideas in practice, which requires adaptation and compromises given the plurality of idea systems and their limitations both at present and in principle.

We start the chapter with some cases, and then a warning: a claim by Bhikhu Parekh that Western ethics, whether Christian, liberal or Marxist, have been mono-cultural and disrespectful of other cultures.

INTRODUCTORY CASES

Inherited norms can be dysfunctional. Some have become outdated, and some always rested on misconceptions, as Partha Dasgupta illustrates:

> In rural communities of the foothills of the Himalayas in the state of Uttar Pradesh in India, women give birth to their children in cowsheds and remain there for one to two weeks. They aren't permitted to return to their homes any earlier because they are regarded as impure. The (Indian) Centre for Science and Environment (CSE, 1990) reports that village folk in these parts believe cowdung

and urine to be good disinfectants. They also believe that the mother and child are protected by the cows from evil spirits. Infant and maternal mortality rates are significantly higher on account of this practice ... The rationale for the practice is not that it offers a brief respite to the mother from domestic chores. Within three to five days of giving birth, mothers are expected to collect firewood and fodder and to leave it in the cowshed for others to collect. (Dasgupta 1993: 216)

[margin note: rejection of cultural relativism]

In contrast, much other inherited knowledge is precious. For example: 'Echinacea (purple coneflower) has been used by the Plains Indians of North America for thousands of years' (WCCD 1995: 208), for a range of medicinal purposes. Sometimes called 'the herbalist's antibiotic' (ibid.: 209) its efficacy as an immune-system stimulant has been confirmed by modern science. It is now increasingly used worldwide.

Such cases seem straightforward. In one case, behaviour rests on beliefs refuted by science about what protects mothers and newborn children; in the other, the beliefs are vindicated by science. Neither case seems to raise difficulties of evaluation, although in the cowshed case careful consideration would be required on how to respond without making matters worse. We should distinguish evaluation, prescription, and intervention. We may condemn a practice, and try to persuade its practitioners to change it, but without necessarily prescribing to them which particular change. Even if we do prescribe a certain change, that does not necessarily imply that we feel justified or obliged to intervene to prevent the current practice, even if we see a way to do so without causing severe reactions and disproportionate harm.

We must also be careful when formulating ideas about ethics and culture not to focus only on easier and extreme cases, such as life-threatening situations or cases concerning children (or both, as in the cowshed example). Adults can better fend for themselves, so judgements that their needs and interests diverge from their wants and agreements are rather more problematic. Nussbaum and Glover's *Women, Culture, and Development* (eds 1995) centres on cases where women who seek employment are discriminated against *and* object to the discrimination. Those situations are widespread and important; but harder cases concern women who are apparently discriminated against but express no objection. In a similar hard case, in some societies (for example, Kerala and Japan) the requirements for women's autonomy of agency appear fulfilled, yet they participate little in much of public life. Does that matter?

We must beware also of looking only South (or East). Neoliberal economic ideology from the North deserves attention as a cultural formation (DeMartino 2000). It presents claims about a few universal core features of human societies: specifically that they consist of rational individuals, with given and very largely selfish desires, which always exceed what is available and motivate a never-ending thrust for more production. It includes an equally unnuanced normative basis. First, an extreme version of the doctrine of consumer sovereignty: that there is no other normative criterion than what consumers want. The never-ending thrust is thus justified. The doctrine is one of inter-personal relativism: that no one can judge what is good for another person, or compare one person's wants and satisfactions with another's. Second, neoliberalism operationalises this criterion in the form of market values – how else, it declares, could one evaluate except by summing individuals' preferences, as measured by the real test of payment? If inter-personal distribution remains a criterion, the existing distribution is commonly adjudged to be justified, for otherwise the polity would have changed it. The polity is presumed legitimate, or else considered too inept and corruptible to ever be assigned redistributive tasks. Third, inter-cultural relativism: if one country allows industrial work without health protection for workers and without environmental safeguards, that is 'its' own lifestyle choice, and provides no grounds for others to impose barriers to trade. The country's rulers' choices are taken as national choices and deemed beyond normative comment. (We analyse this further in section 8.3.) Faith in a set of simplistic fixed assumptions, and in reasoning from these supposed essential truths to a system of definite and emphatic prescriptions, downgrading all else, can be called fundamentalism.

IS LIBERALISM ILLIBERAL?

One strand in the calls to prioritise culture has been resistance to thought-less and often contemptuous Western domination – domination by Western ideas, values and leaders (Tucker 1996a). Slim (1995) warns of the imperialism of the market-liberal model of values and organisation which was enforced worldwide in the 1990s. No choice is allowed about the priority given to choice. We need to be careful, though, of some of the reactions: oversimplified, unbalanced critical pictures of the West and a reverse idealisation of the South and East.

Bhikhu Parekh (1935–), an outstanding Indian political philosopher and public figure long settled in Britain, avoids those dangers yet puts the charge powerfully. Parekh observes:

> During the period of colonial expansion Europe had at least three influential traditions of thought that were committed to the ideals of human unity, equality, freedom and the inviolability of the human person, and which were in principle hostile to the violence and exploitation inherent in the colonial enterprise. They were Christianity, liberalism ... and Marxism ... It is striking that with only a few exceptions, the three bodies of thought approved European colonialism. From time to time they did, no doubt, condemn its *excesses*, but rarely the colonial enterprise itself. (1997: 173–4)

Parekh assumes that they should have, perhaps because he strongly values
– both independently and instrumentally – self-determination and contin-
uity, and queries the ability to evaluate others.

Let us single out the second of the traditions Parekh mentions,
liberalism, since it has the most continuing force.

> In many respects liberalism was secularised Christianity and reproduced many of
> the missionary attitudes to non-Europeans and colonialism … [Liberals] took
> over such beliefs as that mankind constituted a unity and shared a common nature,
> that a single vision of life was valid for all, that those in the know had a duty to
> enlighten the ignorant, and that good had a duty to fight evil. (Ibid.: 180–1)

We saw for example how John Locke rejected the original Spanish
denial of Native Americans' humanness. He 'accepted Indians as equal
objects of concern, but not as equal self-defining subjects entitled to
choose their way of life themselves; that is, [his theory] protected them as
individuals but not as a *community*, and respected their moral interests but
not their way of life and the moral and spiritual interests associated with
it' (ibid.: 184). The Native Americans also had to be judged by the universal
criterion of productive use of God's commonwealth, and could be
rightfully displaced if they did not satisfy it. Immanuel Kant was impatient
with the lives of Stone Age leisure, plenty and pleasure which were
reported of the South Sea islanders. Mankind must be 'industrious, rational,
energetic and purposive' (ibid.: 186). John Stuart Mill similarly justified
European imperialism in Asia, using a universal criterion that collectivities which had misused independence, and were incapable of self-
reform, had no right to keep it.

In modern liberalism, persons must be capable of meaningful conscious
choice. For Will Kymlicka (e.g. 1989), a liberal state should support and
protect minority cultures, on two grounds: for members of minorities to
make meaningful choices about a way of life they must, first, have the
option of their minority's tradition and, second, have grown up with a
secure cultural background, in order to be stable and self-confident
persons. Susan Moller Okin (1999a, 1999b) objects that cultures which
seriously repress some of their members should not qualify for a protection that is based on the principle of fostering independent individuals.
Parekh objects to Kymlicka very differently:

> For Kymlicka deliberate choice is the only proper way to relate to one's culture,
> and all alike must conform to [this]. He does not see that different communities
> might have different modes of conceiving and relating to their cultures, and that
> the liberal way is neither the only one nor the best'. (p.187)

Parekh holds that liberals, like Christians and Marxists, have been blinded
by 'their monistic vision of the good life' (Parekh 1997: 191).

Perhaps Parekh goes too far. We will see an intermediate position, presented by Onora O'Neill. Not everyone must 'step out of [their culture], locate it within a range of options, and choose it as a matter of conscious decision' (loc. cit.), but everyone has the right to do so and to be able to do so. A culture is not required to enforce conscious decision-making by its. members, but is obliged to permit and not block that. This stance responds to the claim that liberal logic suggests that people should be able to choose against liberalism.

Parekh alleges that all major Western traditions of social philosophy rest on a 'belief in moral and cultural monism' which 'carries little conviction' in the contemporary world (p. 192). He agrees, however, that 'the challenge of finding ways to reconcile equality with difference and integrity with openness is one no major intellectual tradition can any longer avoid' (loc. cit.). His discussion of seventeenth- to nineteenth-century liberal thought may not do justice to contemporary work, often led by women and Southerners, which attempts to meet that challenge. We introduced some of the work in Chapters 6 and 7, and now investigate it further.

8.2 CULTURE: THE UNDERLYING ISSUES

Much thinking on the place of culture in development ethics has remained at the first stage of ethics, raising striking examples and concerns, without advancing to a second stage of building more coherent systems. To do so we must clarify concepts, to be able to discuss which aspect of culture has which sort of significance for which sort of development. We need also to draw out assumptions about the nature of persons. We will then consider the proffered syntheses and hidden tensions in the report of the World Commission on Culture and Development (WCCD 1995) which attempted to deepen the perspective of 'human development'.

CONCEPTIONS OF CULTURE

'Culture', suggested Vincent Tucker, is a concept that represents a particular way of theorising: an emphasis that people construct, use and are influenced by understandings and meanings, and are moved by loyalties and feelings (Tucker 1996a). The approach arose in reaction to the anonymous and homogenising forces of a science-based market economy, within and across nations. In central and eastern Europe in the nineteenth century, and in the discipline of social anthropology in a colonial context in the twentieth, the approach has had a tendency to exaggerate local wholeness, self-containedness and the presence of unified 'communities' (ibid.; Guijt & Kaul Shah 1998). We find then at least three meanings of 'culture' in discussions on culture and development: 'culture' as a residual, covering aspects neglected in economistic thought; culture as everything, the entire way of life of a community; and culture as values and attitudes, the glue or genius of that way of living (Gasper 1996a).

The first body of usage (C1) covers those factors which lie outside simple market models – whether the factors are viewed as obstacles to economic development or celebrated as truer sources of value. Emma Crewe and Elizabeth Harrison (1998) note that 'culture' is often the label for whatever is not understood. Seeing the 'culture' category as a residual helps us understand why its contents are so diverse: distinctive local values, local concepts and perceptions of life and the world, local institutions, local knowledge, 'non-economic' values; needs and styles of expression, activity, meaning, identity, dignity and beauty; and more. Making valid statements about such a conglomeration of concerns becomes difficult.

In the second usage (C2), 'culture' is everything: 'by culture, therefore, is meant every aspect of life' (Verhelst 1990: 17); 'culture may be regarded as whatever characterises a community' (BuZa 1991: 190): all values, norms, attitudes, habits, ways of doing, artefacts, and even institutions. However, we are especially interested in finding underlying generative factors, some pattern in the forest of detail.

In the third usage, 'culture' consists of values and attitudes, ways of thinking and feeling (C3). In Geert Hofstede's influential definition (e.g. Hofstede 1994) it is the shared mental programming which distinguishes one group from another. Crewe and Harrison (1998: 152–3) warn as anthropologists that this conception is a management-studies simplification, sufficient to convey that cultures differ and persist, but potentially misleading in several ways. People are active creators of culture, not (only) passively and fixedly programmed. The creation of culture – formation of attitudes, definition of self, presentation to others, representation of others – depends on with whom one interacts and for what purpose, and is influenced by the context of power relations.

Further, to say that groups share some ideas by no means implies that they share all. The WCCD stressed that cultures are internally heterogeneous and marked by internal disagreements; they also overlap extensively. The tendency to reify culture as a cohesive unity is more than a conceptual slip (Tucker called it a 'fallacy of misplaced concreteness'). It is also a political strategy to enforce control over a community.

ROLES PERCEIVED FOR CULTURE

We saw in development studies literature four major types of usage of 'development'. Two were non-normative: (1) development as fundamental or structural change and (2) development as intervention, action; while

Table 8.1 Culture as barrier, instrument or ethical foundation?

	'DEVELOPMENT'	'CULTURAL' ISSUES ARISING

NON-
NORMATIVE
dependent
	1. Fundamental
	   qualitative change
	   MEANINGS
	2. Intervention
		1. a) Culture as engine or brake?
		   b) Culture as independent or
		      variable?
		2. a) Culture as target/instrument
		   b) Culture of the interveners
		   c) Inter-cultural relations

NORMATIVE
MEANING
	3. Improvement	3. Which criteria of improvement?
		   Economistic or wider criteria?
		   Immanent or trans-cultural criteria?

Source: Gasper 1996a

two were normative: (3) development as improvement, good change and (4) development as that which enables or allows improvement (section 2.2). For our present purposes the normative meanings can be combined. For each set of meanings of development, distinct 'cultural' and/or ethical issues arise, as summarised in Table 8.1. (This subsection draws on Gasper 1996a.)

We then see distinct roles which culture may be given in ethical and policy argumentation. One mainstream view takes culture (in usages C1 and C3) as a fully accommodating dependent variable which does not influence (economic) development, and so can be ignored. This is the stance of many economists. An opposite mainstream view sees culture (C1, C3) instead as often an obstacle to economic development. An alternative variant sees the consumer culture of the West as an obstacle to global environmental sustainability and thus to development in the South. Again the concern with culture is instrumental, leading to the question: how to ease the brake by some cultural engineering? Thus a third, connected, type of mainstream instrumental stance takes culture (C1, C3) as a policy tool, to be studied and made use of. The stance arises from an understanding that failures to take into account distinctive local culture, motives and meanings contribute to policy and project failures (Kottak 1991). A more recent conception views cultures (C1, C2, C3) also as a policy resource, but not as a delimited tool to be manipulated, rather as a storehouse of knowledge and adaptive capacity, to be preserved for unforeseen and even unnoticed functions. An analogy is drawn between cultural diversity and biodiversity (WCCD 1995).

A stronger version of the policy tool conception claims that local culture (C1, C3) is an essential means or modality, so that if it is not respected then nothing will succeed. This implies many 'roads to development'

(BuZa 1991: 237); but the development goal itself can here still be viewed as universal in content. In a similar spirit, 'Each Member [of the WCCD] was convinced that ... the enlargement of people's capabilities could be rooted only in a people's ethics and values' (WCCD 1995: 10). This matches the ideas that people have basic cultural needs, and that an inherited societal or group culture is the major vehicle for fulfilment of the needs.

What views exist on how culture relates to the ends of development, not only as a means? In one view, culture (C1) is accorded independent value, making it 'an important part' of development, a separable independent concern. In a second view, fulfilment of cultural needs is not only independently valued but occurs through all the media of social activity, not just through a separate 'part'; this is a constitutive independent concern. Thirdly, there can be an overriding independent concern: inherited culture (C1; sometimes C2) is declared of incomparable and absolute value, and must be preserved. In contrast, in a liberal stance, since local culture (C1, C2) is felt by many people to have independent value, it should be respected, though as just one criterion, not an overriding one.

Next, a foundational concern considers that each culture (in whichever sense: C1, C2, C3) is the source of criteria that define 'the good life' or 'development' for its members, and one can only measure development in terms of a given culture's values. So there are various 'paths of development', with their own goals. Advocates of 'endogenous development' take this position. Thierry Verhelst, for example – in his *No Life without Roots: Culture and Development* (1990) – argues that alternative forms of modernity are possible, and exist, besides Westernisation; and fortunately so, given Western civilisational crises. In a stronger version, culture serves as the oracle: one must refer to 'the culture' (C3) for the answers on which objectives and criteria to adopt.

Some views can be described as 'culture, not development', for they claim that the values propounded within 'development' are culturally unacceptable (for example because deemed individualistic and materialistic) and deserve rejection. '[D]evelopment, as generally construed, is the imposition of a particular notion of human destiny on a global scale. It is the imposition of externally constructed meaning and values on a diversity of peoples and locations' (Tucker 1996a: 11). Sardar (1996) provides an extreme formulation of such a view. 'Imposition' here means unjustified enforced application by those with greater power. Ironically, proponents of such a view use arguments about 'false consciousness' to criticise the adoption of globalised values and meanings by many in their own societies, especially the young, but reject such arguments when used to criticise older practices in their culture.

NATURAL MAN, PLASTICINE MAN, NURTURED NATURAL MAN

The view of culture as a fully accommodating dependent variable can combine with the 'plasticine man' model, that people's natures are determined by their environment (section 6.4). Plasticine men are completely formed in the mould set by their social environment, which in turn might be completely determined by underlying economic conditions. People are deemed plastic, and cultures are plastic too. There is then no problem of felt cultural loss, for people's attitudes readily adjust. At most there is a problem of cultural lag amongst the elderly, as the plasticine gets stiff.

The 'economic man' view of persons likewise implies no problem of felt cultural loss, since such people have no deep culture. This view is a variant of 'natural man': all persons everywhere – past, present and future – share one nature. In the economic-man case they apply means-ends rationality to fulfil their generally selfish and acquisitive desires. Dasgupta (2001) offers a reason for the claim made by economists that values are largely shared and that only ideas on facts differ: that common selective pressures in evolution have led to large cultural commonalities. But economic-man models neglect matters of meaning and identity, and are weak in understanding both people's agency and their well-being.

Chapter 6 presented as a third view basic human needs (BHN) theory: that people have common potentials and needs which can be actualised in many different ways. Here there is room for cultural tension and felt cultural loss. Not all values are universal, and people are not totally flexible. We can ask how far their nurture matches their nature.

We mentioned three views not because these exhaust the possibilities, but to understand the range. The extremes of plasticine man and economic man have special force and influence because of their elegance and analytic convenience; we added an attempted more adequate intermediate position. We saw also doubts about how adequate BHN theory really is. BHN theories make provision for culture, via needs of meaning, identity and expression, and via the culturally specific moulding and pursuit of every general need. They do so in a way that can be grasped by not only cultural theorists. But does the approach exaggerate human unities and understate cultural variety? Let us consider this at two levels, methodological and substantive.

It is best to see explanatory BHN theory as a methodology that helps us to investigate variety in a more structured way, and not as a complete and sufficient picture. Mary Douglas et al. (1998) include basic needs theory in their targets when arguing that most social science has lacked a concept of persons as social beings: 'this means a way of talking about the person who has needs and wants as immersed in a culture co-produced with other persons, a culture arising out of social solidarity that gives an array of entrenched ideas' (ibid.: 250–1). Douglas's own school of 'Cultural Theory' offers a manageable picture of four 'cultural biases' it claims are found in most situations – 'fatalist', 'hierarchist', 'individualist' and 'egalitarian' (Thompson et al. 1990; Rayner & Malone 1998). It is manageable by being, like BHN theory, simplified and incomplete, 'for the sake of having a parsimonious model of social organisations' (Douglas et al. 1998: 255). However, it does give us a methodology with which to investigate cultural diversity and complexity, including through identifying hybrids of the four biases (Hood 1998). It is weak on grasping the motives that drive behaviour in each of its four quadrants. Cultural theory and BHN theory could be good partners, the former providing us with a vocabulary of situations, the latter with a vocabulary for motives.

Substantively, sociology and social anthropology have typically emphasised behavioural variety. Edmund Leach, for example, asserted that 'anthropologists have not discovered a single universally valid truth concerning either human culture or human society other than those which are treated as axioms' (1982: 52); but was also typical in 'naturally' soon contradicting himself, claiming that sectarianism is part of 'the very essence of our human nature' (ibid.: 85). The historical sociologist Barrington Moore agreed that the wide range of different behavioural actualisations of common needs and potentials means that often 'social causes have far greater explanatory power than the elastic biological capacity' (1978: 7). However, he applied criteria for identifying possible moral feelings with universal status: (1) we can share the feeling concerned; (2) other societies besides us and its 'home' also share it; and (3) for cases where it appears absent, one can identify plausible inhibiting mechanisms. He was able to find no society without 'some definition of arbitrary cruelty on the part of those in authority' (ibid.: 26), including the theme of violation of reciprocity. Similarly he identified other posited universals meeting his criteria. Others have undertaken similar exercises with similar results (e.g. Küng 1997), including the international commission on culture which was formed by the United Nations.

THE UNEASY RELATION BETWEEN INDIVIDUAL RIGHTS AND GROUP RIGHTS

In 1992, UNESCO in cooperation with the UN Secretariat established an independent World Commission on Culture and Development (WCCD). It was chaired by former UN Secretary-General Javier Pérez de Cuellar from Peru, and included figures from around the world. Its report appeared in 1995 as the book *Our Creative Diversity*.

Strikingly, the first chapter was entitled 'A New Global Ethics'. The commission asserted: 'There is an underlying unity in the diversity of cultures, which is defined in a global ethics' (WCCD 1995: 16). These ethics draw both from existing local cultures and from the emerging 'global civic culture', which includes principles of human rights, democratic legitimacy, public accountability, and an ethos of evidence and proof (ibid.: 36). The emphasis was evidently on officially acknowledged values, especially higher-ranked values, rather than on every current attitude or practice.

Major elements of the declared universal ethics include (ibid.: 15–17 & 36–45):

1. the principle to 'treat others as one would want to be treated oneself', as found in all faiths (the key question then becomes 'who are included as others?'; here the WCCD was emphatic, citing 'the ethos of universal human rights');
2. 'universalism is the fundamental principle';
3. 'the basic necessities for a decent life must be the foremost concern of humanity', including to 'provide security to each individual';
4. 'to alleviate and eradicate suffering whenever this is possible';
5. 'democracy and the protection of minorities';
6. 'respect for all cultures whose values are tolerant of others and that subscribe to a global ethics should be the basic principle. Respect goes beyond tolerance. It implies a positive attitude to other people and rejoicing at their different ways of life';
7. 'the commitment to the peaceful resolution of conflicts and to fair negotiation, and equity both within and between generations'; the commitment to peace is important because there is no full agreement on the meaning of equity, or rather on the balance of its various aspects.

Item 6 on respect for cultures which are tolerant of others reflects the perennial tension between groups and individuals in discussions of ethics and culture. The clause 'and that subscribe to a global ethics' is found in the Executive Summary (ibid.: 15) but not in the version in the main text (ibid.: 25). Without that clause, a 'respect for all cultures whose values are tolerant of others' can enjoin respect for culture systems which tolerate other cultures but are themselves based on the domination and exploitation of many of their members. The clause on global ethics prevents this, given the report's stress elsewhere on universal human rights.

The commission laid considerable stress on societies as objects and custodians of value. It declared that development requires 'the opportunity to choose a full, satisfying, valuable and valued way of living *together*' (ibid.: 15, emphasis added); culture 'makes the development of the individual possible' (ibid.: 24); and while 'Bonds without options are oppressive[,] options without bonds are anarchy' and can be equally oppressive (ibid.: 41). 'The aim should be a society in which liberty is not libertine … [and] bonds are more than painful restrictions' (ibid.: 41).

At the same time it firmly rejected the claim that the idea of human rights reflects a narrow Western individualism. It presented human rights in low-key fashion: as the right of everyone to be regarded 'in a limited number of ways' as equal (ibid.: 42) and as major factors to be considered, not as immutable constraints but 'taking into account already existing traditions and institutions' (ibid.: 41). But the commission insisted that 'such essential equality outweighs any claims made on behalf of group and collective values' (ibid.: 42) and, as in the 1992 UN Declaration on Minority Rights, that 'human rights take precedence over any claims to 'cultural integrity advanced by communities' (ibid.: 45).

The tension between claimed individual rights and claimed group rights is at its greatest with respect to the position of women and children, and not by chance, says Susan Moller Okin. Regulated group practices typically focus on matters of sexual and reproductive life: 'marriage, divorce, child custody, division and control of family property, and inheritance' (Okin 1999a: 13). 'Nationalism tends to identify the nation with the bodies of its women,' claims Katha Pollitt (1999: 29). In similar vein, Saskia Sassen (1999) warns that cultural assertions that contain anti-women aspects by some immigrant groups in the North are responses to discrimination and rejection. A similar pattern may apply at an international scale (Sassen 2001).

Since group practices have typically been enunciated and interpreted by men and often been male biased, the tension when women in a group, or others claiming to speak for them, assert that they are inequitably treated by existing practices is normal throughout the modern world. Whereas 'multiculturalism demands respect for all cultural traditions ... feminism interrogates and challenges all cultural traditions. Feminists might disagree about strategic issues ... [and even] about what true equality is in a given instance', but its demand for equality for women runs fundamentally counter to cultural relativism, declares Pollitt (1999: 27).

A tension between women's individual rights, and group rights to community management, would not be surprising and does not imply that 'group rights' are a spurious notion, advises Abdullah An-Na'im. People are both individuals and group members. Many aspects of life cannot be organised at individual level. The UN Covenant on Economic, Social and Cultural Rights recognises the rights of peoples to, for example, 'freely determine their political status' – for which a people 'must be able to act collectively as a community' (An-Na'im 1999: 63).

Let us look at two case studies of this widely found tension.

WOMEN'S RIGHT TO EMPLOYMENT?

The volume *Women, Culture, and Development* (Nussbaum & Glover eds 1995) provides a version of Martha Nussbaum's capabilities ethic with special reference to women's interests; commentaries by a range of thinkers, including supportive chapters by women philosophers from low-income countries; and reflections on a central case study provided by Martha Chen (1995). Chen gives examples from parts of India and Bangladesh in the 1970s and 1980s of active opposition to rural women (notably widows) obtaining paid work, although they wanted and needed it to support themselves and their immediate families. The situations did not involve external planners proposing something that was not prioritised by a target group. The study and the commentaries identify a series of claims which were made regarding why women should, however, not receive paid employment.

1. Women don't need paid employment or need it less; or women are unsuited or less suitable for the work concerned. These claims were often made but easily refuted for the women and contexts in Chen's study.

2. Such employment would contravene local culture (as specified by: written tradition/men/law/the local elite/legitimate local leadership/the older generation). This is the main objection to consider here. Alleged prohibition by religion is a variant. A form of communitarian ethics is often cited in support: that morality is whatever a community accepts; there is no other basis for evaluation. We must distinguish this from other possible communitarian views, such as that communities are important and valuable; or the chauvinistic '*my* community comes first, above others'.

3. The third set consists of objections to calculations in terms of women's individual personal benefit. These objections can be part of local culture. One such is that women willingly sacrifice the pleasure of paid work, for the good of others. It can be rejected in Chen's case, if the 'others' means the women's immediate family, because the women wanted paid work in part precisely to help their immediate family; but it might refer to wider family and local community in the long-run. Another objection is thus the claim that the criticised role pattern is necessary for the long run good of society.

Øyhus (1998) presents a comparable case from southern Sudan. Amongst the semi-nomadic pastoralist Toposa people, cattle belonged in men's world and crops in women's world. By the 1970s drought, disease and conflict with neighbouring peoples had led to severe malnutrition. A Norwegian NGO proposed to introduce ploughing with oxen, amongst other innovations. But should it be undertaken by men or women or both? There was no precedent. Further, since cattle had a spiritual significance, and the Toposa declared their system of norms to be complete and for eternity, could such redefinition of worlds be accepted? The NGO consulted the all-male councils of elders. After prolonged discussions these concluded that ploughing by men with oxen was a contingency already included within the Toposa world-view, but previously kept in reserve. When the NGO proposed that ploughing be open to women as well as men, the answer was no. The practice was declared absent from the Toposa world-view. From an assessment of the needs and vulnerability of women, especially widows, the NGO decided to go ahead and offer training in ploughing to women. Many women requested and received it. In effect they rejected the exclusive right of the elders to determine what was culturally acceptable. (The case is described more fully in Gasper 2000a.)

In the rest of the chapter we investigate this type of debate in the area of gender and the broader contestation between universalism and relativism. Section 8.3 examines communitarian ethics. Section 8.4 will touch on the anti-individualistic arguments which sometimes underpin it and possibly have more weight in certain other situations than the two cases just described. It also examines with reference to education the harder case where potential beneficiaries do not, at least in advance, want the posited benefit.

8.3   COMMUNITARIAN ETHICS AND CULTURAL RELATIVISM

The type or aspect of communitarian ethics that concerns us here is the attempt to restrict the scope of morality to national or local communities or culture areas: cultural relativism. We should respect, take seriously, and often build from community values; but cultural relativism goes much further. It does not go as far as full ethical relativism, which asserts that there are no ethical rights and wrongs, only matters of personal taste; instead it holds that values are constructed within communities, each of which is a self-sufficient moral universe.

THE TEXTURE OF COMMUNITARIAN ETHICS

Communitarians argue that an ethic must be based in the values, life experiences, heritage and traditions of a community. It then has a democratic and life-tested validity. This gives a group its own moral space, space for its self-development, in which it learns through living and thus achieves moral adulthood. Different groups grow up differently, and we should be no more against such cultural diversity than we are against bio-diversity. Communitarian ethics in the work of exponents such as Alisdair MacIntyre (e.g. 1981) and Charles Taylor (e.g. 1995) draws in a deeply enlightening way on the history of changing concepts of value and self, showing their social conditioning. This evolutionary rationale contrasts, however, with the attempt by some custodians of culture to define and fix practices for ever, based on an idea that a community has a complete, consensual and consistent moral language.

A group's 'ability to name the world in a way which reflects their particular experience' is key to its autonomy, argues Vincent Tucker (1996a: 4). Yet the autonomy of persons as opposed to groups is seen by some communitarians as a narrowly individualistic ideal. They reject some of the types of participation that liberals propose as necessary, for example for women. Even if they accept *equal* rights for women they may dispute that these be defined as access to the *same* opportunities as men. Bhikhu Parekh agrees that women should enjoy equal dignity and rights, but considers it too non-consensual and also impractically vague to require that they 'be equally autonomous, free to challenge their social roles' (1999: 72).

Nations and culture areas are in fact far too large to be communities, in most senses. The *Penguin Dictionary of Sociology* cites three meanings of 'community' beyond merely 'inhabitants', people living in the same territory: (1) a group having a shared system of social structure; (2) a self-contained operational unit; and (3) a group with a feeling of belonging or community spirit. One can add (4) a group in which all the inhabitants at least form part of a network of interaction, even if it is not self-contained. Each meaning quite often fails to hold for a territory's inhabitants or a culture area. Yet many communitarians like to talk as if nations or culture areas are communities in the same way as a village or small town might be. Sometimes we need then to put the term 'communitarian' in quotes, or to speak instead of nationalists, culturalists or cultural relativists.

WALZER'S WORLDS

In Chapters 3 and 5 we referred to the 'spheres of justice' theory of the American political philosopher Michael Walzer (1935–). It illustrates both the value of an approach to ethics which starts from real, richly detailed, diverse forms of life, and the failings when communitarian thought instead downgrades cross-cultural, and oversimplifies intra-cultural, discourse. That results from a flawed sociology which overstates community coherence and consensus and understates trans-local connections.

Walzer offers two main ideas. Both partition life into zones, both are rejoinders to abstract universal conceptions such as utilitarianism and libertarianism. But the two are separable (cf. Taylor 1995) and should be separated (Okin 1995). One is helpful: the notion of diverse spheres of justice within any society, each sphere having distinct principles. This idea is empirical, an important description which an adequate normative ethics will be aware of. The second idea is normative, and mistaken: that communities are self-contained moral universes, with agreement within a community as the only valid criterion for justice within it.

Walzer uses two important subsidiary ideas about spheres of justice.

Again one is helpful: 'complex equality', which is when the distributions of goods in the diverse spheres each generate different rankings of persons. This requires the absence of 'dominance': power in one sphere of life should not carry over into other spheres. The other idea is exaggerated: that appropriate ethical norms within each sphere in a society can be read off from the nature of the goods concerned – for example that we can know enough about how health care should be allocated by simply reflecting on its nature, namely that it is for the unhealthy. (Miller & Walzer eds. 1995 contains refutations by several authors, notably Brian Barry) This problematic idea has a broader version which underpins the notion of self-contained moral universes: that ethical answers, normative 'shared understandings', reside in each community's language, the seat of its culture. 'We will know what objects we owe to other people as soon as we understand what those objects (really) are and what they are for' (Walzer 1993: 169). But that degree of consensus is less and less likely in complex differentiated societies, which is precisely why they turn to the sorts of universalistic moral theory which Walzer decries (Rustin 1995). Further, consensuses can be wrong, for reasons we will turn to. Knowing the social meanings of goods is relevant but not sufficient (Gasper 2000a).

Walzer asserts that 'A given society is just if its substantive life is lived in a certain way – that is, in a way faithful to the shared understandings of the members ... In a society where social meanings are integrated and hierarchical, justice will come to the aid of inequality' (1983: 313). Here Walzer refers to an Indian village organised on lines of extreme inequality but, according to the account he cites, with no disagreement over the established rules: '[justice] cannot require a radical redesign of the village against the shared understandings of the members. ... To override those understandings is (always) to act unjustly' (ibid.: 313–14) – not simply imprudently but unjustly. The term 'shared understandings' is here stretched to cover two meanings. Recognition of the rules as current social facts, buttressed by precedent and power, is not the same as acceptance of them as morally right. Most Dalits ('untouchables', at the bottom of or even beneath the hierarchy of castes) in India now reject the meanings of caste society. But suppose that they earlier did not and that the downtrodden shared the understandings which excluded and denigrated them. In Walzer's view the resulting situation was just.

Suppose next that some Dalits learn and come to share universalistic conceptions of justice, by which they see their former acceptance as mistaken and manipulated, a product of their lack of power, alternatives and exposure. By Walzer's specification such universalistic conceptions are mistaken, but he also declares that those conceptions become part of local social meanings and enter a local debate for which there is no just substitute. But the fact that every universalist principle has been conceived and presented by a particular person in a particular context does not reduce it to just a 'part of local social meanings'. Universalism is defined by its content, not its origin.

Walzer (1993) accepts that the exclusion of some people from the construction of meanings, and their non-acceptance (even if inarticulate or hidden) of the outcomes, do constitute reasons for rejection of those arrangements as just. Here he tacitly employs universalistic criteria. Indeed he comes to see that his 'theory of social construction [of meanings and values] implies (some sort of) human agency' (ibid.: 173). Hence it requires a basic-needs principle to ensure the requisites for agency. And he must then reject some 'shared understandings' as being unfairly derived, when based not on autonomous agency but on implied threat, indoctrination, or exclusion from relevant information. Walzer tries ineffectually to preserve his theory by saying that agreement in such instances 'would not constitute *agreeing*' (ibid.: 174; his emphasis). He does not discuss agreement through psychological adaptation and resignation (see e.g. Sunstein 1995). In any case his principle of being 'faithful to the shared *understandings* of members' is clearly insufficient. Some shared understandings lack moral weight.

If and when the Dalits do object, Walzer agrees that outsiders can rally to their cause, but not before. He presents this as a point of principle, not of tactics. The position rests on a rigid and excessive contrast between outsiders to and members of 'a culture', indeed a simplistic unitary notion of membership (e.g. Walzer 1994; see DeMartino 2000, Gasper 2000a). It exaggerates local wholeness and neglects the holding of multiple identities, such as 'Dalit', 'labourer', 'citizen' and 'person', in addition to 'villager'.

COMMUNITARIANISM IS BASED ON POOR SOCIOLOGY

We can consolidate the criticisms of communitarian ethics under two headings: its questionable assumptions about societies and, in the next subsection, its inconsistency, both internally and with other strongly held beliefs. Communitarians urge reference to the shared understandings in communities. However:

1. 'Communities' are not consensual, even locally, let alone nationally and in an era of globalisation (Rustin 1995; Benhabib 1995). In Martha Chen's case of female employment the divisions were intra-local. In Partha Dasgupta's case of cowshed childbirth, the divisions of view are intra-national, and in fact intra-local for any level of locality above that of the hillspeople. Recent attention to bottom-up and participatory development has, ironically, often ignored local divisions: 'this mystical notion of community cohesion continues to

permeate much participatory work, hiding a bias that favours the opinions and priorities of those with more power'; '"community" provides a smokescreen for professionals to avoid intra-communal struggles, notably the micro-politics of gender relations' (Guijt & Kaul Shah 1998: 1 & 11).

2. We must always ask: who is representing the culture? Who has the power to make authoritative declarations about what its 'shared under-standings' are? 'Granting non-democratic communities group rights thus amounts to siding with the privileged and the powerful against those who are powerless, oppressed and marginalised, with the traditionalists (often even the reactionary) against the nonconformists' (Tamir 1999: 48), and often thus to siding with patriarchs against women.

3. Cultures are not fixed, they always evolve, especially in the modern world. This is one reason they are heterogeneous. Yael Tamir stresses that evolution of one's way of life does not imply loss of one's identity. He fears that granting special rights to allow undemocratic groups 'to survive' misspecifies their situation. Typically neither the group's nor the individuals' survival is at stake, only the survival in frozen form of an undemocratic version of a particular way of life.

4. Group leaders sometimes defend their practices by reference to fine passages of official doctrine rather than to what actually happens in the group, and without confronting inconsistencies in the bodies of doctrine.

5. Even if there were no disagreements between members, the doctrines and cultures contain ambiguities, internal tensions and inconsistencies, for various reasons. 'Communities' overlap and lack clear boundaries; it would be dysfunctional for cultures to be so fully defined as to remove room for manoeuvre and learning; and no set of social rules can be complete, totally clear and able to handle all new situations. The need for new interpretations arises, and these are debatable, as we saw in the case of the Toposa. Chen adds an example of disputes over what are the requirements of *purdah* in a changing world.

That living cultures always involve debate is often downplayed by group leaders, and by colonial and post-colonial presentations of 'Other' cultures as governed by tradition not reason. Jan Nederveen Pieterse aptly concludes (2001: 60): 'Culture is an arena of struggle'.

CULTURAL RELATIVISM IS INCONSISTENT, INTERNALLY AND WITH OUR OTHER BELIEFS

While communitarians insist on ethical reference to shared or authori-tative meanings in a community, they seek to debar assessments from outside a culture. Rejection of the possibility of external assessments and comparisons suits the convenience of elites in all countries. But frequently in doing so they contradict themselves or other firmly held beliefs. (This subsection builds on Gasper 1997a.)

1. Relativists may inconsistently derive a universal ethical injunction – to accept each culture's values for within its own territory – from an assertion of the absence of universal ethical values.
2. Often proponents assert non-comparability between cultures – there are 'diverse and non-comparable ways of existence', declared *The Development Dictionary* (Sachs ed. 1992) – yet themselves compare cultures and emphatically criticise some (as we saw in section 2.4 on universalism and relativism in definitions of development).
3. The latter inconsistency is unsurprising, for the possibility of cross-cultural criticisms arises from widely and deeply held ideas about common humanity and basic human needs and rights. Those ideas are indeed disputed, but without some such ideas criticism in any direction becomes illegitimate, including one's criticisms of others, not only criticism by others of oneself.
4. Why are universalist ideas widespread and deeply held? They reflect fundamental concerns in ethical reasoning. For example, what if community leaders treat in different ways people who were in exactly the same position? (In Martha Chen's case, leaders interpreted the requirements of *purdah* indulgently for their own families and class members and harshly for other people.) While there can be disputes about what are relevant differences and similarities, the demand for equal treatment of equal cases crosses, and cannot be blocked by, cultural boundaries. What if a community favours some persons vastly more than others, as in apartheid South Africa? Cultural relativism left no grounds for external criticism of the apartheid culture of a majority of white South Africans. Instead it justifies spaces where 'the strong can declare themselves "different" and entitled to pursue their own rationality and the unique values of their own allegedly incomparable way of life, including by consuming the weak' (Gasper 1996a: 633).
5. Even if such ideas of basic rights were unique to Western philosophy, which they are not, they would not be mere tools of Western imperialism. Doctrines differ from practices, and doctrines such as basic human rights are often critical of Western rule and rulers and are used to counteract them.
6. Even if communities had consensual and consistent cultures, they would remain open to external moral evaluation. If consensus were due to indoctrination, even brainwashing, including through lack of information and awareness, it would not be morally convincing. In fact cultures also convince and appeal to members by reference to reasons,

including asserted facts and views about human requirements – reasons which are fallible and corrigible and require examination.

Much of the assertion of cultural relativism is an attempt to protect traditions and certain groups against the forces of markets and Western ideas, and to defend them from ignorant criticism. However the method goes too far. Certainly for deciding 'not just what we *want* as independent persons, but who we *are* as a community and society ... the reasons we give for our desires should be given far more weight than our willingness to pay to secure them' (DeMartino 2001: 80). But while wealth should not determine such choices, nor should other forms of domination, inherited and placed beyond question.

THE CENTRALITY OF INTERNAL CRITICISM

The legitimate version of cultural relativism is not to debar judgements about practices, but to require that proposed judgements derive from thorough understanding of both the context judged and the judger's own context. Criticism from within is likely to be better informed, as well as to have more chance of acceptance. Abdullah An-Na'im (1999) and some of his co-authors add that for external criticism to carry credibility the critics must also apply equal standards to their own societies, and the same norms and degrees of sympathy and indulgence about what are reasonable rates of change. For their own societies, critics usually call for reform, not abandonment.

Martha Nussbaum cites the famous Shah Bano case in India. The Chief Justice of the Supreme Court, a Hindu, awarded maintenance to an elderly Muslim woman who had been summarily divorced by her husband, following Muslim personal law, after forty-four years of marriage. The judge made numerous comments on the deficiencies of Muslim practices and the requirements of Muslim scriptures if properly interpreted. He fell into the tactical trap of emphatically interpreting others' religion for them. The Muslim backlash against his ruling and Rajiv Gandhi's search for votes led to civil legal entrenchment of the regressive Muslim personal law.

The underdefinition, internal plurality, mutual influence and abilities to reason displayed by cultures all give capacity for internal criticism and evolution in the face of new experiences, information and opportunities (Nussbaum & Sen 1989; Walzer 1987). Al-Hibri (1999) and Nussbaum (2000), for example, stress the (occupied) space in contemporary Islamic societies for internal criticism that rediscovers the Quran and its divergence at many points from ideas and practices currently widespread in Islam. Culture is then to be constructed, not just preserved; learning is important. We can link this to needs of expression, choice and inquiry, seen not as 'just a few more items on a long list' of needs – they cannot be handed out like water or medicines – but in the special category which concerns how other needs are handled (Camacho 1991: 76).

There is a danger of a strategy of internal criticism subsiding into permanent reendorsement. Nussbaum adopts a tactical political line for not supporting the Shah Bano verdict. She might fall into another trap, ghettoisation, in her conclusion that withdrawal of state recognition from the dominant, questionable, interpretation of Muslim family law would under present circumstances be 'difficult to dissociate [from] ... a relegation of Muslim citizens to second-class status' in India (Nussbaum 2000: 178); and in her claim that 'any abolition of the system of Islamic law would be a grave threat to religious liberty and a statement that Muslims would not be fully equal as citizens' (ibid.: 211). The proposal is not to abolish Islamic personal law, but to give Muslims the right to opt out into civil law, away from a version of Islamic law which gives half the Muslim citizens a real second-class status. To block that right is the true threat to religious liberty; it transfers those citizens' religious liberty to mullahs. The present situation seems more likely to contribute to a low esteem by other Indians for Muslims than would the Shah Bano verdict.

8.4 CASES AND PROCEDURES

Parekh (1999: 74) offers this statement of the essentials of a multiculturalist stance:

[1.] culture provides the necessary and inescapable context of human life, ...

[2.] all moral and political doctrines tend to reflect and universalise their cultural origins, ...

[3.] all cultures are partial and benefit from the insights of others, ... [thus]

[4.] the liberal view of life is culturally specific and neither self-evident nor the only rational or true way to organise human life; some of its values, when suitably redefined, may be shown to have universal relevance, but others may not; ...

[5.] truly universal values can be arrived at only by means of an uncoerced and equal inter-cultural dialogue ... and liberal relations with nonliberal cultures should be based not on dogmatically asserted liberal values but on a critical and open-minded dialogue.

Such dialogue, observing 'the minimally necessary moral constraints,... cannot but deepen and broaden the hitherto somewhat parochial feminist sensibility' (ibid.: 75). What would be those minimally necessary constraints? Okin (1999b) warns, for example, that dialogue is flawed if leaders of a cultural group are far from representative. Women and the young, whose lives are most at stake, should participate too.

CRITERIA FOR JUST DECISIONS

Different positions exist on the claim that sharp gender divisions and exclusions are necessary for the long-run good of society. Reference to the achievements in for example Scandinavia lead some people to reject the claim, while some others remain unconvinced of the longer-term viability of those societies. Rather than assert a definite answer to the claim, we could adopt a more procedural approach to gender rights, with women to participate equally in setting the criteria by which women's positions can be judged (Wolf 1995). So to answer 'what is acceptable variation in culture?' we would look at how decisions are made rather than check for prerequired outcomes. The British moral philosopher Onora O'Neill (1941–) makes a proposal (O'Neill 1991, 1996, 2000).

Just rules of procedure must, first, ignore differences between persons which are irrelevant in the case concerned, and, second, take into account relevant differences. Communitarian relativism fails on the first criterion. It takes all inherited conventions as defining relevant differences: it has no independent criterion for what are unjustified discriminations against various groups, such as women. The assumption is that communities (or in reality the powerholders in them) never make moral mistakes. This simplifies moral discourse enormously, and too far. Some versions of Western liberalism fail on the second criterion: they systematically ignore, for example, the distinct needs and frequent disadvantages faced by women. Instead rules should be such as could be accepted under reasonable conditions by all those who are subject to them. By 'reasonable conditions' we refer to the sorts of issues and criticisms we saw concerning Michael Walzer's example of uncomplaining acceptance of inequality in an Indian village (see also Sunstein 1995, 1999; Okin 1999b). Let us state them more fully.

- Have people any tolerable alternative to accepting? Will they be punished if they dissent – either directly victimised or left in a situation of serious disadvantage because of lack of good options? Even if an obnoxious practice could eventually be broken by resistance, it may continue in force due to a 'collective action problem' where successful resistance requires the sustained action of many, and potential early dissenters know they would or might sacrifice themselves. In contrast, in the Toposa case the elders could condemn ploughing by women but had no power to prevent or penalise them; so women began to plough.
- Have people adequate and reliable information?
- Have they the intellectual capacities and training to analyse and choose? Or have they been compulsorily moulded into adopting and accepting one set of rules?

- Have they the other psychological capacities to choose, sometimes to dissent? Or have they eliminated the possibility of disappointment from life by adjusting downward their preferences and expectations, so as to be content with their situation? For example, for older people to reject certain practices which they have undergone might perhaps undermine their felt life rationale and self-esteem.

These criteria form a set of constraints regarding what is 'acceptable acceptance'. They do not determine the content of the rules which may be agreed to. As with any set of criteria, they give clear guidance for some instances but are hard to interpret for some others.

To fix ideas, let us take a series of hypothetical cases in which women accept subordinate roles (Gasper 1996a; see also Table 8.2).

- In case 1, the women have no reasonable alternative. Their lives will become too difficult if they do not accept. This would fail O'Neill's requirements for justice.
- In case 2 they have alternatives but no or insufficient awareness of them or their implications. This also fails.
- In case 3 they have alternatives, a well-informed awareness, real choice, and no overwhelming cultural moulding: but they accept subordinate roles, because they accept arguments about the good of following community tradition (including religion) or that they should serve the wider interests of their family, even if they do not adopt the extreme argument that society will not be viable unless they do so devote themselves. By the criteria above, this choice would be accepted.
- In case 4 they have alternatives and awareness, but have been culturally moulded into accepting their roles. This is the hardest of our four cases (Post 1999), but highly relevant. It includes the possibility of adaptive preferences: besides being inculcated with these role models before they are adults, the women's preferences as adults adapt to justify their situation, for otherwise life is hard to endure. This pattern is well established (Elster 1983, Sen 1995, Sunstein 1995). The women are in this sense co-creators of the culture. One possible response is to not object, provided that the women have continuing access to the alternatives and to relevant information, including on new alternatives and ideas. The case is hard to judge, and harder to prescribe for. If one did object to it, on grounds of major damage to individuals' interests, this damage should be weighed against the reasons against intervention, such as possible damage to the continuing functioning of a cultural system (including, for example, its religion; Sunstein 1999).

O'Neill's approach insists on the rights of individuals to choose. This respect for individuals is not the same as promotion of individualism. That it would accept case 3 shows how far it is from a strongly individualistic feminism. Like Susan Moller Okin's, the approach does not reject informed choices but stresses the conditions for meaningful choice. While it is not a 'comprehensive liberalism', Okin (1999b) describes her position as beyond 'political liberalism'. Education, she emphasises, should be multi-cultural and open minded, and make people autonomous and aware of their rights. Ironically, while liberals may support multi-cultural education, the provision of serious exposure to other cultures, this goes too far for some supposed multi-culturalists.

We asked whether women willingly partly sacrifice themselves for the good of others – just as most parents partly sacrifice themselves for their children, perhaps not even conceiving it as sacrifice because not identifying themselves so separately. O'Neill's criteria allow this, if several conditions are met, as in case 3. But children themselves are not yet mature choosers, and we must pay special attention to cases in which their interests are being sacrificed, not served. Devereux & Cook (2000) asks whether basic education is really a priority in very poor countries, compared to food security and livelihood security. In many African countries, for example, primary school enrolments dropped sharply when school fees were imposed in the 1980s or 1990s. Conversely when countries like Malawi, Tanzania and Uganda removed primary school fees in recent years, the response has been vast. Overwhelmingly most poor people agree that education is a priority for their children. But in India, where 'empowerment of non-literates … [implies] empowerment of the rural poor, the women and the Dalits' (Athreya 1999: 255), we encounter culturalist arguments and other doubts expressed out of apparent concern over whether the poor really prioritise education. Is it not more important for them to send their children to work and earn money? (In fact 'a large majority of out-of-school children do relatively little work', and school hours are anyway short; Drèze & Sen 2002: 156.) Majumdar (1999) notes the self-serving logic. Such arguments are used to justify wretchedly low public funding of primary education in India, as compared to funding for the tertiary level, which serves middle- and upper-class children. Such primary schools offer little benefit from attendance. The low attendance is then used to claim that the poor have other priorities, other values. The uneducated continue desperately poor and hindered in grasping the benefits of schooling (Gasper 2001b).

Table 8.2 Objection and non-objection to practices: overview of cases and factors

TYPE OF CASE	INHIBITING FACTORS	ILLUSTRATIONS
SOME LOCAL PEOPLE OBJECT OPENLY TO WHAT IS DECLARED AS LOCAL CULTURE	(*Despite* the factors listed below)	Widows seeking paid employment (Chen) Toposa women wishing to plough Present-day Dalits in India (despite continuing victimisation) Shah Bano case
SOME LOCAL PEOPLE OBJECT BUT ONLY TACITLY	They have no good option: face substantial risks of non-evadable sanctions and even victimisation for open disagreement or divergence (Case 1)	Dalits previously
NO (OR FEW) LOCAL PEOPLE OBJECT	Shortage of information, awareness and perhaps of the capacity to decide (Case 2)	*Cowshed births (Dasgupta) Low attention to basic education? Smallpox case (Marglin) Tanzania bilharzia case*
	Adaptive preferences: people adapt their opinions to justify their situation	Very widespread
	Cultural moulding (Case 4)	Women in e.g. Kerala & Japan?
	Conscious willing acceptance (Case 3)	Women in e.g. Kerala & Japan?

AN OVERVIEW OF CASES

Table 8.2 lists the situations and cases on culture which we have discussed. Highlighted in italics are cases where those affected do not object, because of lack of information and awareness, and could never do so since they are children or babies. Thus in the case of cowshed births, to talk of acceptance of a practice which damages their survival chances is at least not nonsensical for mothers, but is absurd for babies. Frédérique Appfel Marglin (1990) protested against the imposition of Western anti-smallpox vaccination in colonial India. It displaced the alternative practice of variolation, described in *Encyclopaedia Britannica* as immunising patients by infecting them with substance from the pustules of patients with a mild form of smallpox. Variolation was linked to worship of the goddess Sitala as part of a way of life to which Marglin granted fundamental respect. But 'the risk of death from [indigenous] variolation varied from 1 to 3 per 100' (ibid.: 109), significantly higher than from vaccination, and the deaths involved were largely those of children.

In a case in southern Tanzania, a Dutch doctor found that most eight- to twelve-year-old children in the area had bilharzia and so sometimes urinated blood. Those who did not pass blood were considered sick and were treated by traditional doctors. The Dutch doctor concluded that a sustained supply of anti-bilharzia drugs to the area could not be expected. Feeling a genuine dilemma between giving people more awareness and choice or leaving them happy, he decided not to intervene, not even to seek to dispel the beliefs. He feared that information would only make the majority of the children feel ill and their parents feel guilty. (For more details of the case see Gasper 2000a.) Some commentators agreed warmly with the doctor, on the grounds that communities know best what suits their situation and way of life. Yet the 'the community knows best' argument went with a wish to not give them information! Usually interventionists risk being called paternalist; but here other commentators argued that the *failure* to supply medical information and so allow parents to make better-informed choices and seek their own solutions was to treat the parents as children. Would the 'the community knows best' commentators agree that they should not be informed if, say, a Tanzanian doctor visiting their country observed that alternative pharmacists appeared to have misclassified and misprescribed Tanzanian remedies?

We can thus identify cases where the ethical weight of a local cultural stance looks relatively low, such as: some medical cases, where firmly established knowledge is not yet absorbed by the local culture, or the survival interests of children are at stake (Dasgupta 1993); other cases where values rest on identifiably false empirical beliefs (Putnam 1993); and, more controversially, resistance to provision of alternative information and education. These cases involve the ethical claims of basic needs. But they are far from the only cases.

Vincent Tucker (1996b) notes that Western medicine has always been a central part of the discourse and claims of development, explicitly and also indirectly via medical–biological metaphors for societies. Modern medicine was used to build legitimacy and productivity in the colonies, and to buttress self-belief, as proof of the colonists' superiority. In reality, relatively little was spent on health during the colonial era, but eventually life expectancy did indeed slowly increase, after the devastating famines of the late nineteenth century (Davis 2001). In the post-colonial era, the medicine-based legitimacy of development has continued to coexist with dire neglect in many countries of the medical needs of large sections, even the majority, of the population, and with a small and even declining share of health-related expenditure in international aid (Sachs et al. 2001; Mehrotra 2001). Tucker advises that we must study the cultures and political economy of the medical professions (see e.g. Muraleedharan 1999) and the biotechnology and pharmaceutical industries (cf. Le Carré 2001); and also, for seeds of hope, those of their critics.

We must not restrict discussions of culture to commentaries on 'distant strangers'. All the types of case and factor noted in Table 8.2 can apply to acquiescence in Western consumerism. Earlier chapters raised several doubts about parts of Western economics-centred culture: commodity fetishism, victimisation, and damage to both its own and global ecological and social bases (Chapter 3); blaming, excluding and ignoring the victims (Chapter 4); connections to violence (Chapter 5), and to sometimes obsessive and futile consumption, with widespread pathologies such as gluttony, extreme pornography, isolation and alienation (Chapters 6 & 7). Cultural analysis should involve looking in the mirror, including at the cultures in some economics and market operations. They too can be studied and assessed as internalised norms which discriminate invidiously but are fiercely clung to.

These points – the needs to think with cases, including both some clearer cases and some more obscure ones, and to look in the mirror and not only at 'the other' – return us to the issues raised at the start of the chapter.

8.5 CONCLUSION

We began with the question: are there systems called cultures which view development fundamentally differently? The chapter suggested that the answer is yes, but with large areas of commonality and important scope for ethical dialogue and assessment. Bhikhu Parekh warned eloquently of Western ethnocentrism, including in moral and political philosophy. But he himself lays out a picture of dialogue that can confirm some universal values. Critique of cultures is not then inevitably ethnocentric. The World Commission on Culture and Development (1995: 71) cited World Link's picture: 'a set of universal values which we all share, even if their optimal balance may differ from people to people, from religion to religion and from individual to individual and where there is great respect for such a difference'. This recognises both agreements and disagreements.

We saw that 'culture' is an ambiguous label for a vague and diverse set of concerns and issues, and that the fullness, consensuality and uniqueness of definition of group 'cultures' is often exaggerated. Tension inevitably exists between individual rights and group rights. Arguments for the priority of the latter can run in terms of tradition and group 'survival', and against individualism. We looked at these especially in relation to women's rights and, to a lesser extent, children's rights.

We concentrated on relativist arguments in communitarian ethics which hold that cultures must only be judged in terms of their own internal criteria, including extreme versions in which cultures never make mistakes in their own terms. Culture areas are presumed to form communities which share and follow consensual criteria. These relativist arguments protect groups, especially their leaders, from external criticism, some of which is indeed based on ignorance. However, relativism appears a mistaken method, resting on authoritarianism, poor sociology and weak logic. The arguments also often employ poor psychology, such as neglect of the possibility of agreements that are based on some people's exclusion from information and education, and on indoctrination, implied threat, and people's adaptation of preferences in order to reconcile themselves to their lives. A better response is to recognise that internal criticism is commonly intellectually and politically superior, but not to declare external criticism irrelevant or prohibited.

Some proposed criteria for judgement of cultures concern, then, their degree of acceptance by members under conditions not marked by exclusion, indoctrination and such factors; in other words, with respect for basic needs and rights. We can distinguish cases according to which of those conditions are present. Some 'hard cases' are difficult to decide using these criteria of fair procedure, for example due to obscurity over how much ethical weight a group culture has relative to other factors. Cultural relativism offers by contrast an escape into a world-view that claims to have no uncomfortable hard cases – a flight from reality.

DISCUSSION THEMES

1. Cultures are certainly diverse; are they also 'non-comparable' (i.e. are there no reasonable and persuasive ways to conclude that society A does better than society B for matter X), as proposed in parts of Sachs' *The Development Dictionary*?

2. When are (a) local culture (b) individuals' stated views to be relied on or not relied on, in ethical discussions?

3. What is your response to the cowsheds case described by Dasgupta? Would you inform the community that their childbirth practices rest on medical misinformation? Would you seek to intervene on behalf of the endangered mothers and babies?

4. Why should women receive/have access to paid employment? Identify and evaluate various reasons that are put forward for not permitting such access.

5. Comment on cases 1, 2, 3 and 4 described in section 8.4: cases where women accept subordinate roles.

6. What is your response to the bilharzia case described in section 8.4?

7. Examine some issues of *The Economist* newspaper and its website, and for example its supplement on globalisation (September 2001). Essay a cultural analysis of the newspaper (and/or the supplement).

Goulet (1971) remains a stimulating introduction to ethical issues concerning culture and development. The report of the World Commission on Culture and Development (1995) is a readable survey of many development issues – group identity, mass media, gender, children, environment, and more – with reference to culture and 'a new global ethics'. Chapter 5 on gender and culture is recommended. Nussbaum & Glover (eds 1995) is a valuable collection on that area, while Okin et al. (1999) contains a pointed set of shorter papers for a general audience, with a lead essay by Susan Moller Okin, a wide range of comments and Okin's reply, and is revealing even in the misreadings of Okin by some commentators.

Bell (1993) gives an enjoyable exposition of a communitarian viewpoint, written as a conversation. Benhabib (1995) incisively critiques such viewpoints, as do Apel (1992) and Hussein (1992) in a special issue of the *UNESCO Courier* entitled 'Universality: a European Vision?'. Etzioni (1996) replies to criticisms of community-based analysis and action. Parekh (2000) powerfully analyses the treatment of cultural diversity in political theory. Miller & Walzer (eds 1995) contains good discussions of Walzer's ideas and a reply by him. Gasper (1996a) has a fuller treatment of certain issues in sections 8.2 and 8.4; Gasper (2000a) elaborates the picture of three stages in ethics, with examples from intra-cultural and cross-cultural debates.

CHAPTER 9

EPILOGUE

We asked in Chapter 1: Why should there be a field called development ethics? What does it cover? And how can it proceed, with which methods and roles? Here we revisit the questions. First, we underline the motivations behind the field; second, we give an overview of the major themes which we discussed; and third, we reflect on methods in development ethics. Lastly, we note some of the important areas which we did not discuss.

The book has covered selected issues in development ethics, upon what we called the first stage, description of and reactions to experience, and the second stage, the attempts to then build stronger concepts and normative frameworks. It took as central issues the meanings of development as improvement and thus of human well-being. It has not moved fully onto what we called the third stage, of ethical policy analysis and the ethics of policy practice, including professional ethics to guide conduct and choices in pressured real situations. It has not directly considered, for example, on whom specifically fall which responsibilities to act, and how far responsibilities exist across national boundaries. This chapter places what we have covered in relation to those and other uncovered issues.

Consider three statements from the final morning of a mid-2002 conference of development economics. Oded Grajew, a Brazilian businessman and President of Instituto Ethos for corporate social responsibility, highlighted UNICEF's figure that 30,000 babies and children under the age of five die *every day* from poverty-related causes. He observed that this is the equivalent of ten September 11th World Trade Center (WTC) tragedies every day of the year. As for the resources available to address such a mega-tragedy, Finn Tarp of the University of Copenhagen reported that current OECD agricultural protection policies have an effect equivalent to a tax of $62 billion per year on the South. The head of the French development cooperation agency remarked that threats to rich countries' self-interest will have more impact than appeals for altruism. This insight perhaps lay behind Grajew's choice of the WTC as benchmark for grasping the scale of infant mortality in poor countries. Such mortality too, while not chosen in the way that the WTC massacre was, is avoidable.

The conventional recipe for avoidance has been economic growth, although there are, for example, countries with fairly high mean incomes which yet contain large groups with high infant mortality, such as Brazil or South Africa, and countries which have had very low infant mortality despite low incomes, such as China and Sri Lanka. Long-term economic growth has typically demanded substantial sacrifices, enforced rather than voluntary, on the part of earlier generations – especially or specific-ally the weaker groups within them – for the sake of benefits to their successors. In contrast to the uncomplicated, thrilling image of 'take-off', the reality has often been of a period of increased suffering for major groups, due to diversion of resources to investment and wrenching changes in styles of life. Peter Berger's phrase *'Pyramids of Sacrifice'* hinted similarly at mighty structures built upon the lives of victims. It referred to the Aztecs' ritual killings on the steps of their pyramids, to fulfil what the gods were thought to require as the precondition for a better future. Bloodletting was part of conditionality. But when the gods do not exist, or do not keep their promises, or have been misinterpreted or are mistaken, then the future is not better. The stories of much of Latin America and Africa since 1980 sadly bring that analogy to mind. Even if 'take-off' occurs, costs are per-manent for those who are sacrificed; and in some countries costs are borne not by one or two generations only but by a permanent underclass. The direction of 'take-off' requires examination too, but in twentieth-century developmentalism the idea of progress often became largely reduced to economic growth: 'Economists start managing whole societies with the sole objective of achieving growth in economic output, neglecting all other factors ... because they possess no ethical rationale to match,' warned the Brazilian economist Cristovam Buarque (1993: 18).

The central questions we have considered were presented in Chapters 2 and 3: what is 'development' in the sense (or senses) of improvement, desirable change, increase in human well-being? Chapter 2 distinguished four families of meanings of 'development': more neutral descriptive meanings, concerning (1) fundamental/structural change or (2) conscious intervention; and more evaluative meanings, concerning (3) improve-ment or (4) provision of the preconditions for improved achievement. Chapters 3 to 8 investigated issues around the evaluative meanings.

Chapters 3 and 4 examined what are considered as good or bad types of result in development programmes. Typically predominant has been monetised production, but sometimes there is reference also to the inter-personal distribution of the good and bad results, and, increasingly now, to the quality of the processes followed (e.g. how far they respected people's rights or involved their participation and choices) and other aspects. The concept of development has increasingly, and rightly, become distinct from that of economic growth; and, when we use 'development' to refer to states rather than processes, increasingly dissociated from monetary or material wealth in itself. Authors such as Sarah White and Romy Tiongco suggest that the drive to never-ending economic growth in 'the North' partly stems from internal emptiness. This by no means implies that 'development' is predominantly a notion imposed from outside on Brazil, India, China and elsewhere in 'the South'. These are countries at dramatically lower income levels than those in the North, and they generate their own ambitions and aspirations.

Chapters 5 to 7 examined more fully some key types of result and their inter-personal distribution: persons' physical security or insecurity (Chapter 5) and their fulfilment or not of basic needs, notably for health and autonomy (Chapter 6); and more generally their degree of positive freedom, their possession of valued capabilities (Chapter 7). Chapters 6 and 7 thus took up the interpretations of development as provision of valued opportunities or of a platform for improvement. The claims about universal human needs, and the normative frameworks for discussion of human development, centre on universally necessary requirements for pursuing effectively whatever other diverse values people have reason to pursue.

Chapter 8 followed up the issue of universality versus relativism in the meanings of desirable change, with reference to inter-cultural differences. Some values appear universal, but certainly not all; and general values require detailed local interpretation. It argued that relativist positions in ethics typically have problems of inconsistency, both internally and with other beliefs held by their proponents or audiences.

Earlier chapters did not deal head on with such issues of ethical epistemology, namely by what criteria we can say that one ethical argument is better than another. That was not the remit of the book. But the chapters have tried to illustrate relevant criteria and their application: not to establish ethical certainty, but to try to distinguish wherever possible between better and worse argued positions. We are obliged to make or adopt normative arguments, and we do; for we are obliged to make choices, and we do, using – on a basis of conviction and not merely as tactics – criteria for what are better moral arguments, including absence of internal contradiction and of contradictions with evidence. We engage in moral argumentation also because ethics often prove to be not obvious: we find conflicting intuitions within and between persons.

We do not need to go so far as Partha Dasgupta, who asserts that there are no or few real (i.e. pure) differences on values, only differences on what are facts, which then lead to different normative conclusions (2001: 5–6; see Alexander 1967 for one refutation). But we can see that many disagreements on values do arise from disagreements on explanations and data. This weakens Milton Friedman's claim that we quickly run into value differences about which we can only fight (or vote). Further, even with any value differences which are not based on different explanations, there is much we can do to examine the consistency (internal and external), clarity, scope and applicability of different views.

Overall, the book has not presented a comprehensive survey but has preferred to emphasise an approach, a way of linking theory and experience, thought and feelings. For simplicity, we have described this in terms of three stages (see sections 1.3 and 8.1), which can be seen as stages in an ongoing cycle of experience, analysis, and then reflection and decision, leading to action and thus new experience. The third stage, of directly preparing for and making choices of policy and action, has been discussed, but much less than the first and second. It requires a book of its own. However, while this is not a book of policy analysis, we have tried to show connections and to promote an ethically aware approach to policy and practice.

On the first stage, of exposure to experience, nearly all chapters have employed real examples, sometimes extensive. Some of these can be seen as exercises in descriptive ethics, in which we try in a systematic, precise way to describe the ethical stances adopted by various agents. That work flows into the second stage, theorisation. Indeed the main formal work we have done was the careful mapping of positions and probing of concepts; we have not entered highly complex or abstruse ethical theory. Most chapters have provided a map of meanings, often based on analysis of underlying component variables (as in Chapter 4's analysis of equity) or by distinguishing different levels of abstraction (as in Chapter 6's analysis of need).

The interaction of experience, analysis and choice is common to most ethics and practical life. Ethics is not a purely separate sphere, unconnected to empirical analysis of how things work and of how people think and value. Development ethics adds something very significant through the wide range of experience it brings in and the thought-deepening urgency of the practical choices it informs. The field therefore can enrich and has enriched ethics in general, as seen for example in Amartya Sen's work.

Sometimes the conceptual clarifications offered here were what Stefan Körner (1976) called exhibition analysis rather than replacement analysis: deepening the understanding of normative options, their structure and implications (see e.g. section 3.5 on the structure of pro-market arguments and alternative stances), rather than offering a single replacement system.

Table 9.1 A fuller classification of viewpoints in global ethics

VIEWPOINTS IN GLOBAL ETHICS		EXTENT OF VALUES & RESPONSIBILITIES WITH GLOBAL SCOPE		
		EXTENSIVE	*MODEST / SLIGHT*	*NONE*
ARE NATIONAL BOUNDARIES ETHICALLY IMPORTANT?	*VERY IMPORTANT*	1. 'Scandinavian'	2. 'Inter-nationalist' – includes some communitarians	3. 'International sceptic' Plus some other communitarians and post-modernists
	INTER-MEDIATE IMPORTANCE	4. 'Solidarist-pluralist' (Cosmopolitan 3)	5. Transnational corporations (TNCs) with national loyalties/ priorities but some accepted global duties	6. Typical domestic corporation
	NOT IMPORTANT	7. Full cosmopol-itans (solidarist-globalist), e.g. pure utilitarians (Cosmopolitan 2)	8. 'Libertarian-minimalist': I, e.g. TNCs without national loyalties but with some accepted necessary global duties (Cosmopolitan 1 – 'Soros')	'Libertarian-minimalist' II: 9a. Business-only corporations 9b. Robber-baron corporations

respected, just as within countries. These first two positions are found in or near the top right of Table 9.1 (based on Gasper 2003a).

Third, 'cosmopolitan' positions hold that all humanity is the reference group in ethical discussions, some common values apply across humanity, and some responsibilities exist towards all humanity. Three major variants are presented by Dower: libertarian-minimalism, in which individuals and their liberties are all that matter worldwide, not nations/states, which must not interfere with those liberties; secondly, idealist-dogmatism (position 7), better labelled solidarism-globalism in which some more extensive set of values is deemed universally appropriate and to be promoted; and lastly, solidarism-pluralism (position 4), in which global-wide concerns and obligations are emphasised but with acceptance of considerable variation in values and behaviour between settings. These positions are found towards the bottom of the table.

By organizing Dower's positions in terms of the two dimensions, and refining the scale along each – moving from a 2×2 to a 3×3 classification

– we see more clearly the diversity of the 'cosmopolitan' category. The libertarian-minimalists indeed give no special priority to national boundaries, but they deny having large responsibilities to almost any others, not only to foreigners. They are far closer on many international issues to the sceptics and other nationalists than to other cosmopolitans.

This dimensional analysis of the 'cosmopolitan' category leads us also to discern more positions. In the top left corner are positions which have both strong national feelings and strongly felt global obligations. At the borderline here lies a position such as Peter Brown's: with a clearly delimited but still major obligation to give international aid, specifically to promote fulfilment of the basic rights of poor people. Most importantly, we come to distinguish a variety of significantly different positions held by business actors (5, 6, 8, 9a, 9b), within the libertarian minimalist category. The more refined classification is essential to reflect the real range of forces in the world, many of which reject national boundaries as normatively significant yet also reject the global humanist moral community.

A position which genuinely takes individual liberty seriously has at the same time to attend to ensuring the preconditions for such liberty, not only to defend the liberties of the privileged. We can call position 8 'the Soros position'. While the global financial speculator George Soros evinces no national loyalties in his quest for profit, he perceives the usefulness and rightfulness of national and international systems of law and regulation, including the disciplining of states and business by strong civil societies. His Open Society Foundation funds activities to build such society-driven regulation (Soros 2000).

The main operationalisation of the libertarian stance is instead through markets. This leads in a dramatically different direction. The moneyless are not counted, and the rich are counted many times over (position 9a): it is money-tarianism rather than utilitarianism. Corporations carry little social responsibility; accountability in international law is applied to states only. Market perspectives can extend further; they can seek to turn almost everything into a commodity, including human life, human organs, the human genome, even legal rulings (position 9b). A figure as deserving of attention as Soros is the global market raider Marc Rich: the principal supplier of oil to apartheid South Africa, captor of the international aluminium market in the early 1990s, dealer extraordinary, self-styled 'citizen of the world, unencumbered by the laws of sovereign nations' (*International Herald Tribune*, 14 March 2001). The Nietzschean 'Superman' despises mere humanism.

'Development' in the sense of planned intervention to counter or channel the destructive aspects of market forces has been part of our language for two centuries (Cowen & Shenton 1996). The historian Karl

Polanyi (1957) spoke of a 'second movement' from the mid-nineteenth century onwards in Europe, to counter the damaging effects of the 'first movement', the surge of technology-driven markets in the industrial revolution. But the language of development was by the mid-twentieth century largely recaptured by the perspective of economic growth. Development ethics is part of the subsequent attempt to consciously interrogate, assess, and, where, justified, reform this perspective and its institutional embodiments, nationally and globally.

What can it deliver? It uncovers the issue of costs and who bears them, and places the burden of justification clearly on those who advocate paths which involve suffering for real people now, especially for poor people. It raises and investigates questions of conflicting values, priorities, unintended effects, and possible policy alternatives. Some of these roles, though not all, seem like what many economists traditionally saw as their contribution, but they are taken up now with attention to a broader range of human values. And it provides us with a repertoire of evidence, testimony, frameworks, methods and insights. Overall it can contribute, in David Booth's phrase (1993: 52), to 'illuminating choice in development', and to building more democratic and humane national and global politics.

DISCUSSION THEMES

1. Has ethics anything useful to say, beyond categorising the conflicts between different values?
2. What do you mean by 'development'? What do you think is good development, and why?
3. Has international tax-based aid any right to exist at all? If so, from whom, for what purposes, and conducted in what fashion?
4. Suppose you are an academic referee for the *International Journal of Ethics and Development*. Take either a source referred to in this book, or another book on ethics and development, or a chapter of this book, and suppose that it has been offered to the Journal. Write your analysis and advice for the journal's editor concerning the strengths and weaknesses of the article.

READING SUGGESTIONS

Etzioni (1988), Lutz & Lux (1988), Ekins & Max-Neef (eds 1992) and Söderbaum (2000) provide reasons for, and contributions to, the humanistic reconstruction of economics. For discussions of methodology and methods in or for development ethics, see Goulet (1971, 1995), Corbridge (1993), Singer (ed. 1994, 1997), Hamelink (1997), Küng (1997), White & Tiongco (1997) and Gasper (2000a). Good examples of ethically based development policy analysis include Drèze and Sen (1989, 2002) and Haq (1998). On economic, social and cultural rights, see Klein Goldewijk & Fortman (1999), UNDP (2000), and the set of commentaries in Gasper & St Clair (eds 2000). On duties and responsibilities, intra- and inter-nationally, see Aiken & LaFollette (eds 1996), O'Neill (1996, 2000) and Gasper

(1986, 2003a); also Zadek (2001) on corporate social responsibility and sustainable development. For critiques of conventional normative analysis in the study of international relations, see C. Brown (1992), Dower (1998), and P. Brown (2000). On the ethics of international development cooperation and humanitarian relief, see Hamelink (ed. 1997), White & Tiongco (1997), Crewe & Harrison (1998), Moore (ed. 1998), Gasper (1999a, 1999b), Ellerman (1999, 2001), and the work of Hugo Slim (e.g. Slim 1997; Slim & Thompson 1993). For an important extension of the capabilities approach to issues of international justice, see Nussbaum (2002b).

BIBLIOGRAPHY

AGEE (Arbeitsgemeinschaft Entwicklungsethnologie) (n.d.), 'Concept of Development', Development Ethnology Working Group of the German Society for Ethnology.

Aiken, Will and Hugh LaFollette (1996) (eds), *World Hunger and Morality*, Englewood Cliffs, NJ: Prentice Hall.

Alexander, S. (1967), 'Human Values and Economists' Values', in Sidney Hook (ed.), *Human Values and Economic Policy*, New York: New York University Press, pp. 101–16.

al-Hibri, Azizah (1999), 'Is Western Patriarchal Feminism Good for Third World/ Minority Women?', in Okin et al., pp. 41–6.

Alkire, Sabina (2002), *Valuing Freedoms*, New York: Oxford University Press.

Allen, Tim and Diana Weinhold (2000), 'Dropping the Debt for the New Millennium: Is It Such a Good Idea?', *Journal of International Development*, 12, 857–75.

Alvares, Claude and Ramesh Billorey (1988), *Damming the Narmada*, Penang: Third World Network.

Aman, Ken (1991) (ed.), *Ethical Principles for Development: Needs, Capacities or Rights*, Upper Montclair, NJ: Institute for Critical Thinking, Montclair State University.

Andersson, J. O. (1996), 'Fundamental Values for a Third Left', *New Left Review*, 216, 66–78.

An-Na'im, Abdullah (1999), 'Promises We Should All Keep in Common Cause', in Okin et al., pp. 59–64.

Apel, K. O. (1992), 'The Moral Imperative', *UNESCO Courier*, July/August, pp. 13–17.

Apthorpe, Raymond (1997), 'Human Development Reporting and Social Anthropology', *Social Anthropology*, 5(1), 21–34.

Arce, Alberto (2000), 'Creating or Regulating Development', in Alberto Arce and Norman Long (eds), *Anthropology, Development and Modernities*, London: Routledge.

Argyle, Michael (1987), *The Psychology of Happiness*, London: Methuen.

Arneil, Barbara (1996), 'The Wild Indian's Venison: Locke's Theory of Property and English Colonialism in North America', *Political Studies*, XLIV, 60–74.

Arts, Karin (2000), 'Integrating Human Rights into Development Cooperation: Easier Said than Done', in Gasper and St Clair (eds).

Asmal, Kader, Louise Asmal and Ronald Suresh Roberts (1997), *Reconciliation through Truth – a Reckoning of Apartheid's Criminal Governance*, 2nd edn, Cape Town: David Philip and Oxford: James Currey.

Athreya, Venkatesh (1999), 'Adult Literacy in India since Independence', in Harriss-White and Subramaniam (eds), pp. 227–64.

Attfield, Robin (1999), *The Ethics of the Global Environment*, Edinburgh: Edinburgh University Press.

231

Baha'i International Community (1999), *The Prosperity of Humankind*, Wilmette, IL: Baha'i Publishing Trust.

Banana, Canaan (1987), Press Statement 122/87/SK/SN, Harare: Department of Information.

Banana, Canaan (1988), interview, *Moto* (Harare), 65, 4–5.

Banik, Dan (1998), 'India's Freedom from Hunger: the Case of Kalahandi', *Contemporary South Asia*, 7(3), 265–81.

Bannock, Graham, R. E. Baxter and Evan Davis (1992), *The Penguin Dictionary of Economics*, 5th edn, London: Penguin.

Baron, Marcia, Philip Pettit and Michael Slote (1997), *Three Methods of Ethics: a Debate*, Oxford: Blackwell.

Barry, Brian (1995), 'Spherical Justice and Global Injustice', in Miller and Walzer (eds), pp. 67–80.

Barth, Fredrik (1992), 'Objectives and Modalities in South–North University Cooperation', *Forum for Development Studies*, 1992(1), 127–33.

Bauer, Peter (1971), *Dissent on Development*, London: Weidenfeld & Nicolson.

Bauer, Peter (1981), *Equality, the Third World and Economic Delusion*, London: Weidenfeld & Nicolson.

Baxter, J. L. (1988), *Social and Psychological Foundations of Economic Analysis*, Hemel Hempstead: Harvester Wheatsheaf.

Baxter, J. L. (1993), *Behavioural Foundations of Economics*, London: Macmillan.

Bay, Christian (1968), 'Needs, Wants and Political Legitimacy', *Canadian Journal of Political Science*, I(3), 241–60.

Beatley, Timothy (1984), 'Applying Moral Principles to Growth Management', *Journal of the American Planning Association*, Autumn, pp. 459–69.

Bell, Daniel (1993), *Communitarianism and its Critics*, Oxford: Oxford University Press.

Benhabib, Seyla (1995), 'Cultural Complexity, Moral Interdependence and the Global Dialogical Community', in Nussbaum and Glover (eds), pp. 235–55.

Berger, Peter (1974), *Pyramids of Sacrifice*, London: Penguin.

Berger, Peter (1987), *The Capitalist Revolution*, Aldershot: Wildwood House.

Berman, Marshall (1983), *All That Is Solid Melts into Air*, London: Verso.

Blanchard, William (1986), 'What Does Fairness Mean and Can We Measure It?', *Policy Studies Journal*, 15(1), 29–54.

Booth, David (1993), 'Development Research: From Impasse to a New Agenda', in Frans Schuurman (ed.), *Beyond the Impasse: New Directions in Development Theory*, London: Zed, pp. 49–76.

Booth, Ken, Tim Dunne and Michael Cox (2001) (eds), *How Might We Live? Global Ethics in the New Century*, Cambridge: Cambridge University Press.

Bosma, Harke A. et al. (1994), *Identity and Development*, London and Thousand Oaks, CA: Sage.

Braybrooke, David (1987), *Meeting Needs*, Princeton: Princeton University Press.

Braybrooke, David (1991), 'Meeting Needs: Towards a New Needs-based Ethics', in Aman (ed.), pp. 80–90.

Braybrooke, David (1998), *Moral Objectives, Rules, and the Forms of Social Change*, Toronto: University of Toronto Press.

Brittan, Samuel (1983), 'Two Cheers for Utilitarianism', *Oxford Economic Papers*, 35, 331–50.

Brown, Chris (1992), *International Relations Theory: New Normative Approaches*, Hemel Hempstead: Harvester Wheatsheaf.

Brown, Peter G. (2000), *Ethics, Economics and International Relations*, Edinburgh: Edinburgh University Press.

Buarque, Cristovam (1993), *The End of Economics? Ethics and the Disorder of Progress*, London: Zed.

Burton, John W. (1990) (ed.), *Conflict: Human Needs Theory*, New York: St. Martin's Press.

BuZa (Buitenlandse Zaken, Ministerie van) (1991), *A World of Difference*, The Hague: Netherlands Ministry of Foreign Affairs.

Camacho, Luis (1991), 'Some Comments on Peter Penz's Consensual Approach to Basic Needs', in Aman (ed.), pp. 74–9.

Cameron, John (1992), 'Adjusting Structural Adjustment: Getting beyond the UNICEF Compromise', in Paul Mosley (ed.), *Development Finance and Policy Reform*, London: Macmillan, pp. 291–308.

Cameron, John (1999), 'Kant's Categorical Imperative as a Foundation for Development Studies and Action', *European Journal of Development Research*, 11(2), 23–43.

Cameron, John and Des Gasper (2000) (eds), 'Amartya Sen on Inequality, Human Well-being and Development as Freedom', *Journal of International Development*, 12(7), 985–1045.

Carley, Michael (1980), *Rational Techniques in Policy Analysis*, London: Heinemann.

Carmen, Raff (2000), 'Prima mangiare, poi filosofare', *Journal of International Development*, 12(7), 1019–30.

Carty, Anthony and H. W. Singer (1993) (eds), *Conflict and Change in the 1990s*, London: Macmillan.

Cernea, Michael (1999), 'Development's Painful Social Costs', in S. Parasuraman, *The Development Dilemma – Displacement in India*, Basingstoke: Macmillan, pp. 1–31.

Chen, Martha (1995), 'A Matter of Survival: Women's Right to Employment in India and Bangladesh', in Nussbaum and Glover (eds), pp. 37–57.

Chikowore, Enos (1987), speech reported in *The Herald* (Harare), 25 September.

Chikowore, Enos (1988a), Press Statement 243/88/CB/MA, Harare: Department of Information.

Chikowore, Enos (1988b), Press Statement 461/88/CB/SM/SG, Harare: Department of Information.

Chitepo, Victoria (1988), Press Statement 468/88/TC/SM, Harare: Department of Information.

Clark, David A. (2002), *Visions of Development – a Study of Human Values*, Cheltenham: Edward Elgar.

Clements, Paul (1995), 'A Poverty-oriented Cost–Benefit Approach to the Analysis of Development Projects', *World Development*, 23(4), 577–92.

Cohen, G. A. (1983), 'Reconsidering Historical Materialism', in J. Roland Pennock and John W. Chapman (eds), *Marxism*, New York: New York University Press.

Comim, Flavio, Sabina Alkire and Mozaffar Qizilbash (2004) (eds), *Poverty and Justice: the Capability Approach of Amartya Sen,* Cambridge: Cambridge University Press.

Conflict Research Consortium (1998), 'The Denial of Other Human Needs', <http://www.colorado.edu/conflict/peace/problem/needs.htm>.

Connolly, William E. (1993), *The Terms of Political Discourse*, 3rd edn, Oxford: Blackwell.

Corbridge, Stuart (1993), 'Ethics in Development Studies: the Example of Debt', in Frans Schuurman (ed.), *Beyond the Impasse: New Directions in Development Theory*, London: Zed, pp. 123–39.

Costa, Dora (1997), review of Easterlin (1997), <http://www.eh.net/lists/archives/eh.res/aug-1997/0025.php>.

Cowen, M. P. and R. W. Shenton (1995), 'The Invention of Development', in Jonathan Crush (ed.), *Power of Development*, London: Routledge, pp. 27–43.

Cowen, M. P. and R. W. Shenton (1996), *Doctrines of Development*, London: Routledge.

Crewe, Emma and Elizabeth Harrison (1998), *Whose Development? An Ethnography of Aid*, London: Zed.

Crocker, David (1991), 'Toward Development Ethics', *World Development*, 19(5), 457–83.

Crocker, David (1992), 'Functioning and Capability: the Foundations of Sen's and Nussbaum's Development Ethic', *Political Theory*, 20(4), 584–612.

Crocker, David (1995), 'Functioning and Capability: the Foundations of Sen's and Nussbaum's Development Ethic, Part 2', in Nussbaum and Glover (eds), pp. 153–98.

Crocker, David (1996), 'Hunger, Capability and Development', in Aiken and LaFollette (eds), pp. 211–30.

CSE (Centre for Science and Environment) (1990), *Human-Nature Interactions in a Central Himalayan Village: a Case Study of Village Bemru*, New Delhi: Centre for Science and Environment.

Currie, Bob (2000), *The Politics of Hunger in India – a Study of Democracy, Governance and Kalahandi's Poverty*, Basingstoke and Chennai: Macmillan.

Daly, Herman E. and John B. Cobb, Jr (1989), *For the Common Good: Redirecting the Economy toward Community, the Environment and a Sustainable Future*, Boston: Beacon Press.

Dandekar, Natalie (1991), 'Who Decides and for Whom? Some Comments on Braybrooke's "Meeting Needs"', in Aman (ed.), pp. 91–7.

Das, Gurcharan (2002), *India Unbound*, rev. edn, New Delhi: Penguin.

Dasgupta, Partha (1993), *An Inquiry into Well-Being and Destitution*, Oxford: Clarendon Press.

Dasgupta, Partha (2001), *Human Well-Being and the Natural Environment*, Oxford: Oxford University Press.

Davis, Mike (2001), *Late Victorian Holocausts – El Niño Famines and the Making of the Third World*, London: Verso.

Deci, Edward L. and Richard M. Ryan (1985), *Intrinsic Motivation and Self-Determination in Human Behavior*, New York: Plenum.

Deci, Edward L. and Richard M. Ryan (2000), 'The "What" and "Why" of Goal Pursuits: Human Needs and the Self-determination of Behavior', *Psychological Inquiry*, 11, 227–68.

DeMartino, George (2000), *Global Economy, Global Justice – Theoretical Objections and Policy Alternatives to Neoliberalism*, London and New York: Routledge.

Devereux, Stephen and Sarah Cook (2000), 'Does Social Policy Meet Social Needs?', *IDS Bulletin* 31(4), 63–73.

Dietz, Thomas and Alicia Pfund (1988), 'An Impact Identification Method for Development Project Evaluation', *Policy Studies Journal*, 8(1), 137–45.

Dobb, Maurice (1969), *Welfare Economics and the Economics of Socialism*, Cambridge: Cambridge University Press.

Dollar, David and Lant Pritchett (1998), *Assessing Aid: What Works, What Doesn't and Why*, Washington: World Bank.

Douglas, Mary and Stephen Ney (1998), *Missing Persons: a Critique of the Social Sciences*, Berkeley: University of California Press.

Douglas, Mary et al. (1998), 'Human Needs and Wants', in Rayner and Malone (eds), pp. 195–263.

Dower, Nigel (1988), *What Is Development? A Philosopher's Answer*, Glasgow: Centre for Development Studies, University of Glasgow.

Dower, Nigel (1992), 'The Nature and Scope of Development Ethics', seminar paper, Department of Philosophy, University of Iceland.

Dower, Nigel (1998), *World Ethics – the New Agenda*, Edinburgh: Edinburgh University Press.

Dower, Nigel (1999), 'Development, Violence and Peace: a Conceptual Exploration', *European Journal of Development Research*, 11(2), 44–64.

Doyal, Len and Ian Gough (1991), *A Theory of Need*, London: Macmillan.

Drèze, Jean and Amartya Sen (1989), *Hunger and Public Action*, Oxford: Clarendon Press.

Drèze, Jean and Amartya Sen (1996) (eds), *Indian Development: Selected Regional Perspectives*, Delhi: Oxford University Press.

Drèze, Jean and Amartya Sen (2002), *India: Development and Participation*, Delhi: Oxford University Press.

Drydyk, Jay (2000), 'Reflections on the Human Development Report 2000: Human Rights, Development Equity and Inclusive Democracy', in Gasper and St Clair (eds).

Dunham, David (2001), 'Liberalisation and Political Decay: Sri Lanka's Journey from Welfare State to a Brutalised Society', Working Paper 352, The Hague: Institute of Social Studies.

Easterlin, Richard (1997), *Growth Triumphant: the Twenty-first Century in Historical Perspective*, Ann Arbor: University of Michigan.

Easterlin, Richard (2002) (ed.), *Happiness in Economics*, Cheltenham: Edward Elgar.

Edwards, Michael (1996), paper to conference of the International Development Ethics Association, University of Aberdeen.

Edwards, Michael (1999), *Future Positive: International Co-operation in the 21st Century*, London: Earthscan.

Eisenberg, Nancy (1995) (ed.), *Social Development*, London: Sage.

Ekins, Paul and Manfred Max-Neef (1992) (eds), *Real-Life Economics*, London: Routledge.

Ellerman, David (1999), 'Helping People Help Themselves: Autonomy-compatible Assistance', in Nagy Hanna and Robert Picciotto (eds), *The New Development Compact*, Washington: World Bank.

Ellerman, David (2001), 'Helping People Help Themselves: towards a Theory of Autonomy-compatible Help', working paper, Washington, DC: World Bank, <http://econ.worldbank.org/files/2513_wps2693.pdf>.

Elson, Diana (1995) (ed.), *Male Bias in the Development Process*, Manchester: Manchester University Press.

Elster, Jon (1983), *Sour Grapes*, Cambridge: Cambridge University Press.

Elster, Jon (1984), *Ulysses and the Sirens*, Cambridge: Cambridge University Press.

Elster, Jon (1992), *Local Justice*, New York: Russell Sage Foundation.

Elster, Jon (1995), 'The Empirical Study of Justice', in Miller and Walzer (eds), pp. 81–98.

Elster, Jon (1999), *Alchemies of the Mind*, Cambridge: Cambridge University Press.

Eriksson, John et al. (1996), *The International Response to Conflict and Genocide: Lessons from the Rwanda Experience – Synthesis Report*, Copenhagen: Steering Committee of the Joint Evaluation of Emergency Assistance to Rwanda.

Esteva, Gustavo (1992), 'Development', in Sachs (ed.), pp. 6–25.

Etzioni, Amitai (1988), *The Moral Dimension – Toward a New Economics*, New York: Free Press.

Etzioni, Amitai (1996), 'Positive Aspects of Community and the Dangers of Fragmentation', *Development and Change*, 27(2), 301–14.

Eversley, David (1973), *The Planner in Society*. London: Faber and Faber.

Fallon, Sally (1999), 'Nasty, Brutish and Short?', *The Ecologist*, 29(1), 20–7.

Finn, D. R. (1997), 'An Image of the Market as Sphere of Human Interaction', *Journal of Economic Issues*, XXXI(2), 409–15.

Finnis, John (1987), 'The Basic Values', in Singer (ed. 1994), pp. 229–35.

Fischer, Frank (1980), *Politics, Values and Public Policy*, Boulder, CO: Westview Press.

Fitzgerald, Ross (1977) (ed.), *Human Needs and Politics*, Rushcutters Bay, Australia: Pergamon Press.

Forbes, Ian and Steve Smith (1983) (eds), *Politics and Human Nature*, London: Frances Pinter.

Fortman, Bas de Gaay (2000), '"Rights-Based Approaches": Any New Thing under the Sun?', in Gasper and St Clair (eds).

Fraser, Nancy (1989), *Unruly Practices*, Cambridge: Polity Press.

Friedman, Milton (1953), *Essays in Positive Economics*, Chicago: University of Chicago Press.

Friedmann, John (1992), *Empowerment – the Politics of Alternative Development*, Cambridge, MA: Blackwell.

Gallie, W. B. (1962), 'Essentially Contested Concepts', in M. Black (ed.), *The Importance of Language*, Englewood Cliffs, NJ: Prentice Hall, pp. 121–46.

Galtung, Johan (1978/9), 'The New International Economic Order and the Basic Needs Approach', *Alternatives*, IV, 455–76.

Galtung, Johan (1980), 'The Basic Needs Approach', in Lederer (ed.), pp. 55–125.

Galtung, Johan (1994), *Human Rights in Another Key*, Cambridge: Polity Press.

Gasper, Des (1986), 'Distribution and Development Ethics', in Raymond Apthorpe and A. Krahl (eds), *Development Studies – Critique and Renewal*, Leiden: Brill, pp. 136–203.

Gasper, Des (1987), 'Motivations and Manipulations – Some Practices of Appraisal and Evaluation', *Manchester Papers on Development*, 3, 24–70.

Gasper, Des (1990), 'What Happened to the Land Question in Zimbabwe? Rural Reform in the 1980s', *RUPSEA Review*, 1990(1), 38–77.

Gasper, Des (1994), 'Development Ethics – an Emergent Field? A Look at Scope and Structure with Special Reference to the Ethics of Aid', in Renee Prendergast and Frances Stewart (eds), *Market Forces and World Development*, London: Macmillan, pp. 160–185. Revised version in Hamelink (ed. 1997).

Gasper, Des (1996a), 'Culture and Development Ethics – Needs, Women's Rights and Western Theories', *Development and Change*, 27(4), 627–61.

Gasper, Des (1996b), 'Needs and Basic Needs – a Clarification of Foundational Concepts for Development Ethics and Policy', in Gabriele Koehler et al. (eds) *Questioning Development*, Marburg: Metropolis, pp. 71–101.

Gasper, Des (1997a), 'Sen's Capability Approach and Nussbaum's Capabilities Ethic', *Journal of International Development*, 9(2), 281–302.

Gasper, Des (1997b), 'The Logical Framework Approach', Working Paper 264, The Hague: Institute of Social Studies.

Gasper, Des (1997) (ed.), 'The Capabilities Approach to Well-being, Justice and Human Development', symposium, *Journal of International Development*, 9(2), 231–302.

Gasper, Des (1999a), '"Drawing a Line" – Ethical and Political Strategies in Complex Emergency Assistance', *European Journal of Development Research*, 11(2), 87–115.

Gasper, Des (1999b), 'Ethics and the Conduct of International Development Aid – Charity and Obligation', *Forum for Development Studies*, 1999(1), 23–57.

Gasper, Des (1999) (ed.), *Violence and Choice in Development*, special issue of *European Journal of Development Research*, 11(2), 1–140.

Gasper, Des (2000a), 'Anecdotes, Situations, Histories – Reflections on the Use of Cases in Thinking about Ethics and Development Practice', *Development and Change*, 31(5), 1055–83.

Gasper, Des (2000b), 'Evaluating the "Logical Framework Approach"', *Public Administration and Development*, 20(1), 17–28.

Gasper, Des (2000c), 'Structures and Meanings – a Way to Introduce Argumentation Analysis in Policy Studies Education', *Africanus* 30(1), 49–72; and Working Paper 317, The Hague: Institute of Social Studies.

Gasper, Des (2000d), 'Development as Freedom: Moving Economics beyond Commodities – the Cautious Boldness of Amartya Sen', *Journal of International Development*, 12(7), 989–1001.

Gasper, Des (2001a), 'Interdisciplinarity: Building Bridges and Nurturing a Complex Ecology of Ideas'. Working Paper 331, The Hague: Institute of Social Studies.

Gasper, Des (2001b), 'Waiting for Human Development: a Review Essay on *Illfare in India*', *Review of Development and Change*, VI(2), 295–304.

Gasper, Des (2002), 'Is Sen's Capability Approach an Adequate Basis for Considering Human Development?', *Review of Political Economy*, 14(4), 435–61.

Gasper, Des (2003a), 'Global Ethics and Global Strangers – Beyond the Inter-national Relations Framework: an Essay in Descriptive Ethics', *Parallax*, March–April 2003.

Gasper, Des (2003b), 'Nussbaum's Capabilities Approach in Perspective – Purposes, Methods and Sources for an Ethics of Human Development', Working Paper 379, Institute of Social Studies, The Hague, <http://www.iss.nl>.

Gasper, Des and Varkki George (1998), 'Analyzing Argumentation in Planning and Public Policy: Assessing, Improving and Transcending the Toulmin Model', *Environment and Planning B: Planning and Design*, 25, 367–90.

Gasper, Des and Asunción St Clair (2000) (eds), 'Seven Commentaries on the Human Development Report 2000', *Newsletter of the International Development Ethics Association*, December 2000.

Gasper, Des and Irene van Staveren (2003), 'Development as Freedom – and as What Else?', *Feminist Economics*, 9 (2/3), 137–61.

Giri, Ananta (2000), 'Rethinking Human Well-being: A Dialogue with Amartya Sen', *Journal of International Development*, 12(7), 1003–18.

Goodin, Robert E. and Julian Le Grand (1987), *Not Only the Poor*, London: Allen & Unwin.

Goodwin, B. (1994), *How the Leopard Changed Its Spots: the Evolution of Complexity*, London: Weidenfeld & Nicolson.

Gorz, André (1989), *Critique of Economic Reason*, London: Verso.

Gough, Ian (2000), *Global Capital, Human Needs and Social Policies*, Basingstoke: Palgrave.

Gough, Ian and Theo Thomas (1994), 'Why Do Levels of Human Welfare Vary Among Nations?', *International Journal of Health Services*, 24(4), 715–48.

Goulet, Denis (1971), *The Cruel Choice*, New York: Athenaeum.

Goulet, Denis (1983), 'Obstacles to World Development: an Ethical Reflection', *World Development*, 11(7), 609–24.

Goulet, Denis (1995), *Development Ethics*, London: Zed.

Graaf, Martin de (1986), 'Catching Fish or Liberating Man', *Journal of Social Development in Africa*, 1(1), 7–26.

Granick, David (1967), *Soviet Metal Fabricating and Economic Development*, Madison and London: University of Wisconsin Press.

Gray, Jack (1974), 'Mao's Strategy for the Collectivization of Chinese Agriculture', in Emanuel J. de Kadt and Gavin Williams (eds), *Sociology and Development*, London: Tavistock.

Gray, John (1993), *Beyond the New Right*, London: Routledge.

Green, Reginald H. (1978), 'Basic Human Needs', *IDS Bulletin*, 9(4), 7–11.

Griffin, Keith (1990), *Alternative Strategies for Development*, London: Macmillan.

Guijt, Irene and Meera Kaul Shah (1998), 'General Introduction', in Irene Guijt and Meera Kaul Shah (eds), *The Myth of Community – Gender Issues in Participatory Development*, London: Intermediate Technology Publications, pp. 1–23.

Gunatilleke, Godfrey (1983), 'The Ethics of Order and Change: an Analytical Framework', in Gunatilleke et al. (eds), pp. 1–39.

Gunatilleke, Godfrey, Neelan Tiruchelvam and Radhika Coomaraswamy (1983) (eds), *Ethical Dilemmas of Development in Asia*, Lexington, MA: Lexington.

Hacker, Andrew (1989), 'Affirmative Action: the New Look', *New York Review of Books*, 12 October, pp. 63–8.

Hamelink, Cees (1997), 'Making Moral Choices in Development Co-operation: the Agenda for Ethics', in Hamelink (ed.), pp. 11–24.

Hamelink, Cees (1997) (ed.), *Ethics and Development – on Making Moral Choices in Development Cooperation*, Kampen, Netherlands: Kok.

Hampshire, Stuart (1983), *Morality and Conflict*, Oxford: Blackwell.

Handy, Rollo (1969), *Value Theory and the Behavioral Sciences*, Springfield, IL: Charles Thomas.

Hanlon, Joseph (2000), 'How Much Debt Must Be Cancelled?', *Journal of International Development*, 12, 877–901.

Haq, Mahbub ul (1998), *Reflections on Human Development*, 2nd edn, Delhi: Oxford University Press.

Haque, W. et al. (1977), 'Toward a Theory of Rural Development', special issue of *Development Dialogue*, 1977(2).

Harrell-Bond, Barbara (1986), *Imposing Aid: Emergency Assistance to Refugees*, Oxford: Oxford University Press.

Harriss-White, Barbara and S. Subramaniam (eds), *Illfare in India*, Delhi: Sage.

HDR (*Human Development Report*): *see* UNDP.

Held, Virginia (1990), 'Reason, Gender and Moral Theory', in Singer (ed. 1994), pp. 166–9.

Heller, Agnes, Ferenc Fehér and György Markus (1983), *Dictatorship over Needs*, Basingstoke: Macmillan.

Hettne, Björn (1995), *Development Theory and the Three Worlds*, 2nd edn, Harlow: Longman.

Hicks, Douglas A. (2000), *Inequality and Christian Ethics*, Cambridge: Cambridge University Press.

Hirschman, Albert (1977), *The Passions and the Interests*, Princeton: Princeton University Press.

Hirschman, Albert (1986), *Rival Views of Market Society*, New York: Viking.

Hofstede, Geert (1994), *Cultures and Organizations*, London: HarperCollins.

Hoksbergen, Roland (1986), 'Approaches to Evaluation of Development Interventions: the Importance of World and Life Views', *World Development*, 14(2), 283–300.

Hollis, Martin (1977), *Models of Man*, Cambridge: Cambridge University Press.

Hood, Christopher (1998), *The Art of the State*, Oxford: Clarendon Press.

Hussein, M. (1992), 'The Common Ground of Humanity', *UNESCO Courier*, July/August, pp. 20–3.

Illich, Ivan (1992), 'Needs', in Sachs (ed.), pp. 88–101.

ILO (International Labour Organisation) (1976), *Employment, Growth and Basic Needs*, Geneva: International Labour Organisation.

Ingham, Barbara (1993), 'The Meaning of Development: Interactions between "New" and "Old" Ideas, *World Development*, 21(11), 1803–21.

James, Wilmot and Linda van de Vijver (2000) (eds), *After the TRC – Reflections on Truth and Reconciliation in South Africa*, Athens: Ohio University Press and Cape Town: David Philip.

Johnston, Bruce F. and Peter Kilby (1975), *Agricultural Development and Structural Transformation*, New York: Oxford University Press.

Killick, Tony (1981), *Policy Economics*, London: Heinemann.

Kirkpatrick, Colin, N. Lee and Fred Nixson (1984), *Industrial Structure and Policy in Less Developed Countries*, London: Allen & Unwin.

Klein Goldewijk, Berma and Bas de Gaay Fortman (1999), *Where Needs Meet Rights – Economic, Social and Cultural Rights in a New Perspective*, Geneva: World Council of Churches.

Koch, Roland (1993), *Entwicklungsschutz statt Entwicklungshilfe*, Saarbrücken: Breitenbach.

Körner, Stefan (1976), *Experience and Conduct*, Cambridge: Cambridge University Press.

Kottak, Conrad (1991), 'When People Don't Come First: Some Sociological Lessons from Completed Projects', in Michael Cernea (ed.), *Putting People First*, 2nd edn, New York: Oxford University Press, pp. 431–64.

Krog, Antjie (1998), *Country of My Skull*, Johannesburg: Random House.

Küng, Hans (1997), *A Global Ethics for Global Politics and Economics*. London: SCM Press.

Kurien, C. T. (1996), *Rethinking Economics*, Delhi: Sage.

Kurien, C. T. (2000), 'Social Arrangement for Human Rights', in Gasper and St Clair (eds).

Kurien, V. M. (1981), 'Life and Death through Foreign Aid', in M. J. Joseph, *Struggle against Death*, Kottayam, India: The Kottayam Group, Baselius College.

Kymlicka, Will (1989), *Liberalism, Community and Culture*, Oxford: Clarendon Press.

Lal, Deepak (1976), 'Distribution and Development', *World Development*, 4(9), 725–38.

Lane, Robert (1978), 'Waiting for Lefty: the Capitalist Genesis of Socialist Man', *Theory and Society*, 6(1), 1–28.

Lea, Stephen et al. (1987), *The Individual in the Economy: a Survey of Economic Psychology*, Cambridge: Cambridge University Press.

Leach, Edmund (1982), *Social Anthropology*, Glasgow: Fontana.

Lebret, L.-J. (1959), *Manifeste pour une civilisation solidaire*, Caluire, France: Économie et Humanisme.

Le Carré, John (2001), *The Constant Gardener*, London: Hodder and Stoughton.

Lederer, Karin (1980) (ed.), *Human Needs*, Cambridge, MA: Oelgeschlager, Gunn & Hain.

Le Grand, Julian (1991), *Equity and Choice*, London: HarperCollins.

Le Grand, Julian, Carol Propper and Ray Robinson (1992), *The Economics of Social Problems*, Basingstoke: Macmillan.

Lesser, Harry (1980), 'Human Needs, Objectivity and Morality' in Raymond Plant, Harry Lesser and Peter Taylor-Gooby, *Political Philosophy and Social Welfare*, London: Routledge, pp. 37–51.

Lewis, C. S. (1947), 'The Abolition of Man', in Herman Daly (ed. 1973), *Toward a Steady-state Economy*, San Francisco: W. H. Freeman & Co., pp. 321–32.

Lewis, W. Arthur (1955), *The Theory of Economic Growth*, London: Allen & Unwin.

Li, Xiaorong (1996), 'Making Sense of the Right to Food', in Aiken and LaFollette (eds), pp. 155–70.

Little, Ian, Tibor Scitovsky and Maurice FG. Scott (1970), *Industry and Trade in Developing Countries*, Oxford: Oxford University Press.

Locke, John (1988, first pub. 1690), *Two Treatises of Government*, Oxford: Oxford University Press.

Lopes de Souza, Marcelo (1999), 'The Spatiality of Social Development: a Theoretical and Conceptual Framework', mimeo.

Lutz, Mark and Kenneth Lux (1988), *Humanistic Economics: the New Challenge*, New York: Bootstrap Press.

MacArthur, John D. (1976), 'Evaluation of Land Settlement in Kenya', in Maurice FG. Scott, J. D. MacArthur and D. M. G. Newbery (eds), *Project Appraisal in Practice*, London: Heinemann, pp. 235–409.

McCloskey, Deirdre (1996), *The Vices of Economists; the Virtues of the Bourgeoisie*, Amsterdam: Amsterdam University Press.

MacIntyre, Alisdair (1977), 'Utilitarianism and Cost–Benefit Analysis', in Kenneth Sayre (ed.), *Values in the Electric Power Industry*, Notre Dame, IN: Notre Dame University Press, pp. 217–37.

MacIntyre, Alisdair (1981), *Against Virtue*, London: Duckworth.

Mackie, John (1977), *Ethics*, Harmondsworth: Penguin.

MacRae, Joanna (1998), 'Purity or Political Engagement?: Issues in Food and Health Security Interventions in Complex Political Emergencies', *Journal of Humanitarian Assistance,* <http://www.jha.ac/articles/a037.htm>.

Majumdar, Manabi (1999), 'Exclusion in Education: Indian States in Comparative Perspective', in Harriss-White and Subramaniam (eds), pp. 265–99.

Mangwende, Witness (1990), speech reported in *The Herald* (Harare), 13 July.

Marglin, Frédérique Appfel (1990), 'Smallpox in Two Systems of Knowledge', in Frédérique Appfel Marglin and Stephen A. Marglin (eds), *Dominating Knowledge: Development, Culture and Resistance*, Oxford: Clarendon Press, pp. 102–44.

Margulis, L. (1994), review of Goodwin (1994), *Times Higher Education Supplement*, 23 December.

Maslow, Abraham (1943), 'A Theory of Human Motivation', *Psychology Review*, 50, 370–96.

Maslow, Abraham (1954), *Motivation and Human Personality*, New York: Harper & Row.

Maslow, Abraham (1970), *Motivation and Human Personality*, 2nd edn, New York: Harper & Row.

Mathew, G. (1995), 'The Paradox of Kerala Women's Social Development and Social Leadership', *India International Centre Quarterly*, 22(2–3), 203–14.

Max-Neef, Manfred (1989), 'Human-scale Development', *Development Dialogue*, 1989(1), 5–81. Expanded as *Human-scale Development* (1991), New York and London: Apex Press.

Mehrotra, Santosh (2001), 'The Rhetoric of International Development Targets and the Reality of Official Development Assistance', Working Paper 85, Florence: UNICEF Innocenti Research Centre.

Miles, Ian (1985), *Social Indicators for Human Development*, London: Frances Pinter.

Miller, David (1976), *Social Justice*, Oxford: Clarendon Press.

Miller, David (1982), 'Arguments for Equality', in Peter A. French et al. (eds), *Midwest Studies in Philosophy VIII*, Minneapolis: University of Minnesota Press, pp. 73–87.

Miller, David and Michael Walzer (1995) (eds), *Pluralism, Justice and Equality*, Oxford: Oxford University Press.

Mishan, E. J. (1967), *The Costs of Economic Growth*, London: Staples Press.

Moore, Barrington, Jr (1978), *Injustice*, London: Macmillan.

Moore, Jonathan (1998) (ed.), *Hard Choices – Moral Dilemmas in Humanitarian Intervention*, Lanham, MD: Rowman & Littlefield.

Mosley, Paul (1987), *Overseas Aid: Its Defence and Reform*, Brighton: Wheatsheaf.

Mugabe, Robert (1984), 'The Building of Scientific Socialism', address to Zimbabwe Institute of Development Studies, *The Herald* (Harare), 10 July.

Mugabe, Robert (1987), Press Statement 2/87/SK/EM, Harare: Department of Information.

Mugabe, Robert (1991), report by Ziana (Zimbabwe news agency), 7 February.

Muraleedharan, V. R. (1999), 'Technology and Costs of Medical Care', in Harriss-White and Subramaniam (eds), pp. 113–34.

Myrdal, Gunnar (1958), *Value in Social Theory,* London: Routledge & Kegan Paul.

Myrdal, Gunnar (1968), *Asian Drama: an Inquiry into the Poverty of Nations*, New York: Random House.

Nagel, Stuart (1984), *Public Policy*, New York: St. Martin's Press.

Nagel, Stuart (1997), *Super-Optimum Solutions and Win–Win Policy*, Westport, CT: Quorum.

Nagel, Thomas (1987), 'The Objective Basis of Morality', in Singer (ed. 1994), pp. 155–8.

Narayan, Deepa (2000), 'Poverty is Powerlessness and Voicelessness', *Finance and Development*, 37(4); <http://www.imf.org/external/pubs/ft/fandd/2000/12/narayan. htm>.

Narayan, Deepa et al. (2000), *Voices of the Poor*, 2 vols, New York: Oxford University Press; <http://www.worldbank.org/poverty/voices/reports.htm>.

Nederveen Pieterse, Jan (2001), *Development Theory – Deconstructions/Reconstructions*, London: Sage.

Nielsen, Kai and Steven C. Patten (1981) (eds), *Marx and Morality*, Guelph, ON: Canadian Association for Publishing in Philosophy.

Nijkamp, Peter, P. Rietveld and Henk Voogd (1990), *Multicriteria Evaluation in Physical Planning*, Amsterdam: North-Holland.

Nkomo, John (1995), 'Nkomo urges universities to relate to societal needs', press statement, Harare: Department of Information, 19 February 1996.

Norgaard, Richard B. (1994), *Development Betrayed – the End of Progress and a Coevolutionary Revisioning of the Future*, London: Routledge.

Nozick, Robert (1974a), *Anarchy, State and Utopia*, New York: Basic Books.

Nozick, Robert (1974b), 'The Experience Machine', extract from Nozick (1974a), in Singer (ed. 1994), pp. 228–9.

Nussbaum, Martha (1990), 'Aristotelian Social Democracy', in R. B. Douglass et al. (eds), *Liberalism and the Good,* New York: Routledge, pp. 203–52.

Nussbaum, Martha (1992), 'Human Functioning and Social Justice: in Defence of Aristotelian Essentialism', *Political Theory*, 20(2), 202–46.

Nussbaum, Martha (1995), 'Human Capabilities, Female Human Beings', in Nussbaum and Glover (eds), 61–104.

Nussbaum, Martha (1999a), *Sex and Social Justice*, New York: Oxford University Press.

Nussbaum, Martha (1999b), 'A Plea for Difficulty', in Okin et al., pp. 105–14.

Nussbaum, Martha (2000), *Women and Human Development: the Capabilities Approach*, Cambridge: Cambridge University Press and Delhi: Kali for Women.

Nussbaum, Martha (2001), *Upheavals of Thought – the Intelligence of Emotions*, Cambridge: Cambridge University Press.

Nussbaum, Martha (2002a), 'Aristotelian Social Democracy: Defending Universal Values in a Pluralistic World', lecture text, Berlin, 1 February.

Nussbaum, Martha (2002b), 'Beyond the Social Contract: Towards Global Justice', draft text of Tanner Lectures, <http://philrsss.anu.edu.au/tanner/>.

Nussbaum, Martha and Jonathan Glover (1995) (eds), *Women, Culture and Development – a Study of Human Capabilities*, Oxford: Clarendon Press.

Nussbaum, Martha and Amartya Sen (1989), 'Internal Criticism and Indian Rationalist Traditions', in Michael Krausz (ed.), *Relativism*, Notre Dame, IN: University of Notre

Dame Press, pp. 299–325.

Nussbaum, Martha and Amartya Sen (1993) (eds), *The Quality of Life*, Oxford: Clarendon Press.

Nyerere, Julius (1977), 'The Arusha Declaration Ten Years After', in Andrew Coulson (ed. 1979), *African Socialism in Practice*, Nottingham: Spokesman, pp. 43–71.

O'Boyle, Edward J. (1990), 'Poverty: a Concept that is Both Absolute and Relative because Human Beings Are at Once Individual and Social', *Review of Social Economy*, pp. 2–17.

Offerdal, Hans Eggil (2000), 'Whose Rights? A Christian, Humanist Commentary', in Gasper and St. Clair (eds).

O'Kane, Maggie (2000), 'Pain and despair in the land of the dying', *Guardian Weekly*, 13 July.

Okin, Susan Moller (1995), 'Politics and the Complex Inequality of Gender', in Miller and Walzer (eds), pp. 120–43.

Okin, Susan Moller (1999a), 'Is Multiculturalism Bad for Women?', in Okin et al., pp. 7–24.

Okin, Susan Moller (1999b), 'Reply', in Okin et al., pp. 115–31.

Okin, Susan Moller et al. (1999), *Is Multiculturalism Bad for Women?* Princeton: Princeton University Press.

O'Neill, Onora (1986), *Faces of Hunger: an Essay on Poverty, Justice and Development*, London: Allen & Unwin.

O'Neill, Onora (1991), 'Justice, Gender and International Boundaries', *British Journal of Political Science*, 20, 439–59; and in Nussbaum and Sen (eds 1993), pp. 303–23.

O'Neill, Onora (1996), *Towards Justice and Virtue*, Cambridge: Cambridge University Press.

O'Neill, Onora (2000), *Bounds of Justice*, Cambridge: Cambridge University Press.

Øyhus, A. O. (1998), 'Universal Soldiers: the Developers', paper to Conference on Ethics and Development, Norwegian Association for Development Research, Skjetten, 5–6 June.

Palast, Greg (2000), 'Keep taking our tablets (no one else's)', *Guardian Weekly*, 27 July.

Parekh, Bhikhu (1997), 'The West and Its Others', in Keith Ansell-Pearson, Benita Parry and Judith Squires (eds), *Cultural Readings of Imperialism*, London: Lawrence & Wishart, pp. 173–93.

Parekh, Bhikhu (1999), 'A Varied Moral World', in Okin et al., pp. 69–75.

Parekh, Bhikhu (2000), *Rethinking Multiculturalism*, Basingstoke: Palgrave.

Parsons, Talcott (1968, first pub. 1937), *The Structure of Social Action*, New York: Free Press.

Penz, Peter (1991), 'The Priority of Basic Needs: toward a Consensus in Development Ethics', in Aman (ed.), pp. 35–73.

Perez Bustillo, Camilo (2000), 'The UNDP and the Origins and History of Human Rights', in Gasper and St Clair (eds).

Petri, H. L. (1981), *Motivation: Theory and Research*, Belmont, CA: Wadsworth.

Plant, Raymond (1991), *Modern Political Thought*, Oxford: Blackwell.

Polanyi, Karl (1957), *The Great Transformation*, Boston: Beacon Press.

Pollitt, Katha (1999), 'Whose Culture?', in Okin et al., pp. 27–30.

Pontifical Council for Justice and Peace (1987), *At the Service of the Human Community: an Ethical Approach to the International Debt*, Vatican City: Pontifical Council for Justice and Peace.

Post, Robert (1999), 'Between Norms and Choices', in Okin et al., pp. 65–8.

Putnam, Hilary (1993), 'Objectivity and the Science/Ethics Distinction', in Nussbaum and Sen (eds), pp. 143–57.

Pyatt, Graham (1995), 'Balanced Development', inaugural address, Institute of Social

Studies, The Hague.

Qizilbash, Mozaffar (1996), 'Ethical Development', *World Development*, 24(7), 1209–21.

Qizilbash, Mozaffar (2002), 'Development, Common Foes and Shared Values', *Review of Political Economy*, 14(4), 463–80.

Radford, Tim (2000), 'Life in the time of cholera', *Guardian Weekly*, 10 August.

Rae, Douglas et al. (1981), *Equalities*, Cambridge, MA: Harvard University Press.

Rahman, Anisur (1992), 'People's Self Development', in Ekins and Max-Neef (eds), pp. 167–180.

Ramsay, Maureen (1992), *Human Needs and the Market*, Aldershot: Avebury.

Rawls, John (1972), *A Theory of Justice*, Oxford: Clarendon Press.

Rayner, Steve and Elizabeth L. Malone (1998) (eds), *Human Choice and Climate Change*, 4 vols, Columbus, OH: Battelle Press.

Reynolds, Norman (1987), 'A Diagnostic Study of Poverty ... in Chikore Ward', paper to Agritex Conference on Semi-arid Areas, August, University of Zimbabwe, Harare.

Rhoads, Stephen (1985), *The Economist's View of the World*, Cambridge: Cambridge University Press.

Richards, Howard (1985), *The Evaluation of Cultural Action – a Study of the Parents and Children Program*, London: Macmillan.

Riddell, Roger (1985), 'Bauer on Aid', *Development Policy Review*, 3(1), 103–8.

Riddell, Roger (1986), 'The Ethics of Foreign Aid', *Development Policy Review*, 4(1), 24–43.

Riddell, Roger (1987), *Foreign Aid Reconsidered*, London: James Currey.

Robbins, Lionel (1938), 'Interpersonal Comparisons of Utility', *Economic Journal*, 48.

Robinson, Peter (1988), 'Financing Rural Services', paper to ZERO Symposium, Harare.

Roemer, John (1996), *Theories of Distributive Justice*, Cambridge, MA: Harvard University Press.

Rostow, Walt W. (1960), *The Stages of Economic Growth*, New York: Cambridge University Press.

Rothschild, Emma (1994), 'Psychological Modernity in Historical Perspective', in Lloyd Rodwin and Donald Schön (eds), *Rethinking the Development Experience*, Washington: Brookings.

Roy, Ramashray (1979/80), 'Human Needs and Freedom: Three Contrasting Perceptions', *Alternatives*, V, 195–212.

Roy, Ramashray (1994), 'The Concept of Development: Its Implications for Self and Society', *Psychology and Developing Societies*, 3(2), 133–55.

Rustin, Michael (1995), 'Equality in Post-Modern Times', in Miller and Walzer (eds), pp. 17–44.

Sachs, Jeffrey (1999), 'Helping the world's poorest', *The Economist*, 14 August, pp. 17–20.

Sachs, Jeffrey et al. (2001), *Macroeconomics and Health: Investing in Health for Economic Development – Report of the Commission on Macroeconomics and Health*, Geneva: World Health Organization.

Sachs, Wolfgang (1992), 'Introduction', in Sachs (ed.), pp. 1–5.

Sachs, Wolfgang (1992) (ed.) *The Development Dictionary*, London: Zed.

Sachs, Wolfgang (1999), *Planet Dialectics*, London: Zed.

St Clair, Asunción and Des Gasper (2001) (eds), 'Assessing Martha Nussbaum's Latest Version of the Capabilities Approach: Six Reviews of *Women and Human Development*', <http://www.development-ethics.org/document.asp?cid=5007&sid=5002& did=1072>.

Sardar, Ziauddin (1996), 'Beyond Development: an Islamic Perspective', *European Journal of Development Research*, 8(2), 36–55.

Sassen, Saskia (1999), 'Culture beyond Gender', in Okin et al., pp. 76–8.

Sassen, Saskia (2001), 'A message from the global South', *The Guardian*, 12 September.

Schaffer, Bernard and Geoff Lamb (1981), *Can Equity Be Organised?*, Farnborough: Gower.

Schumacher, E. F. (1973), *Small is Beautiful*, New York: Harper & Row.

Scitovsky, Tibor (1952), *Welfare and Competition*, London: Allen & Unwin.

Scitovsky, Tibor (1992), *The Joyless Economy: an Inquiry into Human Satisfaction and Consumer Dissatisfaction,* 2nd edn, New York: Oxford University Press.

Seers, Dudley (1977), 'The New Meaning of Development', *International Development Review*, 19(3).

Segal, Jerome (1986), 'What Is Development?', Working Paper DN-1, College Park, MD: Institute of Philosophy and Public Policy, University of Maryland.

Sen, Amartya (1975), 'The Meaning of Efficiency', in Michael Parkin and A. R. Nobay (eds), *Contemporary Issues in Economics*, Manchester: Manchester University Press, pp. 196–210.

Sen, Amartya (1979), 'What's Wrong with Welfare Economics?', *Economic Journal*, 89, 537–58.

Sen, Amartya (1981), *Poverty and Famines*, Oxford: Clarendon Press.

Sen, Amartya (1982), *Choice, Welfare and Measurement*, Oxford: Blackwell.

Sen, Amartya (1984), *Resources, Values and Development*, Oxford: Blackwell.

Sen, Amartya (1987), *On Ethics and Economics*, Oxford: Blackwell.

Sen, Amartya (1988), 'The Concept of Development', in Hollis Chenery and T. N. Srinivasan (eds), *Handbook of Development Economics*, Amsterdam: Elsevier, vol. 1, pp. 9–26.

Sen, Amartya (1992), *Inequality Reexamined*, Oxford: Oxford University Press.

Sen, Amartya (1995), 'Gender Inequality and Theories of Justice', in Nussbaum and Glover (eds), pp. 259–73.

Sen, Amartya (1998), *Reason before Identity*, Oxford: Oxford University Press.

Sen, Amartya (1999), *Development as Freedom*, New York: Oxford University Press.

Sen, Amartya (2000), 'Social Exclusion: Concept, Application and Scrutiny', Social Development Paper no. 1, Manila: Asian Development Bank.

Sen, Amartya (2002), *Rationality and Freedom*, Cambridge, MA: Harvard University Press.

Sen, Purna (1999), 'Enhancing Women's Choices in Responding to Domestic Violence in Calcutta', *European Journal of Development Research*, 11(2), 65–86.

Serageldin, Ismail and Joan Martin-Brown (1998) (eds), *Ethics and Values – a Global Perspective*, Washington: World Bank.

Shadish, William R., Thomas D. Cook and Laura C. Leviton (1991), *Foundations of Program Evaluation*, Newbury Park, CA and London: Sage.

Shanmugaratnam, N. (2001), 'On the Meaning of Development: an Exploration of the Capability Approach', *Forum for Development Studies*, 2001(2), 263–87.

Shapiro, Ian and Casiano Hacker-Cordón (1999) (eds), *Democracy's Value*, Cambridge: Cambridge University Press.

Shivji, Issa (1989), *The Concept of Human Rights in Africa*, London and Dakar: CODESRIA.

Short, Clare (2000), 'One in Four Lives in Abject Poverty', *Developments*, 9.

Shubik, Martin (1978), 'On Concepts of Efficiency', *Policy Sciences*, 9(2), 121–6.

Sillince, John (1986), *A Theory of Planning*, Aldershot: Gower.

Simon, Herbert (1976), *Administrative Behavior*, 3rd edn, New York: Free Press.

Simonis, Udo (1992), 'Least Developed Countries – Newly Defined', FS-II 92–404, Berlin: Research Professorship Environmental Policy, Science Center Berlin.

Singer, Peter (1994) (ed.), *Ethics*, Oxford: Oxford University Press.

Singer, Peter (1997), *How Are We to Live? Ethics in an Age of Self Interest*, Milsons Point, NSW: Random House Australia.

Slim, Hugo (1995), 'What Is Development?', *Development in Practice*, 5(2), 143–8.

Slim, Hugo (1997), *Doing the Right Thing – Relief Agencies, Moral Dilemmas and Moral Responsibility in Political Emergencies and War*, Uppsala: Nordiska Afrikainstitutet. (Partial version in *Disasters*, 21(3), 244–57.)

Slim, Hugo and Paul Thompson (1993), *Listening for a Change*, London: Panos Institute.

Söderbaum, Peter (2000), *Ecological Economics: a Political Economics Approach to Environment and Development*, London: Earthscan.

Soros, George (2000), *Open Society – Reforming Global Capitalism*, London: Little, Brown & Co.

Springborg, Patricia (1981), *The Problem of Human Needs and the Critique of Civilization*, London: Allen & Unwin.

Stafford, William (1983), 'Utopianism and Human Nature', in Forbes and Smith (eds), pp. 68–85.

Stewart, Frances (1989), 'Basic Needs Strategies, Human Rights and the Right to Development', *Human Rights Quarterly*, 11, 347–74.

Stiglitz, Joseph and John Driffill (2000), *Economics*, New York: W. W. Norton.

Streeten, Paul et al. (1981), *First Things First – Meeting Basic Human Needs in Developing Countries*, New York: Oxford University Press.

Sunstein, Cass (1995), 'Gender, Caste and Law', in Nussbaum and Glover (eds), pp. 332–59.

Sunstein, Cass (1999), 'Should Sex Equality Law Apply to Religious Institutions', in Okin et al., pp. 85–94.

Swedberg, Richard (1991), *Economics and Sociology – Redefining Their Boundaries*, Princeton: Princeton University Press.

Tamir, Yael (1999), 'Siding with the Underdogs', in Okin et al., pp. 47–52.

Taylor, Charles (1995), 'Cross Purposes: The Liberal–Communitarian Debate', in *Philosophical Arguments*, Cambridge, MA: Harvard University Press, pp. 181–203.

Taylor, Paul (1959), '"Need" Statements', *Analysis*, 19(5), 106–11.

Teivainen, Teivo (2002), *Enter Economism, Exit Politics*, London: Zed.

Thomas, Alan (2000), 'Development as Practice in a Liberal Capitalist World', *Journal of International Development*, 12, 773–87.

Thompson, Michael, Richard Ellis and Aaron Wildavsky (1990), *Cultural Theory*, Boulder, CO: Westview.

Tóibín, Colm (1998), 'Erasures – the Great Irish Famine', *London Review of Books*, 30 July, pp. 17–23.

Toulmin, Stephen (1958), *The Uses of Argument*, Cambridge: Cambridge University Press.

Truong, Thanh-Dam (2001), 'Human Trafficking and Organized Crime', Working Paper 339, Institute of Social Studies, The Hague. Later published as 'Organized Crime and Human Trafficking' in Emilio Veriano (ed.), *Organized Crime, Myths and Profits*, Burlington, VT: Ashgate.

Tucker, Vincent (1996a), 'Introduction: a Cultural Perspective on Development', *European Journal of Development Research*, 8(2), 1–21.

Tucker, Vincent (1996b), 'Health, Medicine and Development: a Field of Cultural Struggle', *European Journal of Development Research*, 8(2), 110–28.

UNDP (United Nations Development Programme), 1990–(annually). *Human Development Report* (HDR). New York: Oxford University Press.

Unger, Peter (1996), *Living High and Letting Die – Our Illusion of Innocence*, New York: Oxford University Press.

Ushewokunze, Dr H. S. M. (1985), 'Introduction', *Zimbabwe at Five Years of Indepen-*

dence, Harare: ZANU(PF).

Uvin, Peter (1999), 'Development Aid and Structural Violence: the Case of Rwanda', *Development*, 42(3), 49–56.

Valaskakis, K. and I. Martin (1980), 'Measures of Development and Measurement of Happiness', reprinted in *Journal of Social Development in Africa*, 1986, 1(1), 81–91.

van Staveren, Irene (2001), *The Values of Economics – an Aristotelian Perspective*, London: Routledge.

Verhelst, Thierry (1990), *No Life without Roots: Culture and Development*, London: Zed.

Verwoerd, Wilhelm (1999), 'Individual and/or Social Justice after Apartheid? The South African Truth and Reconciliation Commission', *European Journal of Development Research*, 11(2), 115–40.

Wade, Robert (1976), 'Culture of Poverty Revisited', *IDS Bulletin*, 8(2), 4–7.

Wallerstein, Immanuel (1991), *Unthinking the Social Sciences*, Cambridge: Polity Press.

Walzer, Michael (1983), *Spheres of Justice*, Oxford: Blackwell.

Walzer, Michael (1987), *Interpretation and Social Criticism*, Cambridge, MA: Harvard University Press.

Walzer, Michael (1993), 'Objectivity and Social Meaning', in Nussbaum and Sen (eds), pp. 165–77.

Walzer, Michael (1994), *Thick and Thin – Moral Argument at Home and Abroad*, Notre Dame, IN: University of Notre Dame Press.

WCCD (World Commission on Culture and Development) (1995), *Our Creative Diversity*, Paris: World Commission on Culture and Development. 2nd edn, 1996, Paris: UNESCO.

Weigel, Van B. (1986), 'The Basic Needs Approach: Overcoming the Poverty of *Homo Oeconomicus*', *World Development*, 14(12), 1423–34.

Weigel, Van B. (1989), *A Unified Theory of Development*, New York: Praeger.

White, Sarah and Romy Tiongco (1997), *Doing Theology and Development*, Edinburgh: Saint Andrew Press.

Whitelegg, John (1999), 'Debates Missing Life', review essay on the journal *Environment and Development Economics*, 1996–99, *Times Higher Education Supplement*, 8 October.

Wiggins, David (1985), 'Claims of Need', in Ted Honderich (ed.), *Morality and Objectivity*, London: Routledge.

Williams, Bernard (1972), *Morality*, Cambridge: Cambridge University Press.

Wisner, Ben (1988), *Power and Need in Africa*, London: Earthscan.

Witkin, Belle Ruth and James W. Altschuld (1995), *Planning and Conducting Needs Assessments*, Thousand Oaks, CA: Sage.

Wolf, Susan (1995), 'Martha C. Nussbaum: Human Capabilities, Female Human Beings', in Nussbaum and Glover (eds), pp. 105–15.

Woodward, Susan (1995), *Balkan Tragedy: Chaos and Dissolution after the Cold War*, New York: Brookings.

Yunus, Muhammad (1998), 'Credit where credit's due', *Guardian Weekly*, 6 November.

Yunus, Muhammad and Alan Jolis (1998), *Banker to the Poor: the Autobiography of Muhammad Yunus, Founder of the Grameen Bank*, London: Aurum Press.

Zadek, Simon (2001), *The Civil Corporation – the New Economy of Corporate Citizenship*, London: Earthscan.

INDEX

247